W9-CCM-499

SAPP
ATTACK

SAPP ATTACK

My Story

WARREN SAPP

with

DAVID FISHER

Thomas Dunne Books
St. Martin's Press
New York

THOMAS DUNNE BOOKS.
An imprint of St. Martin's Press.

SAPP ATTACK. Copyright © 2012 by Warren Sapp and David Fisher. All rights reserved.
Printed in the United States of America. For information, address St. Martin's Press,
175 Fifth Avenue, New York, N.Y. 10010.

www.thomasdunnebooks.com
www.stmartins.com

Design by Omar Chapa

ISBN 978-1-250-00438-3 (hardcover)
ISBN 978-1-250-02200-4 (e-book)

First Edition: September 2012

10 9 8 7 6 5 4 3 2 1

I would like to dedicate this book to everyone who has put on the pads, bought a ticket to a football game, turned on the television, or picked up a newspaper—and by doing that became part of the world of football. The love of this game is what we all share—most of us with a passion—and the game could not be what it has become without all of your contributions. This book is for you.

On the day that Tampa Bay's brand-new Raymond James Stadium opened in September 1998, I called my mother to see if she was coming to my game that afternoon. The Chicago Bears were in Tampa. "Oh," she asked, "ya'll got football?"

"Yeah, Mama," I told her, "we definitely got football."

"Okay. Well then, I'll be there."

I asked her if she intended to go to the game with my wife, JaMiko, but she said no, JaMiko was never ready early enough. "What difference does it make what time you get there?" I asked. "Long as you get there before the game starts."

She paused for a few seconds and then said, as if it was the most obvious thing in the world, "I like to get my mouth all ready for football."

Like mother, like son.

ONE

When I was growing up in Plymouth, Florida, my mother sometimes worked four jobs, but still my family didn't have much. We didn't even have a paved street in front of our house. We did have one small air conditioner, but the only time we were allowed to put it on was when our pastor was coming for Sunday dinner. Then that thing'd be blasting out cold, and I'd be standing right there in front of it thinking, now this is just like the rich people—least until one of my brothers or sisters yelled at me to get out the way, I was blocking their cool air.

I was born on December 19, 1972. When your family doesn't have much money and your birthday is six days before Christmas, the one question you get used to hearing is, "Do you want your birthday present or your Christmas present?" Or? Did you say *or*? Whatever happened to *and*? Where my presents were concerned there never was an *and*. So I definitely grew up appreciating the value of things. When I wanted something I had to work hard to get it, and when I got something I learned how to take care of it. Since I was a child I can remember the thing I wanted most of all was the football. When I had a football in my hands I held on tight to it, and when somebody else had it in his hands, I would do whatever it took to get it from him. That was the way I always played the game of football: It's my football, you're just holding on to it temporarily.

For me, playing defense has always been just this basic: Gimme my ball.

A football is a pretty small, strangely shaped object to have played such a big role in my life. Nobody ever knows which way it's going to bounce—or what the result is going to be. For me, it sure has taken some unexpected bounces. For example, it led to me forming one of the most talked about personal rivalries in football: Sapp v. Favre. At the end of the 1999 season, we were playing the Green Bay Packers, and the winner was probably going to the NFC Championship. One time early in the game I hit the great Packers quarterback Brett Favre and he fumbled. That ball was bouncing around on the ground, and I held him down on the ground so he couldn't grab it. There was nothing he could do but watch it bounce away from him. And maybe while I was holding him down I pushed his helmet down into the turf a little bit too. Okay, maybe I pushed him a lot. When Favre got up he was kind of angry that he'd lost the ball and put his hands on me. Really? You really want to do this? Do you actually believe that is a sane thing to do? I slapped his hands away and turned to go to the sideline. After I took a few steps he screamed at me, "Hey, Big Boy, how much you weigh? The program says 276."

I stopped and turned around to face him. "That was when I checked into camp last July. I weighed 307 last Thursday. Why you want to know?"

This is on the field, you understand, with the entire stadium standing and screaming, thinking we were about to go at it. Favre smiled at me and boasted, " 'Cause I think I can outrun you," he said.

"Oh, don't you worry none," I told him, "You're gonna get a real good chance to try." Maybe two plays later I grabbed him by the jersey, and he made the serious mistake of trying to get away from me. I chopped him right on the bridge of the nose.

Right away he started screaming, "Oh my God! Oh my God, you broke my fucking nose."

"Goodness me," I said. "I'm sorry, but didn't I hear you say you could outrun me?"

I had a great game. I sacked Favre three times, I had five tackles, I forced two fumbles and recovered one of them myself, and we won 29–10. The second sack I got a clean shot at him from behind; the poor man never heard me coming. Heaven, I'm in heaven. . . . My job was pretty straightforward: Inflict as much possible human pain on the opposing quarterback—within the rules. Now, I admit that I liked hitting running backs, but I loved hitting quarterbacks. Absolutely loved it. A running back is okay to tackle, but he's going to fight back a little. But hitting a quarterback is like tackling a pillow. Quarterbacks are all soft and cushiony, and then when you got him down on the ground you get to lay on him for a few seconds and whisper in his ear that you'll be right back. The quarterback has always been the biggest prize—that's who the pretty girls come to see play, that's who the camera focuses on—so when you sack that quarterback they just naturally have to pay attention to you.

Brett Favre was the biggest prize of all. He was building his the legend and the Green Bay Packers were our biggest rival. I always said before we played the Packers that I intended to get so close to him that I'd know what his kids had for breakfast and spilled on him. On this particular play Favre's arm was in the air when I hit him like a ton of Sapps. I blew the air right out of him. I hit him so hard his shadow decided to retire. He laid on the ground face down for a few seconds until he remembered to breathe, and then finally he turned his head and looked up at me. I gave him my biggest grin and asked, "Who you think it is?"

And then he smiled right back at me and responded, lying right there in the dirt, "You got to love it, Big Boy."

He got that right. I do love the game of football. I loved playing it, I love watching it, and I certainly love talking about it. I love the feel of a football in my hands, I love stopping by a schoolyard and watching little kids play a pickup game, I love reading the newspaper and magazine stories about the game. Football is the simplest, most complex game ever created. It's a beautifully violent game. And it never has failed to bring me joy.

At Apopka High School I played on both offense, or as my mama called it, "the winning side," and defense. I was recruited by the University of Miami as a tight end but was switched to defensive tackle. In professional football, for nine years at Tampa Bay and then four more years with the Oakland Raiders, that was my position. I was on the D-line. The job description of a defensive tackle is pretty basic: Knock people out of the way until you find the man with the ball. Keep him.

I played 13 seasons in the National Football League, which sometimes I also referred to as the *No Fun League.* During my career I knocked down so many people that I am one of only six players in pro football history to play in multiple Pro Bowls (seven consecutive games), be honored as the Defensive Player of the Year (1999), and win a Super Bowl (2002). I got known by fans for being a very rough player on the field. Reporters described me as "an every-down demolition man who blew up plays from the inside out" and a "300-pound monster truck with deceptive speed who rode roughshod over double and sometimes triple teams, collapsing pockets, stuffing running backs, and demoralizing quarterbacks." But as my mother would say about that, a *nice* monster truck.

Sometimes I was accused of being too rough. Too rough for the NFL? Really? Okay, if the media and the officials say so it must be true, 'cause now that I am a football analyst on the NFL Network and ESPN I know that we in the media never get it wrong. The truth is that I never cared a bit what other people thought or said about me. I know who I am, I am a descendant of greatness, so I have never feared to do what I believed was right. For example, I had one move on the field that was called "rock bottom," where I grabbed a ball carrier running laterally down the line of scrimmage around his legs, picked him up, carried him a few steps; and then put him down. I mean, I. Put. Him.

Down. *Whomp*! When I did that to Marshall Faulk in a *Monday Night Football* game against the St. Louis Rams one of the broadcasters said, "I think Warren Sapp just spiked Marshall Faulk."

Both on and off the field I earned a reputation for doing things my way. No one ever accused me of holding back. That is the only way I know how to be. I was pleased to offer my opinion to officials, to the league, and to fans, sometimes even before they asked for it. So much so that the *New York Times* wrote that I was "pro football's biggest blabbermouth, known as much for his dominating play as his entertaining trash talk."

I played hard, I played tough. That was my football! But I never played one game with malice or mean intentions. Well, admittedly there were a few plays from time to time when I got riled, but never a whole game. I only knew one way to play and that was all-out, and I played it that way in practice as well as in the game. I actually had to be taught by the great coach Rod Marinelli not to go all-out every play. Football fans either loved me or loved to hate me, but they always knew I was there. For years my no. 99 jersey was among the top-10-selling NFL team jerseys. I was given the honor of being a character on *The Simpsons*, and the year I retired I was invited to be a contestant on *Dancing with the Stars*. I've been a judge on the Miss USA Pageant, I've been "Punk'd," and I've even been slimed on Nickelodeon.

There are people who claim they were born to play football; that wasn't me. My mother always told me I was born because she went to the witch doctor. Apparently my mother had been pregnant a long time, and people were beginning to wonder about it: "Annie still pregnant? That child must be real comfortable in there." There was a lady in the neighborhood who decided my mother had been pregnant too long with me, so she gave her the $5 she needed to go see the witch doctor. This witch doctor, a fortune-teller, told her I was going to be born the next Tuesday. But if she didn't have that baby by Tuesday, then she was to come back and see her again. My mother didn't have five more dollars, so I was born at 4:32 a.m. the next Tuesday morning. One time after I had become a Pro Bowl player in the National Football League a reporter asked our preacher, Deacon McCraroy, what he remembered most about me when I was little. He smiled and said, "What I remember is that he was never little." I weighed 9 pounds 14 ounces when I was born and after that I just kept going.

When I was a kid my brothers used to tell me that I didn't have the same mother as they did. My mother, Annie Roberts, would say the same thing. "Before you were born," she admitted, "I was something else. I was a tough fighter, I was partying and cussing, and off and on I was married. I turned my life around because the Lord let me know if I kept going like I was, I was gonna kill somebody or somebody was gonna kill me, so I'd better see about my spirit.

"What changed me was a visitation from the Lord. I was just lying in bed one morning, and all of a sudden this big light was coming toward me. I threw the cover back and told the Lord I would do whatever he wanted me to do. I turned my life over to the Lord and nothing was ever the same again."

My mother was a church-going, Bible-reading woman who raised me to be prideful and value the proper things in life. Everything I have accomplished I owe to that woman. Everything. That was my world right there. You talk about hard work, I saw that old girl do it all for 36 years. She was an assistant teacher and worked in the cafeteria at the Phyllis Wheatley Elementary School. When she finished there she'd go on over to Quincy's restaurant and work as a waitress and then finish the day at a local nursery where she potted plants. And never complained about it one word. She did it for her children. I watched her and I wanted to emulate her. She taught me to chase knowledge, to treat all people the same, and to be myself. "If a person can't accept you for who you are," she said, "don't go changing to please them. They weren't your friends to begin with."

She had high expectations for me and set strict rules. Trust me, you did not break my mama's rules. Those times I did, if she could catch up to me she'd whup me with whatever she could get her hands on first. If she couldn't catch me, she'd throw something at me. She had a good arm for a mother. By the time I got to high school I was 6'2" and weighed 220 pounds, so that stopped right there. I remember her telling me proudly, "I ain't gonna be hurting myself swinging no bat at you."

My mother was the only person I ever feared. I wasn't afraid she was going to hurt me; I was afraid I was going to let her down. So I listened to her. I used to take a quarter out of her purse and go down to Al's Supermarket to play video games. When you've got only one quarter, you get good at those games. One time I was playing a video game named Kicker, a martial arts game. I was going for a million points, which meant I would flip the game; it would go back to zero, and I got to start all over again. Flipping a game was the ultimate goal. I had never done that before on this game. I was about 6,000 points short when Al told me, "Your Momma's on the phone and she wants you to come home right this minute." Oh my God! This was a choice no kid should ever have to make: Listen to my mother or flip Kicker! None of my friends were with me so I had nobody to pass it to either. Al was looking at me with serious pity. He knew. I will never forget the look on his face as I walked away from that game and out of the store. I was sick, sick. But I had to leave. When Annie Roberts said it was over, it was over. That score did hang up there for a long time, though.

Money was always a little bit short. When handheld video games first came out, oh did I want one. My cousin was getting one for Christmas and he didn't even want it. I knew what I was getting for my birthday-Christmas present: Every poor kid knows there is no Santa Claus, there is no person to send a list to. We all knew that no jolly white guy was coming around our neighborhood at night to drop off presents. Even the pizza delivery guy wouldn't come into my neighborhood at night. Every year I asked my mother for a bike for Christmas—I never got it, but I kept asking for it. But this year I told her, "I don't want a bike, I want a video game."

The very last thing she was going to spend money on was a video game. She thought video games were a waste of time. She said no and then explained her reasoning to me: " 'Cause I said so."

I had to find a way to get that game. I was walking out of the washroom in our house and I looked down and . . . oh my goodness. A $100 bill was just laying there in the corner. I figured all those Sundays I'd spent going to church were finally paying off. I did the figuring; the game was $63. I had $100. They were going to give me back $37. Thank you, Lord, I'll never doubt you again.

I told my mother, "Mama! Look what I found! I found $100!"

That woman snapped that money out of my hand faster than Elastic Man. I'd never seen anybody move that fast. "You don't find money in my house. It's in my house, it's my money."

Don't I even get a finder's fee, I thought. Not in my mama's house. Santa Claus did not bring that video game to me that year. She taught me early that the value of a dollar is 9-to-5. That $63 was either going to buy me a video game or put food on the table. I learned the difference between a need and a want.

I had my moments though. I was an usher in the church choir. Part of our job was to make sure that no one chewed gum in church. One Sunday I was walking down the aisle and I saw my mother chewing gum. I knew I had her. "Give up the gum, Mama," I said. She just looked at me, trying to find a loophole. I gave her a big smile and held out a piece of paper to wrap it in.

My mother was always more concerned about my education than my tackling ability. It never occurred to any of us that playing a game was going to put food on the table. I was a good student, but I was lazy in class. I did what I had to do to get by. One time I got a bad progress report, and I knew that would make her unhappy. The last thing I wanted to do was make my mother unhappy, which is why I hid the report from her. At least that was my story; I only did it for her. I never destroyed a bad report; that would have been wrong. Instead I hid it in my pocket or the back of my notebook, so I could claim that I just forgot to show them to her. Of course, that way she had a fighting chance of stumbling over it.

Which she did one time. I was at football practice when I heard somebody say, "Uh oh, Sapp's mother coming." I looked up and she was coming across the field—fast. Somebody asked, "What'd you do, man?"

The only question was how much trouble I was in. "I'll bet she found my progress report," I said. There was anger in every step she took. She didn't even stop at the coach. She came right up to me, slapped me on the back of my head, and said, "Go."

I started walking. As I walked past our head coach, Coach Gierke, he said softly, "Oh yeah, guy." It was like I was hearing his last words. I walked about another 20 yards and turned around for one final look before meeting my doom. "Turn around," she ordered. "You keep looking forward."

The very worst part of that day was that during the entire drive home she didn't say one word. Not one word. That was awful, worse than being yelled at, because I knew I'd let her down. She was working all those jobs so I could get my education, and I was playing with it.

Of course, when we got home the yelling started. It seemed like the entire world was against me. The next morning I was back in school, and the first thing I heard as I walked in the door were those incredibly embarrassing words, "I heard your mother took you out of practice yesterday . . ."

The fact is that she cared about me like nobody else in the world. My biggest dream was that one day I would be able to provide a place for her to finally sit down and just be comfortable. And maybe have somebody work for her. The proudest day of my life came about three weeks after I signed my first professional contract with the Tampa Bay Buccaneers and drove my mother in her new Mercedes to her new house.

In addition to my mother's rules, as the youngest of six children, I had my three brothers' and two sisters' rules. My brother Parnell felt that I had no discipline, so he was going to help me find it. He was still living at home, so his rent consisted of washing the dishes and taking out the trash. I was the baby, 12 years old, and I didn't have to do anything. Turned out he thought I could find discipline by cleaning the bathroom. First he wanted me to wash the dishes, telling me, "Mama lets you sit around doing whatever you want to. You gotta get some discipline. If you ain't disciplined there is nothing in your life that ever will work. You got to have discipline, discipline, discipline. Now go ahead and start washing all those dishes."

I knew that washing the dishes was his job. I told him, "I'll wash the dishes after I'm 13. I'm not supposed to wash dishes when I'm still 12." That was a rule I made up.

But there was no rule against cleaning the bathroom and the toilet. Every day Parnell would come home after work and tell me, "That bathroom must be cleaned. You need discipline."

"I'm not cleaning the bathroom for you."

"You're not cleaning it for me, you're cleaning it for everybody. You need some discipline." When I complained about it he told me, "You don't have to like it, you just got to do it." I developed my own technique for cleaning an entire bathroom: Always start in the four corners and work inward. At first I didn't clean the base of the toilet; I'd do the top but not underneath. He checked me on that. I cleaned underneath. A few years later when my mother was cleaning houses for the white ladies I'd go and help her. Bathrooms were my specialty, because I had experience. You learn from that when you're growing up; you learn that you have to work hard to get what you need. The way I always say it is, work is a disease, but not everybody can catch it.

After my junior year at the University of Miami I was awarded the Rotary Lombardi Award, which is given annually to the best lineman or linebacker in college football. It's not a particularly attractive trophy; it's a 40-pound piece of granite, mostly it just looks like a fancy rock. But after Vince Lombardi II handed it to me I noticed that on the top of it there was one word engraved: *Discipline*. Just that one word, *discipline*. Whoa. I saw that and it shook me like a bell. Discipline. Of the awards I've won, that trophy is my proudest possession.

I definitely did not have the same father as my brothers, although one of my sisters and I had the same biological father. My biological father's name was Hershey Sapp. I had his name, but he never was any bit a real father. Like many of the people I've played with, and too many of my friends, I grew up in a single-parent home. I used to tell my mother, "Like it or not, you're my daddy and my mama." There were too many times that man was supposed to pick up my sister and me for the weekend, and we just sat there waiting until all the hope was gone from us. When he walked out of the house and left my mother he had agreed to send her like $25 a week in child support for each of us, but he didn't do that either. At most, he was a once-in-a-while shadow that cast darkness over our lives.

I was asked once if I ever missed my father. Miss him? I said the truth, "You can't miss something you never had."

There are some things that people can do to children that are just unforgiveable: My sister's birthday is in early August, and a couple of weeks before then he came to see us. I was 11 years old, and she was about to enter her senior year in high school. The three of us sat at the kitchen table, and he started telling her about the wonderful present he was going to give her for her birthday. My sister's eyes just lit up listening to him. She was dreaming about that present. I remember sitting there thinking, you lying motherfucker. He was selling that lie to my sister and she was totally falling over into it. I was so damn mad. I was only 11 years old, and I knew he was lying, but there was nothing

I could do to soothe my sister's pain that I knew was coming. I had the choice of confronting him at that table or letting my sister have her joy for at least a few weeks. I was 11 years old and I chose to let her be happy. No little kid should have to make that choice. I remember that day so vividly.

What I did have, what so many poor kids have, was sports. Baseball, basketball, throwing railroad rocks at cars, green-orange fights in the groves, and football. I played them all, all the time, but for me all the other sports were just a way of filling time till we got to football. Mostly I played with my brothers and their friends. So no matter what sport we played I was always the youngest. And they had a rule: Carlos—that's what they called me—Carlos never wins. We'd play in the backyard, in the lot across the street, neighborhood against neighborhood, but no matter who we played against or where we played, I was always the youngest. For example, the Williams family had 12 boys. I played with them every day, and every one of them was older than me. They would push me to the limit of my ability because they were at least six or seven years older than me. I was always chasing older people.

When I played against my brothers I used to pray, c'mon Lord, be fair, let me beat them one time. Just one time. Just let me strike them out one time; just let me score more points one time; just let me score a touchdown one time. They would just beat on me until I couldn't take it anymore. Finally I'd go in the house to cry, but I would never let them see me crying. They knew though, "Go ahead, go in the house with Mama and cry like a baby."

"I'm just going to get some water."

Mama would ask, "What'd they do to you?"

I'd tell her, but I wouldn't let her see me cry.

"It's okay," she'd say, "You ain't gonna win 'em all."

"Win 'em all? I ain't won none!" I hadn't won a damn one ever, and nobody but me seemed to mind.

So when I finally had the opportunity to play against kids my own age . . . whoa! How long has this been going on? It was so easy for me it was a joke. I had been playing against people 10 years older than me; how was a kid my own age going to be better than me?

My brothers were all good athletes. In football they were all running backs. I always said that I met my first superstar in my own living room. It was my brother, Arnell Lykes. When he was living with my aunt in little bitty Redwood, Texas, his high school team won the state championship and he was the star running back. He once ran for 348 yards in a game against Bishop Moore. His old high school coach showed me his game films. Oh man, Arnell would be hit four times, five times on a play, and they couldn't hold on to him. He was a beast, a monster. When I was seven years old I can remember watching him step out of a car wearing his state championship jacket, and I thought, it does not get better than this. When he wasn't home I'd take that jacket out of the closet just so I could wear it around the house.

It wasn't a big secret how great Arnell Lykes was. When I used to play in the Dust Bowl with my friends the rule was that soon as you got the ball you had to call out who you were: I'm Drew Pearson. I'm Tony Hill. We were playing one day and my friend caught a pass and screamed, "I'm Arnell Lykes."

"Hold it." I stopped the game. "You can't be him, man. That's my brother. You can't be my brother." But that was who he called. Arnell could have been a great college player. He was recruited by Pitt to take Tony Dorsett's place. They offered him a full scholarship, but he turned it down. The reason was that he was afraid to leave home. That was the country boy mentality.

Nobody ever left Plymouth. Plymouth was the typical small southern town. We had a few hundred people, one restaurant, two stoplights, and not a lot of future. The most famous person who ever lived in Plymouth was Joe Frazier's brother, and Frazier visited there a few times. It was near the bigger town of Apopka, which was known as the "indoor foliage capital of the world," so there was always work for us in the nurseries, and Zellwood, which was famous for its corn festival. Plymouth wasn't known for anything; the biggest business in the town was the muck farm.

The social center of Plymouth was the tree, a big old oak tree out by US 441. It was the only shady place around during the heat, so everybody hung out there. There's where people would meet: "See you down at the tree." And while they were enjoying the shade, maybe they were playing some cards, or throwing some dice, drinking a few beers. The tree was our honky-tonk. So when I was young my mama didn't allow me to hang out there. I could go to the block and stand on the outskirts, but she was clear about it: "I do not want you at the tree. 'Cause I said so!"

But it seemed like eventually everybody who grew up in Plymouth ended up at the tree. You grew up there, maybe you ended up working in a nursery, maybe you moved to Apopka, maybe even all the way to Orlando, but you didn't go far from the tree. That's the way it had always been: We were supposed to do the same things people from Plymouth always did. Going to the same spot, doing the same things over and over again, knowing that our children were going to do it too. The same thing over and over. We weren't supposed to experience anything different.

For most of the people I grew up with it was a black and white world, and we were the black part of it. The first time I visited New York City was before my junior year in college, at the Big East Conference preseason press conference. We went all over the city and finally took the boat out to see the Statue of Liberty. We were standing out there on the deck as the boat approached the island. I was with a white friend, Paul Kerzner, and he looked at it with awe. I did not get real nostalgic about it. My people did not take that route. We took the southern route.

I didn't experience a great amount of overt racism growing up, but we were always aware that there were certain places we were not supposed to go. Growing up in the South you just understand that. It's bred into you by the older people who surround you. It's just not your place. If you don't listen, it can be a hard lesson.

When I was 12 years old I went fishing with a friend on the other side of the lake one afternoon; "their" side of the lake. We were on the way home when one of those huge 4x4s with the light rack on top—we used to call them n----r hunting lights—and the gun rack in back stops right next to us. "Don't you move, n----r boy," he said. Then we heard *click, click.* I knew that sound. We didn't wait. We took off right into the woods and ran through those trees. That was the last time I ever fished on that side of the lake. Fish weren't no bigger on their side. Now, did I really think we were in danger? Probably not, but that wasn't his point. He made his point.

So we knew we didn't go to places like the Plantation House restaurant, down by the Burger King. That was their little spot. We didn't even drive through the Herald Estates, though everybody knew that one black couple lived in there. We went to the tree.

My high school, Apopka High School, was a racially mixed school, and I don't recall ever having any difficulty there. In school it was never about the color of your skin or what you had in your pocket. Especially on the sports fields. My football coach, Chip Gierke, was the closet thing I had to a father figure—and he was white. And I liked to say that he treated me just as badly as he treated everybody else, regardless of color. I learned from my mother: Don't stereotype people. Judge people by their actions, not by the color of their skin. Treat each person as an individual. She never permitted me to allow race to become a factor in my world. When I complained that she spent seven hours cleaning a white woman's house and got paid only $30 she stopped me. "It ain't about that $30. It's about the clothes, the introductions to other people, the extra $5. That woman did so many things for me; it ain't about the $30." I didn't understand it at the time. There are a lot of other people in this world who would benefit from knowing my mother.

About the only rule I got left over from growing up in the Deep South is that I will never walk into a Cracker Barrel restaurant. At that time the dictionary definition of a *cracker* was "any male born in Florida or Georgia." Maybe that really is what it means in polite conversation. In fact, I was told that originally they considered naming the Tampa Bay football team the "Crackers," but we knew it meant something a lot less civil than that, that it described an attitude. So while my mother loves Cracker Barrel restaurants and tells me how nice they are and how good the food is, I just cannot go there. I cannot.

Probably the biggest difference in the races wasn't where we came from, but where we were going. This part of the story is the same in just about every black and low-income community in this country: Too many of my friends got shot, killed, or went to jail. Dead and gone before you were 24 was the rule. There were drugs on the street, we all knew where the crack houses were, and we saw the AIDS epidemic up close. Most of us didn't have the positive role models in our lives; most of us didn't have two parents in our home. The difference for me was sports. My homies knew I had a chance to get out, so when they were doing what they were doing, they wouldn't let me get in their car. I can't tell you how many times I heard that same story from other NFL players. "They wouldn't let me get in the car." They understood that we had a chance for a better future, and they were not going to take it away from us.

I always knew there was something bigger than Apopka out there waiting for me. Something that would sustain me for a long time. I was never satisfied with doing the same thing over and over. I needed something different. The only way out that any of us knew, really, was sports. I knew that was possible because Teddy Booger's—that was Preston Weaver's nickname—older brother went to the Baltimore Orioles. I didn't know exactly how I was going to do it, but I knew I was getting out of there. I didn't know where I was going, but I was leaving, and my mama was going with me. We were getting out of there; we definitely were getting out of there.

My brothers made me an athlete. For example, they taught me how to swim. We were standing on the dock out at Rock Springs, and I was watching everybody dive into the water. I was about six years old, trying to get up the nerve to dive in. My brother walked up behind me and pushed me in. I came up out of that water flapping my arms. "Can you swim?" he yelled.

I was flapping my arms. "I can now."

My mother was furious, screaming at my brother, "You pushed my baby off the pier." I yelled back, "Don't worry about nothin', Mama, I'm swimming. Look at me, I'm swimming." Maybe that was the worst way to learn how to swim, but I didn't have a lot of options.

As I got a little older my brothers let me play with them on the town baseball team. They needed a ninth. But even though I was the youngest player on our team I had the fourth highest batting average. Now being truthful, I also was the best at math, so they let me keep the statistics. "You sure that's right, Carlos? You really hitting .500?"

"Here, look at the book. It's right there in black and white." You write it down, it's there.

One time we played against Rock Raines and his kids in Sanford, Florida. I was playing second base. My brother was playing first. Raines was with the Montreal Expos, a future Hall of Famer, and he hit a shot right past my brother. I dived for it, and the ball hopped right into my glove. I scrambled to my feet and threw him out at first. Oh yeah, oh yeah, that was me. After the game Rock Raines stopped me and said, "That was a great play, son." Oh my goodness. That was the best memory I ever had on a baseball field.

I didn't play in any organized leagues. Pop Warner football for kids was based on weight, so bigger kids like me were excluded. When I was eight I weighed more than most 12-year-olds, and you can't put an eight-year-old against a 12-year-old. At least most eight-year-olds. As far as I was concerned that wouldn't have been fair to the 12-year-olds. I was already playing with much older people. Instead I would play with my brothers and my friends. We would go at it every day, all day long. Plymouth had four neighborhoods, the Quarter, the Blacktop, Across the tracks, and the Hill. We'd play against each other in every sport. You go get your four friends, I got my four friends, and we'll meet you in the park. We'd play in the street or at the Dust Bowl, a dirt lot down the block, until it was too dark to see. It didn't stop till somebody got hit in the eye with a pass, and then that was it, game suspended. But even then it was, "Come on, one more play. I know you can see, you still got one good eye." We'd always play close games too, 77–70, maybe 84–79. Everybody wanted to be on offense. Nobody wanted to play defense.

The very first time I played organized football was in high school. My mother did not want me playing football. She had seen my brothers come home all broken up, and she would have to put them together for the next game. She'd had enough of that; I was her baby and she was going to protect me.

I knew the game of football—there was no rule, no route that I didn't know. I'd learned it from playing it, from watching the Tampa Bay Yucks, as we called them, on television, watching my brothers play, and from reading their playbooks. I practically memorized their high school playbooks, and they would teach me how to catch the ball, how to block and tackle, how to play the game. I absorbed knowledge. I couldn't get enough of it. I wanted to learn everything possible about the game. But if not for Troy Rainey I never would have played.

Troy was my best boy, and at the end of our first day at Apopka High School we were walking toward the door with two girls, and he looked at me and asked, "Where you going?"

"I am getting on the bus, I got to go home."

"You crazy?" he said. "We're gonna play football."

I wish. My mother had specifically told me I could not play football, but suddenly I saw a loophole. It was always much better to ask my mother for permission rather than forgiveness. My mother and Troy's mother Lois were friends. She was like my second mother. I figured maybe if I put Troy into it my mother would let me play. I called her at work and told her Troy needed me to play, "You know, Lois's son."

Maybe I caught her busy, but she didn't think about it. "Oh, okay. Go ahead."

Slam! I slammed down that phone so fast she didn't have time to change her mind. We ran to the gym. That day was the first time in my life I had ever put on football pads.

People were serious about their football at Apopka. The Blue Darters—a darter is a predatory bird, like a chicken hawk, and some of them are blue—had produced several Division I college players and about six NFL draft choices; including the 15th pick of the 1988 draft, the Pittsburgh Steelers' first pick, Aaron Jones. And Sammie Lee Smith, who was the Miami Dolphins' first-round draft pick in 1989, played four seasons in the NFL. High school football in Florida isn't a religion; it's much more serious than that. I've heard it said that the only reason certain people go to church on Sunday is to pray for the local high school on Friday night. In Apopka, when people talk about my playing career, they might mention that I *also* played professional football. But as far as they are concerned, the greatest play of my career was the catch I made against our biggest rival, Evans High School. Sammie Smith's brother, Danny, was our quarterback, and we were down a touchdown late in the fourth quarter. His pass led me too much, and I stretched out full length and caught the ball in the air just before I hit the ground. It led to the tying touchdown. Talk to my people about football and that is the play they will remember.

But that first year when Troy and I reported for the junior varsity it didn't even occur to me that this was the first step to a professional football career. I was just hoping I would get to play on the junior varsity.

Until the day before our first game I was second-string linebacker behind Scott Rutherford. JV games were played on Thursdays, and on Wednesday Coach Lombardi—that was my first coach, Coach

Lombardi, isn't that great?—told me that Scott Rutherford was going up to the varsity and that I was starting. Then he started going crazy on me. "How can they take him away from me right now? What do they expect me to do!" We took football seriously at Apopka, even JV football.

I told him, "Relax Coach, I gotcha."

"You don't understand," he said. "That was my best player."

"I gotcha," I repeated. "Don't worry about it."

On my first play of my life in an official league game Coach Lombardi called a blitz. Gimme the ball! I just roared through the line. The quarterback was rolling to his left and I started chasing him. I don't think he knew I was there, because suddenly he stopped and braced himself to throw the ball. I hit him square in the chest. Cracked his sternum. They had to cart him off the field. The very first play of my career, a sack and a cracked sternum. One play, one quarterback. Maybe this game was a little easier than I thought. Soon as I got to the sidelines I said to Coach Lombardi, "Told you."

He responded, "Well, I guess you are gonna hold it down for me."

I had the natural talent, the size, and the desire. I was raw, but I was bigger and faster than anyone else on the field. I remember Coach Lombardi giving me his best compliment, "Son, you stand out like a turd in a punch bowl!"

That made me proud, a turd in a punch bowl. After I'd played three or four games with the JV they decided to promote me to the varsity, but I told them I didn't want to go. This was the first time in my life I'd played against people my own age and I was loving it.

I made the varsity as a junior. My first game was against our big rival, Lake Brantley. Cablevision had just started showing high school football in Florida, and Apopka vs. Lake Brantley, the poor kids vs. the rich kids, was their "Game of the Week." They were bragging that this was Lake Brantley's best team in 20 years, and supposedly we were going to be a good test for them. They failed. We beat them 55–14. We had so much talent that year that 18 of our 22 starters eventually were offered Division I scholarships, so I only played one way, tight end on offense. My first game I had two receptions for 30 yards and two touchdowns. I beat the future Boston Red Sox player Jason Varitek for both of them. I ran right over him and then stepped on his chest as I was going into the end zone.

I also played against another future baseball star, Johnny Damon. He was a little bitty safety. I caught a pass coming across the middle and this kid was coming at me. Really? You're gonna tackle me? Little guy like you? Get out of my way. He got himself a concussion.

Even with all that talent we finished the season 5–5. My coach liked to change our offense every week. He was constantly experimenting with new plays. The first week we ran the Miami offense that featured three wideouts, one running back, and a tight end, and we scored 55 points, so naturally the next week we lined up in a Power-I and got beat 14–0.

Eventually I ended up playing both ways and even doing the punting. If they had wanted me to sell hot dogs at the concession stand I would have done that too. Anything to do with football is what I wanted to do. We didn't have a punter so I tapped Coach Gierke on the shoulder and asked, "You want me to punt the ball for you?"

He lit me up. "You think you can do everything, don't you? I'm getting a little sick of this."

Even back then no one ever used the words *shy* and *Sapp* in the same sentence. I told him, "Don't worry, I'm gonna save your ass." My first punt ever was against Lake Brantley. We were back in our own territory and I was going to blast us out of there. I took the snap and laid into it. That ball took right off—straight up into the air. Eight yards. My first punt, eight yards. Oh my God. Good thing I was playing both ways that season so I didn't have to go to the sideline. I didn't even look at the sideline. There was nothing good waiting there for me. Eight yards.

But I finished the season with a 43.5-yard punting average, mostly because I had an 80-yard punt against Lake Mary. That's right, 80 yards.

Eight-0 yards. We were backed up on our own 10-yard line, and this time I got into it. It went sailing over the returner's head and took a big bounce. Lake Mary loved their soccer, so their field was hard as rocks. That ball hit and just kept bouncing, bouncing, ending up on their 10-yard line. Of course, I did the natural thing, went right over to our sideline to get a little water. Smiled at the coach, how you doing, Coach. I gotcha.

Even though my mother hadn't wanted me to play, she came to every game. Never missed one. No matter how loud the crowd was, I always could pick out her voice cheering for me. In those days she didn't really understand the game that well. She'd sit in the stands with her hands over her eyes until the friend she came with told her the play was over. Then she'd start screaming at the other team, "Get off my boy, get up off my boy." Many years later Keyshawn Johnson came to play for us in Tampa Bay, and at our first home game, he came over to me and asked, "Who's that lady over there yelling like that?"

I knew. "That's my mother." Two million people in the stadium cheering, and above it all my mother's voice stood out. That woman took her cheering seriously.

I also played basketball at Apopka. I'm not telling no lies here: I could play. I was six feet tall at 14 years old and I could dunk. I mean, *dunk*! *Whoomp*! Two points, Sapp. One time I was arguing with Michael Jordan about playing basketball, and I explained to him, "When I played anything within 15 feet of the basket was mine. You could stand out there all day shooting that raggedy-ass jump shot of yours, but you come inside 15 feet I promise you, you're going down."

Michael thought I was kidding, until the great coach George Raveling heard us arguing and came on over. He told Michael, "I went down to Orlando to see this boy . . ."

"Willy Fisher," I said. You bet I remembered it.

"Willy Fisher," he agreed. "His team was playing Warren's team. And I'll tell you what, Michael, Warren isn't kidding. One on one he was unstoppable." Then he turned around and walked away.

I scored 1,000 points and grabbed 1,000 rebounds in high school. Senior year I even got a basketball scholarship offer—from Mars Hill College, a Baptist school just outside Asheville, North Carolina. I appreciated that offer, but I turned it down. There are not too many 6'2" power forwards in the NBA. And honestly, my version of a blocking foul and every basketball official in the world's version of a blocking foul was probably a little different. Oh, basketball's *not* a contact sport? Really?

My best subjects in school were sports and girls. In addition to all the sports awards I received, I was voted Apopka's "Most Flirtatious Male." It wasn't that I couldn't do my academics, I was just lazy about it. But when something got my attention I was good at it. Chemistry, for example. I loved chemistry. My theory of chemistry was simple: Get the periodic chart and let's mix stuff up. For example, I will never forget the day our chemistry teacher taught us how to make an exploding sulfur ball. He made a sulfur ball, took the whole class out to the lake in front of the school, and tossed it in the water. Big deal. The ball sank a few feet and then . . . *poom*! Few seconds later a fish comes floating up to the surface. *That's* chemistry? Oh my God! I glanced at my friend Maurice, our eyes met, and together we saw the future. Sulfur ball fishing!

That teacher actually taught a class of teenage boys how to make fish-killing sulfur balls. You had to believe that man had supreme confidence that we all really liked him. But like I said, when something in school got my attention, I was good at it. I played in the band too. When I started they looked at me and said, "You're a drummer." I guess they figured I liked to hit things. When I told them I didn't want to play the drums they gave me a trumpet, a baritone, and then a trombone. Blow, Warren, blow! I played them all, trumpet, trombone, tuba—everything except the French horn, I did not do French horn—under the direction of band coach Warren C. Barrett. Made second seat in the band, although because I was growing bigger it actually was second and third seat.

My real difficulty in school came from the fact that the work the teachers wanted me to do and what I wanted to do were not necessarily the same. I loved reading, for example. My senior year I read 52 books, but probably not one of them was a book the teachers required me to read. What I like to refer to as "my independent studies" caused a real problem for me about college.

When my brother Parnell was being recruited for college we kept a bucket by the front door, and it got filled up with letters from the top football schools in the country. Michigan, Notre Dame, Pittsburgh, Florida, Alabama, they were all writing to my brother. I'd pick those letters up and run my finger over the embossed logo on the envelope. I couldn't believe the same teams I was watching on television every Saturday wanted my brother to come play for them.

After an athlete becomes a successful professional player, people sort of assume he was always a star—Warren Sapp was so strong that five minutes after he was born he sacked the doctor. Warren Sapp was the greatest defensive tackle in the history of second grade. But that wasn't me. Until my junior year I wasn't exactly on the big-time college radar. It was more like I was under the table the radar was sitting on. But suddenly I started getting those letters my brother had gotten: "We're watching you, and we've got the greatest football program in the whole history of college football. We'd be doing a great favor allowing you to come play for us . . ." By the time that season ended I had my own bucket sitting by the door. I could have pretty much gotten a scholarship from any major program in the country.

At the beginning of my senior year I was ranked the number one tight end in Florida high school football. What none of those people doing that ranking knew was that it didn't look like I was going to be playing football that year. I had quit the team at the end of my junior year. I have had a lot of highlights in my football career, but you never forget the low moments. It's overcoming those rocks that gets you to the top of the mountain. After you become an All-Pro, win a Super Bowl, receive a lot of honors, most people would assume those high school football games lose a little bit of meaning. That isn't true at all for me. I still bleed blue and white. I am a Blue Darter for life. The fact is that those lessons I learned about life while playing football at Apopka are what made me an All-Pro.

In the last game of my junior year our star running back, Roscoe Griffin, needed 350 yards to win the state rushing title. Coach Gierke really wanted him to win that title. Our game strategy was to hand off to Roscoe and block for him. Every play. Every damn play. Hand off to Roscoe. Roscoe runs left. Roscoe runs right. Roscoe runs up the middle. The other team finally figured our strategy. They lined up 19 guys to stop him. At the end of the first half he'd only gained 150 yards. I told Coach Gierke that the only possible way Roscoe's gonna get those 200 more yards he needed was for us to open up this game. We needed to start throwing the football so they couldn't key on him every damn play. Throw it a little, loosen it up, then get Roscoe running again. Coach told me directly, "Shut up."

Shut up? Really?

Really. Coach Gierke was stubborn. Apparently Roscoe was going to keep running the ball till the cows came home and tackled him. No thank you. In the third quarter I told Coach, "You don't throw the ball this next series, you're gonna play the rest of the game with someone else at tight end." Roscoe, Roscoe, Roscoe, punt.

That's it. I walked off that damn field, threw my pads down, and told my mom, "C'mon, we're going home." I walked out of that stadium listening to the cheers fading behind me. I don't know that anybody even realized I was missing. It hurt. It was not my proudest moment as an athlete, but I had to stand up for what I believed was right. There probably was a better way to make that point, but I was 16 years old, and I allowed my pride to get out in front. Right or wrong, it was stupid for me to take that stance.

As some football fans may be aware, this was not the only time in my career that this happened.

Just the first and memorably painful time. I figured that was the end of my football career, except for playing in the Dust Bowl across the street. Instead I focused on basketball, and Mars Hill College started looking mighty good.

The first day of football practice of my senior year I was getting ready to go home. Coach Will Carleton saw me leaving with my girl-friend and stopped us. He told her to go on home and told me to go to football practice. I asked, "Are you gonna take me back on the team?"

"We are, but you need to apologize to the man. Maybe he's wrong, but you can't do what you did. You got to learn how to be a soldier in the army and listen to orders, even if you don't like them."

I walked into Coach Gierke's office with an apology in my mouth, but it never got out. He looked up at me and asked, "You ready?"

"Coach . . ." I started.

"No, I just want to know if you're ready. I'm going to ask you to lead my team. You think you know football, well, I'm putting in a whole new offense, and I need somebody to take charge on the field. I'm gonna ask a lot of you because I think you can handle it. Can you do that?"

"Coach, I . . ."

"Good. Go get ready." He slapped me on the shoulder. On the way out I passed Coach Carleton. Told him, "I didn't even get a chance to say I'm sorry."

"I know. That's his way of letting you know he had some wrong too."

I had a monster senior season. Not only was I playing against kids my own age, a lot of them were even younger than me. Are you kidding me? It was like taking a football from a baby. First game, again versus Lake Brantley, on offense I had three catches for 108 yards and a touchdown. On defense I had 10 tackles, an interception, and a forced fumble. And I punted. The next morning the newspaper called it . . . the *Sapp Attack*!

After our next game the local newspaper, the *Apopka Chief*, described me as "a one-man doomsday machine who played tight end on offense, outside linebacker on defense and also handled the punting while catching a 67-yard touchdown pass and a two-point conversion. In between he intercepted a pass, knocked down two others, forced two fumbles and tackled anything near the ball."

That bucket of scholarship offers was overflowing.

Among the first letters I received was one from the University of Michigan. My English teacher, first period, Miss Katzenberger, was a big Michigan pusher, and I think she wrote to them about me. They sent me the standard letter: We're watching you, we'll stay in contact, maybe we'll even invite you for a visit. Good luck, have a great season. Oh my God! Coach Bo Schembechler writing directly to me! The Big Blue! Playing in the Big House with 100,000 people cheering and everybody in the country watching on TV. I touched that big *M* on the envelope and felt a jolt of electricity shooting through me. I went directly to my guidance counselor to figure out what I had to do to go there. Sapp, Michigan; Michigan, Sapp. It even rhymed.

Well, least in my mind it rhymed.

Then I heard from the University of Maryland. The Terrapins. Loved that little turtle on the envelope. The letters kept coming. One of my high school coaches had accepted a job at Mississippi State and he was recruiting me. Eventually I heard from all the Florida schools, the whole Southeastern Conference, most of the Big Ten—our poor mailman was a little more bent over each week. This was maybe the biggest decision I'd ever had to make in my life. For a young man from a little bitty town I had a very sophisticated way of judging these schools. I eliminated the University of Notre Dame, for example, because they didn't put player names on the back of their jerseys. When I caught a pass how was anybody gonna know it was me? The weather was also an important factor. The only cold I liked came out of that air conditioner when the pastor came for dinner. I had never even seen snow. My man Brad Culpepper, who would be my teammate at Tampa Bay, was another Florida boy who considered going to Notre Dame. He was all set to accept their scholarship offer when he went for his official visit in February. Coach Lou Holtz guaranteed him a national championship if he went there. But it was freezing cold, it was snowing, and the girls were . . . less than attractive. The next weekend he visited the University of Florida. The sun was shining and the girls were beautiful. "I promise you," he told me once, "I had two reasons for going to Florida. The girls there were twice as pretty as anyplace else."

Culpepper and I were both very fortunate to have been born in the great state of Football. I read all the letters I got, I imagined what it would be like playing in those great stadiums around the country, but the truth is when you're already living in the best place in the world to play football, there wasn't no need to go anyplace else. With the University of Florida, Florida State, and Miami all playing in that beautiful Florida weather, I was already living in tight end heaven.

I grew up a Florida State fan, loved those Seminoles, but Miami coach Dennis Erickson had been one of the first people to try to recruit me. Coach Erickson liked to take quick high school tight ends and linebackers and turn them into college defensive ends and tackles. Quickness is different than straight-out speed, quickness is moving laterally, getting out of your stance, attacking. I was quick, I have always been quick. Quicker than most everybody else. Here's an example of how quick I am: I'm already in the middle of the next page and you're still reading this paragraph. That's how quick I am.

Coach Gierke had a relationship with an offensive coach at Miami, Greg Smith, who had originally asked him about me, "He's an athlete, idn't he?"

And Coach told him, "Greg, you ain't kidding."

C'mon, what did I know about choosing a college? Everything I knew about college came from football magazines and TV commentators. I wasn't thinking about eventually playing professional football; I didn't think that was possible. My dream was playing college football on TV. Most high school athletes have absolutely no understanding about the recruiting process. For the universities football is a total business. It's all about the Jeffersons: Winning games, filling the stadium, TV revenue, and invitations to a New Year's bowl game. Meanwhile the young player is running his finger over the embossed logo on the envelope and dreaming about the glory. The universities recruit hundreds of kids every single year; meanwhile that kid gets one shot at making the right choice. Who's gonna get the best deal?

I wasn't just making this decision for myself. I was carrying Plymouth with me. That's the way it is when you come from a small town. People would sit there under the tree debating the best place for me to go to college.

I made my permitted three recruiting visits. I've heard all the stories about the way recruits are treated on their visits. Money, girls, promises; I'm still waiting. Maybe it's true, but that wasn't my experience. The only so-called illegal offers I got were invitations to bring my mother or my girlfriend with me on my sanctioned visits. Nobody put one of those balls of cash I've heard about in my pocket. Culpepper was one of the most highly recruited players in the country in 1987, and no matter what people like to believe, his experience was similar to mine. In addition to the pretty girls, he told me once, "I went to Florida for all the right reasons—to get paid! And they never paid me a cent."

I saw snow for the first time in my life at Michigan State. The ground was covered with it when I landed. I'd never seen anything so white. I got off the plane and told the coach, "I don't have a coat." They put me in a Michigan State jacket, gloves, a skully, and I was good. Good? There is no greater red carpet than the one a university lays down for a blue-chip prospect. By the time I left, the way they treated me I was convinced I was king. And as I got back on that airplane they made me give back the jacket, gloves, and skully.

The University of Florida was the next visit. My mother and my girlfriend drove up there with me. Coach Steve Spurrier picked me up at the Big Lake, which is where everybody gets together in the evening, and asked my mother if he could take me to his office. Me and my new best friend Coach Spurrier went to his office, and he put on tape of Kirk Kirkpatrick, the tight end who caught 66 balls his senior year. That's me, I thought. There I am right there on that tape. The door opened and someone walked in, but I couldn't see who it was. It was the quarterback, Shane Matthews, just happened to be stopping by. He said, "Son, you come to Florida and I'll throw you six balls a game. Guaranteed. You might have to make a play on one of them, it might be behind you, but the rest of them'll be right where you want it."

I looked at Spurrier and said, "Where do I sign?"

"You're sure?"

"Your quarterback promises me he's throwing me the ball, you told me I'm gonna play. I'm going to be a Gator."

We went to get my mother and went back to the office. Coach Spurrier wanted us to meet his tight end coach, Dan Reeves. My mother was standing at the end of the hallway. Coach Reeves came out of his office and said, "Hi M'am."

My mother stepped in front of me and said, "No." That was it. They handed us a check for gas and we left. No explanation, nothing, just "No," and we left. I didn't bother to ask why. Long time later she explained, "I just didn't like the atmosphere. Walk in the door, there was this big ole' stuffed Gator sitting there. Looked liked it was smiling. I can't explain my feelings, but it was not a place I thought was comfortable."

I wasn't going to be a Gator.

Florida State was my first choice mostly because my girl was going to Florida A&M, an historical black college that was right down the street, to be a pharmacist, and because it was Florida State. This was my team growing up. I met Coach Bobby Bowden in his office, and he told me he had two tight ends on the team: "Lonnie Johnson can't catch a cold butt naked in Alaska and Warren Hartz's a fat ass. Son, you come to Florida State and you got my word on it, you'll play as a freshman. You'll have to fight for the job, but I just told you about the competition."

I sat there thinking, two years from now when I'm a sophomore and some hot-ass recruit is sitting in this chair you gonna call me a fat ass like you just did to those two players? I wouldn't play for you to save my mother's life. I said, "Thank you very much, I'll think about it and let you know."

When Coach Gierke called me to ask me about my visit I told him that Coach Bowden sat there and cussed out his own players. "I never heard you talk that way about none of us." I told him the whole story. Finally Coach Gierke got me to agree that if Coach Bowden came to visit my mother I would reconsider Florida State.

Instead of coming to my house, Bobby Bowden met my mother at her job at the elementary school. Coach Gierke told me, "You won't believe this, but this guy thinks you live in the hood, and he was worried about somebody coming by for a drive-by shooting. I told him he was crazy."

Wasn't going to be a Seminole either.

I hadn't seriously considered Miami because it was in Miami. My mother used to watch *Miami Vice* so she knew that Miami was too big and dangerous. If Miami had been someplace else, going there wouldn't have been a problem. But still we went up there to visit the campus. Practically the first person my mother met was Dr. Anna Price, who explained that she would be my academic advisor. She told my mother her job was to make sure I went to class and got an education. Then she explained that the University of Miami actually wasn't in Miami.

Not *Miami Vice* Miami. The campus was in Coral Gables, she said. "Your son doesn't have a car, and you know we don't do public transportation very well down here. He isn't going anywhere."

My mother gave her our phone number.

Coach Erickson was completely honest with me. The first thing he told me was that I wasn't going to play my freshman year. Had to be the greatest salesman ever: Recruiting me by telling me that if I went to Miami I wasn't going to play my freshman year. "We've got five tight ends already," he said. "We'll probably redshirt you your first year, but that'll give you a chance to get acclimated to college life."

He sold me. I was thinking, little country boy like me, I'd have a whole year to get my schoolwork down, get the campus down, get the girls . . . get the campus down without the weekly pressure of big-time college football. And I was a raw talent; I knew there was no way I was ready to play right away at the University of Miami.

I was going to be a Hurricane.

There was only one thing standing between me and the University of Miami: Geometry. I was strong in every part of math—except geometry. I couldn't write a proof. I knew it, I could say it, but I couldn't write it. You start talking geometry, I'm a dead man. You can't block a postulate. I flunked geometry twice and finally made a D in summer school. My senior year I needed a B in Algebra II to get my scholarship. Algebra was easy for me; know the formula and plug in the numbers. I had an A right up till the end, when Algebra II suddenly turned into . . . geometry. I struggled. Finally I went to see Miss Perry and told her, "You know I'm more than competent in math, but I just can't write a proof. I don't know why, but I can't do it."

"Young man," she said, "I've watched you sitting there with smoke coming out of your ears trying to write a proof. I know how hard you worked. Don't worry, you are going to college."

Under the tree that was big news.

TWO

The University of Miami was one of America's greatest institutions of higher football. Trust me on this, there was no better place to go to school and play big-time college football than Miami. I always said that if they could have figured out a way to pay my rent and utilities and give me a little spending money, I would still be there. That'd be me, Sapp the Super Senior.

There is a tradition at Miami that represents how we played the game. Every week, the last thing that happened before we went out onto the field was that the coaches would leave the locker room to the players. They would run out of there and close the door behind them. Slam! Players only. Then one of us would stand up in front of the room, my last year it was me, and say, "We came here to do three motherfucking things!" The team would respond, "Hit! Stick! And bust dick!" And then the leader would shout, "What else?"

The answer to that was pure Hurricane: "Talk shit."

And we did. Oh, we definitely did. That was our reputation. We hit hard, we stuck tackles, and busted dick—and talked big-time shit.

There were no other college football program in the country that were as tough as the Miami Hurricanes. Every practice, every day, was a battle. Our center, K. C. Jones, played five years in the NFL and he remembers listening as his teammates would brag about their toughest days at their college, and he'd think, "That's all you got? That was a Tuesday afternoon at Miami."

It was an unbelievably demanding, competitive, intimidating situation. There were no days off. We were tested every day, and we were playing against the toughest players in college. If we went a few days without a fight in practice we began to wonder if we were losing our edge. We didn't just trash talk, we made death threats. K.C. likes to tell people that on his very first day of practice of his freshman year he was doing one-on-one drills against Mark Ceasar, who was a senior that year. "This was my first day," K.C. says. "My first day. I had no idea what to expect. I thought I would have a little time to get used to the culture. But I ended up locking up with him and I put him on a knee. He didn't like that so he got up and shoved me. A half hour into my first practice and I was being tested. I shoved him back. Next thing I know I'm in the middle of a melee between the offensive line and the defensive line. People were going toe to toe, it was like being in an Old West bar fight. I looked around at what was going on and I thought, what have I gotten into here? They had to separate the offense and defense for the rest of the practice.

"After practice defensive tackle Pat Riley, who was 6'6", 300 pounds shredded, called me over to his locker and asked, 'You going to lunch, Rook?' I said that I was and he smiled and said in a very matter-of-fact voice, 'Good, I'm going to stab you at lunch.' Then he went back to taking off his cleats. The thing that I remember most is that at that moment I believed it was possible. But I knew I had no choice; if I didn't go to lunch I could pack my bags and leave. I'd played high school football in Midland, Texas. I thought we were Texas tough, but in one practice I learned I had stepped into a whole new culture. My parents had asked me to call home after my first practice to tell them how it went. I decided that I'd better not. I figured if I told them that the practice had turned into a brawl and then another player had threatened to stab me they'd be concerned. The culture at Miami was amazing, and being part of it, with all the tradition of excellence, was so much bigger than any individual. By the end of that day I had surrendered to it completely."

As my future Hall-of-Famer close friend Ray Lewis explains it, "Every day at practice was going to be a battle and we all knew it. We weren't just coming to practice to get some practice, we were coming to make whoever was on the other side of the ball better and at the same time making ourselves more dominant. That was the goal and if we pissed each other off, so be it. And if we went into the locker room and somebody wanted to fight, okay, buckle up, move the furniture out of the way, let's go and then let's move on. It didn't carry over, we had another practice the next day.

"No disrespect to any other college program, but what I was introduced to was a brotherhood that taught you how to be a man. That taught you how to go out everyday and put yourself on the line for what you believe in. We would sit there surrounded by all this greatness and we knew, we knew absolutely that we would be able to play on the next level, because we were preparing for it every day."

That's the way it was at Miami. There was no backing down to anybody at any time for any reason. There was no difference between our practices and our games. Long before Dwayne Johnson became "the Rock" he was a D-lineman at Miami, playing behind me. One time we got into a brawl with San Diego State and he tried to pull this other guy's tongue out of his mouth. When the reporters asked him why he did that, he explained, "Well, I couldn't really pull his lips off.

"I was choking him and my hands went from his neck to his mouth. That's when I learned that the human tongue is somewhat slippery. Especially when it's still in the mouth." He didn't stop there either; eventually he chased their mascot, the Aztec, right up into the stands.

And he was considered one of the sane guys on the squad.

Rohan Marley, Bob Marley's son, was a 5' 8", 200-pound linebacker. Rat-boy, we called him, and pound for pound nobody hit harder. In a game against Boston College he hit a running back named Darnell Campbell so hard that Campbell's helmet went flying straight up 10 feet in the air. Rohan didn't back down to anybody. The first play of our 1992 game against West Virginia he got into it with their 6', 270-pound center, and punched him in the face mask. That player turned around and walked away. Rohan Marley had the U attitude we all shared: "The best feeling in the world is when you hit someone so hard that you get a jarring headache."

That was the thing, we had the talent to back up every brag. That was the tradition I walked into. Coach Dennis Erickson had won the national championship in 1989 and 1991 and was in the conversation every other year. I didn't know what position I was going to play when I got there. The coaches told me I could play either linebacker or tight end. Some choice: They already had six tight ends on the roster—and the offense didn't even feature tight ends. We ran three wide receivers. The linebackers I was looking at were Micheal Barrow, who was an All-American and played 13 years in the NFL, Jessie Armstead, who played 11 pro seasons, and Darrin Smith, who was the 1991 Big East Co-Defensive Player of the Year and played 12 NFL seasons.

When Jessie Armstead tore his ACL I figured I'd better go after his position. Later we became good friends and I told him, "I was coming for your job that year you blew your knee out."

And he pointed out, "Maybe, but you ate your way off my position."

That was the most amazing thing. That summer after I graduated from Apopka I put myself on a serious diet. I weighed about 232 when I left high school. I knew I needed to lose some weight to play linebacker so I dedicated myself to slimming down. From June to August I starved myself—I never ate more than 3,000 calories a day. I was real careful about it. I woke up in the morning and ate a little salad, jelly on wheat toast, and a hard-boiled egg. At lunch I had a salad with an egg and five olives. For dinner, two veggie burger patties without bread. Oh, my whole body was mad at me.

And I worked out hard every day. I have always been a hard worker, but that summer I really pushed myself. I sweated in that Florida sunshine, just imagining that weight melting off my body. I intended to show up on campus slim and trim and ready to play linebacker.

When I got to Miami I got on the scale—I weighed 267 pounds. I gained 35 pounds eating 3,000 calories a day! That can't happen. That had to be the worst diet in history. It was like Weight Watchers—I was watching my weight get bigger and bigger. I had outgrown my mirror. I still can't figure out how that happened. But it forced me to rethink my plan. At that time there weren't a lot of 270-pound tight ends. The coaches looked at me and asked, okay son, now what are you intending to do here?

I was worried about keeping my scholarship. The only thing I could do was go over where the defensive line was practicing. D-line coach Bob Karmelowicz asked me to play with his people, but he only allowed me to pass rush. I had no idea what I was doing, no technique at all, no strategy, it was just sandlot football—gimme my ball. I was grabbing and pushing, but nobody could stop me from getting into the backfield. I ran inside, outside—they couldn't stop me. And for me, it didn't feel bad. I fit right in. Those people on Karmelowicz's D-line were crazy. If he told them to move the Great Wall of China they would've asked, how far? I liked that—on the football field I did crazy.

When we finished the scrimmage we started doing drills. If you ain't done drills at the U, you ain't done drills. You had to be able to run 110 yards in 16 seconds, and after you crossed the finish line you had to turn around, stand on that line, and show no signs of discomfort. No bending over, no hands on your hips, no sucking wind. No signs of discomfort. Just standing there rocking and ready. Inside you could be dying, but outside, no signs of discomfort. The idea was that when the offense breaks out of the huddle in the fourth quarter with the game on the line, they see the D-line standing there ready to play. Ball is ready, I am ready. No signs of discomfort.

At the end of that first day Coach Karmelowicz was punishing the D-line. We were eating dirt when he tapped me on the shoulder and said nicely, "Son, you're not one of us yet so you don't have to do any of this. When you decide you want to be one of us, then you can do this. But for right now why don't you go stand over there and watch."

I couldn't eat dirt with the D-line? First time in my life anybody made suffering seem desirable. What a motivator, oh my God: You want to be one of the big dogs around here, you want to eat rats and howl at the moon, you let me know. But right now you're nothing but a stray dog, so go stand over there in the corner.

As we were walking off the field after practice I caught up with Coach Karmelowicz. I asked him, "Coach, you really think I got the knack to do this?"

He said, "Son, these eyes don't see nothin' but right tackles and *you* are a fucking right tackle." I was thinking about that when he asked me, "Let me ask you this, how many 300-pound tight ends you know?"

I said, "Eric Green."

Shook his head with sadness. "Digging his own grave with a fork," he said. "Every time that fat ass sits down at the table he is digging his own grave." Then he asked me, "And you know how many million dollar defensive tackles I've made?"

"Well, I know how many you've coached; I don't know about made." Coach Erickson's defense keyed on the tackles. Everything good started down there in the trenches. I did know that Miami's last three defensive tackles, Russell Maryland, Jerome Brown, and Cortez Kennedy, were absolute beasts. Monsters. All of them had become stars in the NFL. It was hard for me to see myself on their level.

"Right tackles are born," he continued. "You can't make 'em. You get real lucky to come across one. I think I just found one, but hey, who knows." He turned away from me and then stopped, "You wanna come join us, you let me know." Only Coach Bob could get you angry by being so nice.

This was my redshirt year, which meant I could practice with the team but not play in games, and the year didn't count against my eligibility. It also meant I had a little time to make a decision. Finally I told Coach Bob that I would play on his D-line, just not that year. "I came here as a tight end," I said. "And that's what I'm going to do." I wanted to showcase what I could do.

I went back to my boys on the scout team, the group that runs the next opponent's plays in practice, to play tight end. But I also put in some time practicing against the first-team D-line, playing tight end, running back, whatever they needed. And I was eating them up and spitting them out. This was the number one ranked defense in the entire country, and I was driving them crazy in practice. I used to tell them, "Watch out for me, I'm going to dump on you the next reps just for the hell of it," and when they knocked me down. I'd get up and ask, "That's it? That's all you got?"

Our job was to service their needs. But that didn't mean we had to play pussy football. One afternoon I got yanked around the neck by defensive tackle Anthony Hamlet. I warned him, "When you tackle me I don't give a damn how hard you hit me, just don't put your hands around my neck." Then he did it again. I turned and fired on his ass. We brawled. The team brawled. We had piles on top of the pile. This was a team that took no shit from anybody—including ourselves. I got in more battles with my own teammates than I ever did against opponents.

If you're going to be a man you have to draw a line. One Thursday afternoon we were running through our plays and tight end Dietrich Clausell came across the middle of the field. Okay, I set up to block him, which evidently he did not appreciate. He took the fight to me. The man challenged me. Really? You sure? I had drawn my line and he had crossed over it. I had to let him know I was there. I turned and grabbed his ass, dropped him on the ground, lifted his helmet, and *pop! Pop! Pop!* Then I caught myself and stopped. He got up fast and angry. I told him, "Make your decision now. You want some more or you want to stop?" He stopped.

I picked up my own helmet and went on over to the sideline. As I was jogging over there I started thinking, we're the number one team in the country, fighting for the national championship, and I'm punching out my own teammate? Suddenly that didn't seem like such a great idea. Coach Erickson was waiting for me when I got there. Uh oh, I thought, here it comes. But instead of screaming at me he had a big smile on his face, and all he said was, "I saw what you did. Nice one-two, but never on Thursday."

"I got you, Coach," I said. "My bad."

Coach Erickson encouraged that competitiveness. He had us so tuned up that we were like rabid dogs, and all he had to do was throw the meat into the middle and we'd go at each other. I mean, you'd look over at him on the sidelines and he'd be foaming at the mouth just like we were.

The hardest part of redshirting is not being able to play in the games. We had the option of watching the game from the stands or in uniform on the field. The first week we played Houston and I decided to sit in the stands. Oh yeah, nice and comfortable. Where's that hot dog guy? A group of cute girls were sitting right near me and I thought, this is definitely going to be nice; football, females, and food. The jackpot. Then they looked down on the field and started cheering for Rohan Marley. Hey, wait a second now. As I figured out, in the stands I was just a regular guy; but on the field I was a member of the Miami Hurricanes football team. Where's my uniform? Every home game after that I put on my jersey and got on the field. I am proud to say that when we won that national championship that season I was standing right there on the sideline waving my jersey!

I didn't get to play in any games, but I did get to practice every day against the best college football team in America. The coaches would just throw you out there to see if you could play. You do that and you're either going to get better or get gone. I got better. So when I came back for the next season I was a 300-pound defensive tackle. That move had major consequences. Changed my life and turned Dwayne Johnson into a movie star. I walked into my first meeting of the D-line and he asked me, "What are you doing here?"

I told him, "You go sit on the sidelines. I'm here to kick some ass."

He had real talent, but he got hurt. As he once told a reporter, "It's surprising how things work out. I'm making movies because of the grace of God. God put Warren Sapp, no. 99 in your program and no. 1 in your heart, in front of me. That's when I knew I wasn't going to be a pro football player and started looking for another career."

Unfortunately Coach Bob Karmelowicz had left Miami to become the Cincinnati Bengals' defensive line coach. So Coach Erickson put me on the line, pointed at the quarterback, and told me, "Go get him." That was about the full extent of the training I got. I think most people just assume that in a big-time program like Miami there is a tremendous amount of detailed instruction. That would be wrong. Basically, it came down to: You're now a tackle. Go tackle somebody.

I didn't know how to play the position. I didn't know about the double team, slip, rock, scoop. I didn't know about gaps, grabbing, holding—I didn't know nothing! I didn't know how to read plays, I didn't know how to study tendencies, about intimidation—I was more raw than sushi.

I developed my own technique, which I called the Walter Peoples Special. Walter Peoples was one of the Tuskegee Airmen, the black fighter pilots unit formed during World War II. Walter Peoples just made it up as he went along; he did what he had to do to survive. That's what I had to do, give 'em the old Walter Peoples Special. I relied on my size, speed, strength, and instinct. Mark Caesar, who was playing in front of me, taught me the basics of the position, using my hands, eyes, hips, and footwork.

Our linebackers coach, Randy Shannon, helped me learn how to think on the football field. Very few fans really understand or appreciate what actually takes place on the field between plays. That's the game within the game. There is so much that goes on every minute that can help you gain an advantage if you pay attention to it. Football is a physical game that's about 85 percent mental—although it helps if your brain is inside a 6'2", 300-pound body. Shannon was smart. I'd go to see him and ask, "Okay, what have you got for me this week?" He'd close the door and we would sit there for hours looking at films and analyzing our next opponent. He taught me how to look for keys: "Look at that running back," he'd tell me. "Look at what he's doing. If he sets up with his hands on his thighs he's getting ready to block so you know they're throwing the ball, but if he's got his hands on his knees he's getting ready to move forward so it's a run." I learned that by looking at a lineman's feet I was sometimes able to determine what direction he was going, or by looking at the amount of pressure he was putting on his fingers I could tell whether he was run blocking or pass protecting. I learned how to interpret the code words the offensive line was throwing around. I even learned how to read a quarterback's lips.

So I did have some instruction. But mostly I learned by trial and error.

The other advantage I had was my long arms. I am long in all the right places. One time I was with Michael Jordan, who is five inches taller than me, but when we reach straight up my palms are just about even with his. Those long arms enabled me to reach out and control an offensive lineman before he could establish his strong defensive base. A defensive lineman has the major advantage of moving forward, attacking, so he can generate momentum, while an offensive lineman is often moving backward to establish a blocking position. The coaches used to tell us that in some ways it's like dancing. Fred Astaire's famous dancing partner in the old movies, Ginger Rogers, used to tell people that she had to do everything that Astaire did—except she had to do it backward and in high heels. Believe me, I could have knocked Ginger on her ass. My speed and arm length, my quickness, allowed me to grab hold of the defensive player before he could get ready and move him in whatever direction I wanted him to go. The fact is that playing D-line came easily to me. I always thought of myself as a safety stuck in a 300-pound body. The good Lord gave me natural ability, and my mother and my coaches taught me how to develop it and use it.

What they did teach at the U was a work ethic. When I was in the NFL I often used to remind myself that on every play I was only six seconds away from the end of my career. One play, one injury, and my career was done. At Miami they told us we were six seconds from being down on the bench, six seconds away from your scholarship being gone, six seconds from being back home under the tree. I can still hear the coaches yelling at Pat Riley, who was on the D-line, that he was six seconds away from shoveling shrimp back in Marreo, Louisiana.

Every morning we were supposed to look at film taken in practice. During one meeting D-Line coach Ed Orgeron asked the team who hadn't watched the film of the previous day's practice. One player actually raised his hand. Afterward I pulled him aside and asked, "What are you doing? You were there, remember? You know what you did in practice, you don't need to watch the film." Now, I didn't watch the film—but I definitely didn't raise my hand either. Once his hand went up he was done. It was like watching Col. Sanders asking a chicken coop for volunteers. When Coach Erickson heard about this he asked him why he hadn't watched the film. The player made the mistake of saying, "I had class."

"What time did that class start?" Coach Erickson asked.

"Ten o'clock." *In the morning?* Well, that left a lot of hours in the morning before class started. Coach nodded pleasantly, "Okay, I understand." One thing absolutely guaranteed: When Coach Erickson said he understood in a pleasant tone, he didn't understand at all. He continued, still in a pleasant voice, "Now, of course we wouldn't want you out of bed before nine o'clock, would we? I mean, you need to get your sleep. Believe me, I understand that." He looked at his coaching staff and they all agreed with him, but finally he added, "But there is just one thing I want to point out to you." I could hear this one coming. "Did you know that in Melbourne, Florida, the fucking garbage truck starts running at 4:30!"

At the U they let everyone know that the day you didn't want to do your work there was somebody waiting right behind you to take your place. I learned that playing behind Mark Caesar in 1992. Mark was 6'2", 340 pounds, and he was from the rough part of Newark, New Jersey. Right tackle was his position; he didn't just play it, on that team he owned it. And he wanted me to play. At times his ass would get tired, and as soon as he trusted me to replace him without too much of a drop-off, he would let me come in. There are players on every team who earn the right to decide when they are going take a break. The coaches know that they care enough about the team to make that decision. They're not going to come out of the game if it might affect the outcome. No matter how much Mark liked me, he wasn't going to let me sub for him if it was going to hurt the team.

Mark knew I could play. He knew it before I did. He told me once, "You're going to be way better than the others. Trust me. I know what I'm looking at."

Maybe it wasn't as big as the Lord telling his first begotten son, "I got a big job for you, and I know you can handle it," but it definitely felt good. I wanted to believe him. I worked hard learning my craft. I felt I had to prove to the coaching staff that I was worthy of the spot they had given me backing up a player like Mark Caesar, and I had to prove to him that I was worthy of his praise. The way I looked at it, I could work my hardest for a few hours every day or I could clean toilets for the rest of my life.

Mark looked out for me both on and off the field. He wanted me to know more and be more. He had joined the Black Muslim nation and took me with him one day to meet them. Mark exposed me to a culture

I hadn't seen before. It didn't fit me, but it expanded my knowledge of the world. My mother's rule was to try to learn at least one thing every day. It didn't matter what it was, the tallest mountain in Sweden or Pam Grier's greatest films, so long as you went to bed at night just a little bit more informed than you were when you woke up that morning.

So when I was on the sidelines I watched Mark very carefully. He understood the game and could teach it, sometimes better than he could play it. He knew what he had to do, but sometimes he couldn't make his body do it. His hips were just a little too wide for that position. He had an awkward body—he was built like a pear—while I was round like a ball. It was sort of like trying to fit a square peg in a round hole—with a sledgehammer. I could fit into a hole he couldn't get through. For a defensive tackle the initial objective is to find a way to get through the offensive line into the backfield and then set up camp in the backfield. Mark would come off the line and hit the offensive lineman, then swing around and hit the tackle. He'd have to readjust himself and then go again; he could do it, but it took time and power. The difference was that I could swing around and miss the tackle and just slide through the hole. I learned from him how to do what he couldn't quite do.

Initially I missed playing offense. To me, playing offense was the real fun part of the game: Offense was touchdowns, catching the ball, making a first down, and jumping up and all that other foolishness. But then I discovered the beauty of . . . the sack. I found the sack for a loss, I found the sack for a fumble. I found the sack. And I never felt a need to play on offense again.

Like the song goes, there ain't nothing like a sack, nothing in the world. Just for an instant, you are King Kong. The term *sack* was created by the legendary Deacon Jones, a Florida boy from Eatonville, who played in what I have always called the aspirin and ice era. Whatever hurt you had, you put ice on it and took two aspirin. That was about the extent of medical expertise. A few beers probably helped—that part hasn't changed—although players no longer drink those beers in the locker room during halftime. Deac was my idol. Without him it would still be called "a tackle for a loss," but by giving it a name he put the glory into it. For a defensive player, it became the measure of greatness. The offense had touchdowns, we had sacks.

I met Deacon Jones for the first time in a hospitality suite at the 1997 Super Bowl. I introduced myself, we started talking, and naturally the subject of quarterbacks came up. By that time he'd been retired almost 25 years so you'd figure some of his emotional intensity would have mellowed. Instead, he looked at me and his eyes got cold and he said passionately, "I *hate* those sons of bitches." I loved it! He came up with the word *sack*, he explained, because he used to dream he could put quarterbacks in a big potato sack, close it, and then beat it with a baseball bat.

Okay, Deac, but tell us how you really feel.

Deacon Jones is also credited with being the first pass rusher to use the head slap, although *slap* doesn't really convey the impact. A *slap* from Deacon Jones is like a *nip* from a pit bull. He began doing it, he said, "Because anytime you go upside a man's head he may have a tendency to blink his eyes or close his eyes. That's all I needed."

I got my very first college sack on September 19, 1992, against Florida A&M University. I remember it so well because I got my ass chewed out for it. Mark had been injured, hurt his ankle or something, so I was starting in his place. Before the season I had been wearing no. 99, the same number that had been worn for six seasons in pro football by the great Jerome Brown. But after Jerome died in a car accident, to honor his memory, Mark wanted to wear his number. I ended up wearing no. 76, Mark's usual number.

As we got set for the first play of the game I lined up opposite an offensive lineman who obviously had played against Mark. He looked at my number, looked at me, looked at the number 76 again, and then he finally said, "Hey Caesar, what happened? Did you go all dark on me?"

This was more of a scrimmage for us than any kind of real test. It just gave my mother a chance to warm up her mouth for my college career. She came to every game wearing her Sapp jersey, usually with her sister Ola. Whatever my mother didn't know about the game she made up for in volume. FAM U never had a realistic chance against us. Our scout team probably was a little better than them. We were winning by two or three touchdowns when the call came in from the sidelines for me and Pat Riley to run a game, meaning a designed defensive play in which one lineman makes a move that allows another lineman to get a shot at the quarterback. Pat looked at me and said, "I don't want to run that shit."

"Me either," I said. "Let's just go." So instead of doing that designed dipsy-doodle, I went one on one with the offensive lineman, grabbed him by the jersey, and discarded him. Then I hit the quarterback chest high and drove him into the ground. I got my sack. My first sack. I leaped up and started screaming, I pounded my chest, I high-fived the referee. I celebrated. My first sack. I was pumped. After we held them on third down I sprinted off the field, ready to accept congratulations. In baseball when you get your first hit they give you the ball; in football when you score your first touchdown they give you the ball. I didn't know what they did to celebrate a first sack, although I figured they weren't going to give me the quarterback. But I was primed to be told how smooth I was.

I got to the sidelines and sat down on the bench. I took my helmet off. And waited. Nobody said one word. They just ignored me. Okay, I figured, I get it. Around here one sack is no big deal, they expect it from you. That's what I thought until we went into the locker room at halftime, when D-line coach Ed Orgeron opened up on me. He'd waited so he could do it in front of the whole team. He was all over me like Trump on money. "You motherfucker, who the hell you think you are?"

Hello? Didn't you see what I just did out there? I got a sack.

Orgeron was definitely not impressed. In fact, he was practically irate. "Motherfucker, you listen to me if you want to play on this team. When I call a game you better motherfucking run it."

It was really confusing to me. How could you get a sack and get cussed out for it? Wow, I thought, just think how bad it would have been for me if I'd gotten two sacks! Orgeron went off on me for the whole 10 minutes. At the end he was shaking a finger at me and said, "If this was Florida State it would mean something to you."

I got it. From that moment on I never went rogue again. That was my first sack ever and I learned from it. I began to understand that on that level football is the ultimate team game. It's a chess game played with big strong pieces. If one player breaks down, or decides to do his own thing, even if he does an effective job, the whole unit suffers. I learned that when I studied a playbook I didn't just look at my position, I looked at every player on the field. I knew what each player was supposed to do on every play. How it all fit together. While to the fan each play looks like organized chaos, everybody playing his own version of gimme the ball, in fact it is a highly structured system completely dependent for success on every cog playing his assigned role. Every player has an assignment that connects him to every other player. If a linebacker knows I'm going through the B-gap he understands his responsibility. If I change my mind without letting him know and go through a different gap I've broken down the system. The ball carrier might find the gap I didn't fill, and the linebacker wouldn't be there to stop him. There are very few fans who understand the real game of football. To the fan watching on television it might look like that linebacker blew his assignment allowing a good gain, but in fact it would have been completely my fault. Here: Imagine what would happen to a symphony orchestra if the tuba player decided to start bomp-bomping to his own time. Years later, at Tampa Bay when the defense broke down and we gave up yardage, we would all stand there on the field looking up at the replay on the Jumbotron. Most of us knew instantly who had missed his assignment and caused the breakdown.

I was getting my higher education in football, but still I had to go to my regular classes. Or at least I was supposed to go, although I have to admit I wasn't fanatical about it. There were some people there who majored in eligibility. At Miami they didn't let you hide, but they also didn't push you to your limits. Participating in a big-time college football or basketball program is practically a full-time job. It requires a minimum of three, four hours a day practicing, working out, or studying a playbook. Try adding to that a full load of academic courses and 10 hours a week of supervised study hall. The advisors made suggestions about which academic courses to take, but athletes were free to make their own decisions. The advisors were not going to put us into anything too heavy. There were professors at the U who didn't want athletes in their classes, which made it a mutual decision. At that age I didn't fully appreciate the importance of my education—like so many African American athletes I was the first person in my family to go to a university. Besides, I've always believed an education isn't only what you learn in a classroom, it's also the people you meet and the experiences you have. It's what you can touch, and what touches you.

There was a tradition at Miami that the upperclassman on the team opened up the eyes of the younger players. I knew very little about the world outside Plymouth when I arrived at the U. But Jessie Armstead, the man whose position I was determined to take, taught me, "There's a wide-open highway out there son. You just got to know how to get in the proper vehicle and drive." He showed me that the world was a little bigger and a little wider if I opened myself up to the possibilities. At Miami I was exposed to so much more than the weight room and the practice field. I made good friends with people outside the football program, people who are still close friends, whose world was so much bigger than mine. My boys took me for sushi, they took me fishing, they showed me art.

When my turn came I took a skinny, little, happy-go-lucky 18-year-old kid named Raymond Lewis and showed him that he needed a bigger canvas because he'd already filled up the one in front of him. Ray Lewis was this nice little lanky linebacker, the boy barely weighed 200 pounds, who had grown up a lot like me. He came from Bartow, Florida, a little town outside Lakeland about 90 minutes from Plymouth, and his father had walked out before he ever got to know him. I've been to the trailer he grew up in, I know his brothers and sisters, I know his heart, so the two of us just naturally fit together. In the opening game of the 1993 season against Virginia Tech our middle linebacker, Robert Bass, tore a ligament, and Ray Lewis had to replace him. He wasn't really ready for that—he just a little football baby. All he did was jibber-jabber; I had to teach him how to take command. In practice the week before a big game against Colorado he walked into the huddle to call the defensive signals, and he said, "Uhh, uhh, uhh." Well, I don't know what he said because nobody could hear him. He broke the huddle and we all just stood there. "Hell no!" I said, "Get your ass back in this huddle and call a play like a man. Let me hear you say something."

He looked at me and I told him, "Yeah, you heard me. You are now the middle linebacker at the University of fucking Miami. This is your huddle, so you call the fucking play like you fucking mean it." He figured it out quick enough—that next Saturday we went to Boulder and he had 20 tackles and an interception.

I took him with me wherever I went. We educated him to the world. I remember one weekend we all drove down to Key West for a party. Without going into any details, I can tell you that after that weekend Ray Lewis never had trouble calling signals again. Just like Jessie Armstead had done for me, I said to Ray, "Ray, meet the real world; real world, met Ray Lewis." Neither one has ever been the same since.

All of that was as much a part of our college education as sitting in the classroom. In many ways it was the most important part of it.

I majored in criminology. While my dream was to play professional football, I figured if that didn't work out I could always find work somewhere within the justice system. One thing I knew for absolute sure, the world was never going to run out of criminals. And as long as you had criminals you were going to need law enforcement officers. So if I couldn't earn a living in football I knew I had a job for the next 100 years.

Classes taught by the head of the Criminology Department, Dr. Wolf, were probably the most popular on the whole campus, because he would show us the most gruesome stuff. It was the type of material that was so awful to look at that you couldn't wait to see more of it. Oh my goodness, I don't want to look at that, so please pass it to me. We went on field trips to crime scenes with the Miami Dade Homicide. I couldn't go with the police because they couldn't stuff my size-14-shoe and 300-pound ass into the back of one of those squad cars, but I did get to ride with the fire department in a rig. The fire department let me sit right there in the back with those big boys and roll with them to fires.

If I read something I remembered it, so school wasn't hard for me. But it was that *if* part that was my problem. It wasn't the work that got to me—as long as there was no geometry in college I could do the work—it was the hours. I actually flunked one course at Miami. Ready for this? I flunked public speaking. I flunked talking. If James Brown, my partner on Showtime's *Inside the NFL*, reads this he is never going to let me speak again. I never told my family, because I don't think they would have understood: "You flunked talking? How could you do that? That was the thing you was best at, all you had to do was open your mouth and the words pour out." None of my high school teachers, coaches, or officials would have believed that was possible: "Warren flunked public speaking? He didn't seem to have any difficulty speaking in public when he was with us."

The problem wasn't the material, it was the time. Who knew that Miami had 8:00 a.m. classes? The teacher said, "You only came to class five times, how am I supposed to pass you?" She was mad that I scored a 90 on her final exam, which seemed to indicate that you didn't actually need to listen to her annoying yapping that early in the morning. She wondered if I might have been cheating. I pointed out to my advisor that the course syllabus did not require mandatory attendance, and I'd completed all my assignments.

To satisfy the teacher that I had learned about public speaking I took her written test again. This second time I scored like an 88. She still flunked me. Didn't bother me, I haven't stopped speaking in public since.

The first time in my life I even began to consider the possibly that I might be good enough to play in the NFL was at the beginning of my second season. I was hoping to be good enough to replace Mark Caesar. I was lying on my bed reading a sports magazine preview and suddenly there's my name. "Sapp could come out after this season." I read it several times. Come out? Give up my college eligibility and enter the pro draft? Until that very moment I hadn't even considered that possibility. But there it was, in print, so somebody had to believe it was true. Not me personally, I knew I wasn't ready to do that, but maybe the writer knew more about my ability than I did. If he was writing about it, somebody must've been talking about it. Reading that was thrilling for me.

Right before the season began our sports information director, John Haun, showed me a photograph of all the major trophies given annually to college football players sitting neatly on a table. It included the Heisman Trophy for the outstanding player, the Outland, which is given to the best interior lineman, the Lombardi Award, which goes to the best lineman or linebacker—all of the trophies a college player can win. He asked me, "Okay, which one do you want?"

"What do you mean?"

"I mean which one do you want?" he repeated. I wasn't naïve, I knew I had talent, but I hadn't even played first team the previous year.

I poked a finger at the Lombardi. "That one." I didn't know what trophy it was, who awarded it, and for what it was given. I didn't take Haun seriously; I didn't seriously believe I had a chance to win any of them.

Of course, if Haun had come to me a season later and asked me the same question I probably would have told him, "I'll take everything on the table. In fact, I'll take the table too." That's how much I improved in one season. I didn't play against a single offensive lineman who could block me one on one, and I didn't have to do much to beat him. It was natural, and it was easy. Other teams began coming up with schemes to try to stop me. Boston College pulled the weak-side guard and had him come across to help the strong-side guard. Virginia Tech used their tight end to try to block me. It didn't work. We held them to −14 yards rushing, and I had two sacks and forced three turnovers as we beat them 24–3. Most every team double-teamed me, and some of them even threw in a running back as an additional blocker. Rutgers' offensive line coach said that the best way to slow me down was to hope: "You got to hope for a rainstorm so he can't get traction."

All of that attention was great; any time you force a team to change their system you gain a big advantage. I never minded taking on two blockers, three blockers, a brick wall; it didn't matter to me, I loved the challenge. Once I finally got on the field I never wanted to come off. I wanted to play every down. That's how I turned Dwayne Johnson into a professional wrestler. He was real talented but I never let him play so the scouts never saw him. Even when we were dominating I played deep into the fourth quarter, and by the time I took a break the scouts were gone home. This is my job, I thought, and I didn't know any other way to do it.

One of the biggest problems we had at Miami was scheduling teams who competed on our level. A sports columnist once wrote that "Miami really isn't as good as everybody seems to believe. In fact, if they were playing in the NFL they'd probably be a second division team!" We played in the Big East, which meant that at most we would only face three or four really competitive teams during the season. At times it wasn't fun. There were games in which I literally could see fear in my opponent's eyes. One time against West Virginia the ball was snapped, I put my hand on the offensive lineman's pads, and he just rolled over. I mean, he quit. Oh my goodness, that was awful. I looked at Kenard Lang, our defensive end, and said, "You saw that?"

He shook his head, "Big dog, that's a shame."

That game I left after that series of downs. I didn't want to play against someone who didn't want to play against me. I always wanted to compete against the strongest, the baddest, the best you can throw at me. Put it out there and let's go at it.

No matter who we were playing, I tried to prepare for every game as if it were the national championship. My room was on the edge of a golf course, and the night before every home game I would walk the 18th hole visualizing the game, seeing myself playing well. My room-mates thought I was crazy—when I came back they'd ask me if I'd played a good game tomorrow—but it cleared my mind.

Our trainer, Todd Toriscelli, who was also with me as a trainer in Tampa Bay, used to say we had two locker rooms at Miami. When we were playing a team that had little chance of beating us we were casual, guys going to work to get the job done, but when we were playing a team on our level our locker room was intense. We were all business. That's when tradition kicked in, and also some of our former players kicked in. After the coaches left the locker room before a big game we set up a pot; we each threw our weekend stipend in, all $32. It paid so much for each sack, so much for a touchdown, so much for a big hit, a pick, a caused fumble, a recovered fumble, for winning the game. But before an important game that pot could grow pretty quick. Before we played Florida State, for example, Michael Irvin was in the locker room, and he reached into his pocket and tossed $5,000 in that pot. Cortez Kennedy wasn't going to be outdone so he threw in five thousand more. Jessie Armstead, Jim Kelly, it added up to a nice pocketful of money.

This was our own money that we were splitting among ourselves. We put it in a backpack and locked it up. Then we went out to earn it.

On Sunday or Monday the whole team would lock the doors and watch the game films together—without the coaches—and hand out the awards. That's $200 for a sack, $200 for that interception, $100 for a tackle for a loss, $400 for recovering that fumble. Linebackers were rewarded for the hardest hit of the week; interior lineman split the pancake pot—for putting a player on his back. Whatever was left paid for the party, and if there was anything left it rolled over till the next game. I knew that if I got two sacks I was set for a month. I never played for the money. There wasn't enough money in the world to compare with the thrill of running out of the tunnel, out of the smoke, onto the field at the Orange Bowl into the loudest cheer I had ever heard. It was like running inside a speaker with the volume turned up high. But it was more cash than I had ever had in my pocket in my life, and it made a huge difference to me.

All kinds of stories have been told about athletes playing revenue-producing sports at major universities being secretly paid. It would be hypocritical of me to claim it didn't happen. That's the worst-kept secret in sports. The whole system is ridiculous. The university is making money, the coaches sometimes are the best-paid employees at the university, but the young people who generate all that money aren't supposed to be given a free meal? All I knew is that on Sunday we'd get in the car and go over to someone's house for a few hours to watch a pro game on television, and they would give us a nice pat on the back, and when we got back to the dorm we could buy KFC for the whole team.

The only money we were legally entitled to receive was to pay for weekend meals, when there was no training table. If you were on the traveling squad you ate with the team so you only got $32, but if you were redshirted and stayed behind you got $63 a week! For me that was like $2,000. If I saved it up at the end of the month I had almost $250.

Believe me, nobody was getting rich. Maybe we could afford the extra-crispy bucket.

But if the NCAA—which was being paid billions of dollars by the TV networks for the broadcasting rights to the games we weren't being paid to play—ever found out we were getting the extra-crispy the university could be penalized: "My God! An alumni bought a football player a super-sized bucket of extra crispy, *with fries*! Take away all their victories."

I admit it, I did have a car—it was an old Honda Accord that had been passed down through my family. But to me it was like a NASCAR. It was a party on wheels. Four or five of us would pile into that car and take off. Although we wouldn't go very far. It was a pretty old car.

The system was ridiculous. Students who didn't earn a dollar for the university had the time to go out and get a job to earn spending money, but playing football was my job. The most I could do was work in the summer. At a nearby university I knew that the football players worked as salesmen—selling fire extinguishers and anything else they had to boosters who would buy whatever they were selling. I worked for an alumnus at Oppenheimer, learning all about mutual funds, variable funds, investment strategies, and a lot of other things I couldn't afford. Went to work and earned my salary, but no one complained if I took time to go to the gym to get my lifting done. Everything was within the rules, although maybe the rules had to be stretched a little bit to make it all fit.

I believe strongly that college football players should be paid. It seems to me that everybody is making money on college football—the TV and radio stations, the university, the coaches—everybody except the college football players. I know a scholarship is worth a small fortune, but it isn't going to pay for breakfast when you're hungry or buy you a new shirt when all of your hand-me-downs are torn. I'm not suggesting salaries or substantial payments; $200 goes a long way in college. It pays for a movie with a date, admission to a concert, a hamburger at a dinner. But the situation as it now exists is set up to encourage cheating.

In 2011 a former Miami booster who pleaded guilty to creating an almost billion dollar Ponzi scheme claimed he had been illegally providing benefits for Miami athletes—including money, women, and gifts—for several years. The man invited players to pool parties on his yacht—who isn't going? We are talking about kids. When I was 20 years old if anybody invited me to party with women on their yacht, I was there. To me, this is entrapment. Okay, it is really nice entrapment, but the players didn't invite him, he invited them.

If you're stealing a billion dollars in a Ponzi scheme you're a pretty sophisticated con man. You're fooling a lot more experienced people than kids. In my experience the alumni didn't stand on corners handing out $100 bills. And anybody who believes this type of behavior is limited to the U probably invested their money with this guy.

By the beginning of my junior year I was a preseason All-American. The reporters were writing that this was going to be my last season at Miami, that I was going to go pro, but I hadn't made that decision yet. I loved playing for Dennis Erickson. Without him I was just another country boy that did not make it. I was close with the defensive coordinator, Greg McMackin, who would talk to me about implementing new concepts. And I loved my teammates. I wasn't in any big hurry to leave. We were top ranked in every preseason poll and definitely had a chance to win the national championship. At the U a championship was considered a rite of passage. Leaving there without a ring was like walking around naked. And I hadn't earned my ring yet. I'd been on the sidelines for the 1991 championship, which we had shared with the University of Washington, but that wasn't my team. This was going to be my national championship season; this was my team. I was a captain. The D-line called ourselves "Death Row," because, like I told the reporters, "When you stare at us, death is what you see." Whoa, still makes me shiver.

Two games that season I will never forget. Never, ever. Our third game was against the University of Washington at the Orange Bowl. Three weeks earlier we'd beaten Georgia Southern to set the all-time college record with our 58th consecutive home victory. Miami hadn't lost a game at home since 1985. That was so long ago I hadn't even weighed 200 pounds! I don't think there was one single person associated with the program that had ever experienced losing a game at home. Our alumni would remind us all the time about the streak they had built and told us they expected us to continue it. It was one of the greatest winning streaks in all of sports history and we were carrying it on.

We were two-touchdown favorites against Washington. Even with all the honors I've received, even after winning a Super Bowl and playing in all those Pro Bowls, this game still makes me angry. We were winning 14–3 at halftime, but they came out and scored 22 points in the first five minutes of the second half to beat us 38–20 and break the streak. And part of that was my own damn fault. It was my fault we had to kick off twice.

That doesn't happen in football. Just like the sun rises and sets every day, one team kicks off at the beginning of the game, the other team kicks off at the beginning of the second half. That's the natural order of football games. Except this one time. As the captain, I went out to the middle of the field for the coin toss. We won the toss and the official asked me what I wanted to do. How hard is that question: There were only two choices, we could either kick off or receive. We wanted to start the second half receiving the ball, so that meant kicking off in the first half. I said "Kick it that way."

Turned out there were actually three choices: Kick, receive, or defer. Defer? What the hell is a defer? This was a football game, not a multiple choice test. Nobody had ever told me about any *defer*.

I found out about it at halftime when Coach Erickson came running up to me and told me we had to kick off again. "What'd you say when they flipped the coin?"

I told him, "What you said, 'Kick it that way.'" That's when I found out I should have said *defer*, which meant we had the choice at the beginning of the second half. That would have allowed Washington to receive, and I would have said my, "Kick it that way." But by making my choice, they had the option to begin the second half. That was the last time in my entire career I ever went to the center of the field.

But even then, it shouldn't have been a problem. We were playing well and seemed to be in control of the game. We hadn't given up one touchdown the whole season, 10 quarters. I figured, what could happen? We'd been holding them all day, no reason for that to change. This was probably my first personal encounter with the Football Gods. That was the day I learned what happens when you anger them. I understand that there are a lot of intelligent people who don't believe in the existence of the Football Gods, and they would be wrong. I've seen what happens when you screw up the natural order of football. The Football Gods are always watching and they will humble you if you fail to play the game the way it is supposed to be played.

I never saw anything like what happened. The Huskies broke a screen pass for 75 yards and made a two-point conversion. Okay, that can happen to any team. We got the ball, and three plays later our quarterback, Frank Costa, threw a pass toward Jammi German. The Football Gods must have tackled him because nobody else touched him. He fell down, slipped on nothing, and their cornerback intercepted the pass and took it 34 yards to the promised land.

Now we were behind, but we knew we were coming back. We'd won 112 consecutive games when we were ahead by at least seven points, and we knew we were going to put up more points. All we had to do was hold them. Somewhere the Gods were laughing. On the next kickoff Jammi got hit deep in our territory and fumbled, and they recovered. We held them for six plays, and on third down at our 2-yard line their quarterback, Damon Heard, fumbled the ball—right into the end zone where their tackle fell on it for a touchdown. It was the most amazing five minutes of football anybody had ever seen. We gave up more points in that quarter than any Miami team had given up in a whole game during the streak. In less than five minutes everything we had known and worked for was gone.

Every possible play went against us. Late in the third quarter our cornerback took a pass away from their receiver, but the officials missed it, and Washington kicked a field goal. On three straight field-goal attempts they had bad snaps, but somehow they managed to convert all three. We couldn't do anything right; they couldn't do anything wrong. At the end people on our bench were crying. Chris Jones told reporters, "I'm ashamed." Ray Lewis called it "a sick, sick feeling, and unless you've been a part of this you don't have any idea how it feels."

I was upset and angry. That was the day I decided that I definitely was leaving school at the end of the year because we were playing people who did not deserve to be on the field. These were people who were not ready to play, and the only reason they were in the lineup was that when they were being recruited they were promised they would play. Made me so angry. Rohan Marley was told he would only start on the road, because another player had to start at home so his parents would continue to donate money. Let 'em leave, I told one coach, if they can't play they don't belong here.

One time later in the season we had a sophomore replace a defensive back who'd gotten hurt. He was talented but didn't put in the work. He didn't know his assignments, and he didn't seem to care about that, so as far as I was concerned he hadn't earned the right to be on the field. I just couldn't stand to be around people who didn't show respect for the game. I got so upset one game that when the defense came off the field I went right over to Erickson and told him, "Coach, if I'm in the huddle and this guy comes in I'm coming off." Erickson knew I wasn't kidding; even then I never said anything that I didn't mean. I don't think that kid played again that season.

After losing that game to Washington it looked like we had no shot at a ring, but we ended up ranked number three in the country, with the number one defense, and played Nebraska in the Orange Bowl on New Year's Day for the national championship. I had already decided I was going to enter the NFL draft, so for me this game was like my final exam.

What I was pleased about was that the game was being played on a Sunday night. One of my closest friends, Michael Bierg, was an Orthodox Jew, and because he'd spent every Saturday in synagogue he had never seen me play. I told him, "It is on! Trust me, my good man, it is on."

Nebraska had three first-team All-Americans on the offensive line, but the player I was lining up against wasn't one of them. So they switched Brenden Stai from right to left guard to try to block me. I devoured him. Ate him up and spit him out. But it was a play at the end of the second quarter of that game that convinced me I had nothing more to learn in college football. It was the best hit of my Miami career.

It was a draw play, the quarterback dropped back to pass, but instead he shoveled the ball forward to the running back. The key to making that play work is selling it to the defense as a pass play so we would continue attacking the quarterback. The ball was snapped, and I was taking Stai up the field, trying to read his body language. He was pass blocking, but I just sensed that it was a run. It didn't feel like Stai was committed to stopping me; instead he just wanted to make me go wider. That would have opened up the hole and enabled their freshman running back, Lawrence Phillips, to go up the middle. I just felt that; it was instinct—and maybe 10,000 snaps in practice and games. If this game was my final exam, I aced it. CSI Miami football. So instead of going around the corner and being out of the play, I pushed back on Stai and buttoned up the hole in the middle. It got me close enough to grab Phillips by the back of his jersey as he raced by. His feet kept moving forward, but the rest of him wasn't going nowhere. I snatched him right off his feet. He looked like Wile E. Coyote when he runs off the cliff, his legs churning but nothing underneath. I grabbed him by the arm and lifted him up—and then dropped him like he was a geometry course. I didn't put him down gentle, I dropped him.

Hand me my diploma, please.

It was a rough game. On the opening kickoff Nebraska's Cory Schlesinger hit one of our special teams players in the neck and knocked him out cold. Really? Okay, this is our type of game. That's the way we'd been playing in practice since I got there. Line up the ambulances. We led most of the game, up 17–9 going into the fourth quarter. Fifteen minutes from my ring. Nebraska had just about stopped running any plays to the right side, my side of the line. They tied it with a touchdown and two-point conversion. Our offense didn't do nothing in the whole second half. In the fourth quarter we never even got the ball across the 50 into their territory, so they had a short field that whole quarter. Seemed like the defense was on the field the whole half, so that was when all that work we'd done to show no signs of discomfort took over.

I learned right then that a lot of broadcasters have no idea what they are talking about. Just before the network cut to a commercial late in the game they showed me down on one knee, my head bowed, and later I found out that Bob Griese said that I was exhausted. Exhausted? I wasn't even tired. I was in my comfort zone—I was down on one knee because I'd gotten hit right in the nuts. Right there, right where it hurts. My whole body was vibrating like a tuning fork. And there was nothing I could do about it. I wasn't about to ask the trainer to rub it. I mean, c'mon, Todd was a friend, but . . . I wasn't coming out of the national championship game so I just had to wait till the bells stopped ringing. Tired, my ass. Let Griese get hit there and he'd be broadcasting in soprano.

We had a chance to win the game. With the score tied our wide receiver Taj Johnson was running up the sideline completely open. Put the ball in his hands and the game is over. It is over. The only person between him and the end zone was the official, and that official couldn't tackle worth a damn. Our quarterback, Frank Costa, threw it right over Johnson's head. Oh, that one hurt.

With about four minutes left in the fourth quarter Nebraska was on our 14-yard line. In those situations, tie game, late fourth quarter, your opponent in field-goal range, the best strategy is strong prayer and hard hitting. The best hope is cause a fumble and get back that ball. In those situations everybody has to do his assigned job. You can't go freelancing. A defense is a chain that is only as strong as its weakest link. Nebraska liked to run the quarterback option: The quarterback rolled out and he could keep the ball, hand it to the fullback, or pitch it to a running back. In our system the middle linebacker was responsible for the fullback, the defensive end got the quarterback, and safety covers the pitchman. Over and over we practiced that, the key being stay home, stay with your man; there ain't no security system on a football field so keep your ass home.

Nebraska called a play designed to beat me. Their fullback, Cory Schlesinger, said after the game, "Warren Sapp would often charge upfield so hard and so quickly, so we had practiced a play all week where I'd get a quick, simple handoff and run right up the middle." They ran Schlesinger right up the middle. I turned and looked, and there was no reason for me to chase the ball; he was running right where the middle linebacker was supposed to be. Except the linebacker thought the quarterback had faked the handoff and so he left home, left the front door wide open. Schlesinger hit his head on the goal post. I watched the national championship go running untouched right up the middle of the field. We never tackled the damn football. Football 101, tackle the man with the ball. It's no more complicated than that. That can't happen. I thought, that's it, I'm out of here. I'm out of here.

I can tell you from my personal experience that losing that game hurt worse than getting punched in the balls. Mentally, at least. Definitely mentally. I'd grown up as a person and a football player at the U, and my class was leaving without delivering a national championship.

I've watched tapes of that game, and I don't have any problem with it all the way to the end. I can't watch the end, when we lost our discipline and didn't tackle the damn fullback. But I don't need that tape to remember that game. I can close my eyes and I'm back on that field. My only regret about my college career was that we didn't win our national championship.

At the end of the season I was nominated for all the player awards, the Heisman, the Outland, the Lombardi Award, the Bronco Nagurski Award. I was a consensus First Team All-American. One strange thing did happen that I have never understood. The *New York Daily News* was doing a whole-page article about me on Christmas Day, 1994. The writer told me he was doing the story because I was going to win both the Outland Trophy and the Lombardi Award. He told me he had been allowed to listen to the conference call with the 12 Outland voters, and after I received my ninth vote he hung up and started writing his story. "Dandy Cane," it was headlined, and later he told me that originally he'd written that I'd won both trophies—but had to go back and change it.

When I went to the awards banquet in Orlando I believed I was going home with three trophies, the Lombardi, the Bronco Nagurski, and the Outland. Usually the winners of awards are not a big secret. They tell you beforehand to make sure you show up. But before the banquet a member of the awards committee told John Haun that the Outland Trophy was being awarded to Zach Wiegert of Nebraska. What happened between the voting and the ceremony I will never know. Maybe that was an example of new math; instead of nine maybe they said *none*. There is no other reason that I can figure out. John asked me what I wanted to do. When the winner of the Outland Trophy was about to be announced I got up and started applauding before they even mentioned his name.

That was a long time ago, and being awarded that trophy would not have made a little bitty difference in my life. But I still remember it. I had been taught that respect is earned, and I had worked hard to earn it.

Something happened there, and I felt disrespected. As anyone who has ever had any dealings with me will tell you, being disrespected can become a big deal to me.

It still was a wonderful night for me. That was the first time they awarded the Nagurski Trophy, which is given to the best defensive player in the country. It's a huge trophy, glass and wood, with a gold football on top. My grandmother, Rosia Lykes, was there that night and she had been sick. I came down from the stage, and I placed it right next to her and said, "Grandmother, this one is for you. You take this one home with you."

That trophy sat in her living room until the day that she passed. She was so proud of it. Anybody who came into her house, she'd point at it and say, "My grandson gave me that trophy." Tell you what, my grandmother looking at that trophy, maybe with a coat or something hung over the football—she was a practical woman—and smiling with pride brought me more joy than receiving the Outland ever would have provided for me.

After the season I officially withdrew from the university. Leaving before I graduated was a business decision. I was going to the graduate school of football, the NFL. I spoke with Coach Erickson and my academic advisor, Dr. Price, and both of them supported my decision. I didn't want to get the university in trouble by being enrolled and not going to class, so I officially withdrew. Reading the papers and the magazines it was obvious I was going to be a high draft choice, and there was a big check attached to that pick. It was time for my mother to finally sit down.

THREE

This is what one NFL scout predicted before the 1995 draft: "If 'Big Daddy' Wilkinson was the number one pick as a defensive lineman last year, then even Ray Charles can see that Warren Sapp is the number one pick this year."

Oooh, that's nice. Say it again, please.

"If 'Big Daddy' Wilkinson was the number one pick as a defensive lineman last year, then even Ray Charles can see that Warren Sapp is the number one pick this year."

Thank you. But that was before the NFL draft, which turned out to be one of the worst days of my whole entire life. Apparently blind Ray Charles can see better than at least 11 NFL teams.

The first thing I had to do to prepare for the pro football draft was hire an agent to negotiate my first professional contract. This is one of the most important and difficult decisions an athlete will ever make; there's no preparation for it, and you got to get it right the first time. At that time there was no set fee for agents; some of them were asking and getting 10 percent of the contract and higher. I had a lot of agents running at me making all kinds of crazy offers. I got a lot of advice from people who had been through the system. Ryan McNeil, who had been a business major, told me I should hire a lawyer and instead of giving him a percentage of my contract I should pay him by the hour. Micheal Barrow told me that whoever I picked I should name the price

I was going to pay, because my contract was slotted, meaning it was determined by how high I was picked, and the agent had nothing to do with that.

Russell Maryland, who had been the number one a few years before, was represented by Leigh Steinberg and thought I should sign with him. I was with Russell when he got a message to call Steinberg's office. He called and asked to speak with Steinberg. The assistant asked, "Who's this?"

"Russell."

The assistant said, "Russell who?" Whoa. The man had been the number one pick in the entire draft. You can be damn sure it wasn't no "Russell who?" when they were negotiating his multimillion dollar contract. They got their money and it was "Russell who." I knew right then I was never going to be "Warren who."

I met with several agents. I went to dinner with one of the better-known agents. I had my big lobster dinner sitting there in front of me when he explained that he was only going to charge me 5 percent. Really? "Oh yeah," he said. "That's our standard fee." Okay. I cut my lobster and took a big chunk out of it. Then I took another chunk, scooped up some cream of corn, sipped my wine, and stood up. "Get that check please," I told him, and walked out. He wasn't going to tell me how "little" of my money he was going to take. I'd learned from all those people who had been through this process. I wasn't a fool.

Robert Bailey, who holds the NFL record for the longest punt return, told me I should get together with his agent, Drew Rosenhaus. But I had heard some stories about Rosenhaus. I thought being on the field was rough—these agents played nasty. Other agents told me that Rosenhaus was stealing millions of dollars from his clients, but when I asked Robert about it, he shook his head and said, "Sapp, if I was standing in a pile of shit, you think I'd pull you in? I'd tell you to run the other way and get myself out of it."

That was as strong a recommendation as I'd ever heard: I like my agent, he's much better than standing in a pile of shit! I said, "You know what, that makes a lot of goddamn sense." Which is how Drew Rosenhaus became my agent.

In February, I was invited to participate in the NFL Scouting Combine in Indianapolis. This is where all the teams get to push, pull, probe, and everything else all the potential draft picks. Basically they measure every single part of your body—hand size tip-to-tip, wing span, vertical jump, everything—put you through extensive psychological testing, drug testing, and then test your physical skills. I figured as long as there was no geometry test I'd be fine. If you were projected to be a top-round pick you didn't have to participate in the physical drills, but if you decided not to they would glare at you like you stole their first born.

The whole concept of the Combine never made a lot of sense to me. The players invited to participate already had played two, three, or even four years of college football. There were miles of film of them actually playing in games against opponents trying to kick their ass. Is a team really going to draft a player because he has a great vertical leap? Really? "Maybe he can't block worth a damn, but he sure can jump!"

The reality is that the Combine is nothing more than a meat market. Literally you're supposed to take off your shirt and turn around so they can see your whole self. Hmm, now where have I seen that before? The whole concept of a black man standing in his shorts in the front of a room being measured and examined makes me nervous. I refused to take off my shirt, pointing out that the Combine was a job interview, and I had been working at $3.35-an-hour minimum-wage jobs since I was 13 years old, and there wasn't one time I had to take off my shirt for a job interview. It seemed to me that the Combine was mostly designed to promote failure and maybe bring down your value. Football fans love reading about it, but for the higher-ranked players nothing good comes out of it.

When I was 18 years old my family somehow managed to scrap together enough money to send me and my cousins Geo and Tywan Jones to Bermuda as our graduation gift. Oh my goodness, the three of us in Bermuda! But instead of being able to go, I got selected to play in the Florida-Georgia All-Star Game. I had very mixed feelings about it; my cousins were going to be on the beaches while I was sweating in the trenches. The morning they were going to drop me off, my grandmother, Rosia Lykes, took us all out to the IHOP for breakfast. For me, this was like heaven. I studied that menu. The stack I wanted to order, with sides, was $3.79. I put down the menu and looked at my grandmother. She had that look on her face with her lips turned up. I didn't know exactly what was troubling her, but whatever it was I knew it wasn't good. The lady comes over to take our order and my grandmother asked, "What do I get for this $3.79 right here?"

The lady said, "I'm going to give you a stack of our buttermilk pancakes."

"How 'bout sides? I get any sides for that?"

"No m'am," the lady said politely, pointing to the menu. "The sides are down here."

With that my grandmother slammed down her menu and said, "Ain't nobody gonna rob me without no gun."

My mother put her hand over my grandmother's hand to keep her from getting up and said, "Don't worry about it, Momma. I'll pay for it."

Grandma looked at her like she was crazy, "I ain't gonna let them rob you either!"

We were not eating at the International House of Pancakes. We got up and went down the street to the Village Inn for the $3.99 breakfast special. We got the whole skillet, a biscuit, and bacon for $3.99. "See, told you," Grandma pointed out. That's exactly the way I felt about the Combine. I'd spent three seasons playing major college football. The scouts could look at game films, talk to my coaches, I was willing to take a medical, but I wasn't about to do drills without sufficient rest that might give them a reason to offer less money. My grandmother was right; ain't nobody gonna rob me without no gun.

The Combine is completely private: They have total control over you. You are not allowed to bring in anything at all. They give you whatever equipment you need, socks to jocks. You are not allowed to talk to anybody; your agent, your mother, nobody. The gates are locked, the doors are locked, there are no telephones. It was the most degrading experience of my whole career. They assign you a number, I was DL 33, and that's who you are for the next few days.

It is not set up for the players to do well. They keep you up till one o'clock in the morning and then wake you at 4:30 to give you a piss test and then make you run and perform—and expect you to beat your best. I told them no thank you. Several teams told me they were disappointed that I wouldn't work out for them. "Let me ask you this," I responded. "If you were paying me a million dollars a year would you like me to stay out till 2:00 a.m., wake up at 4:00 a.m. and come to the job with no sleep? You think I could do my best with no sleep? I am not about to put my future on the line without getting the proper rest." Instead I invited them all to come down to Miami to see me work out after I'd had a good meal and a good night's rest.

It wasn't just me; they tried to beat down on everybody. If your elbow was messed up, for example, all 32 teams would examine your elbow, which guaranteed that if it wasn't sore when the day began it definitely was sore at the end. They definitely found problems with me: By their measurement my hands were too small. They never told me too small for what, just too small. Of course there was nothing I could do about that; I couldn't make my hands grow.

There was one test I couldn't do. No one explained its purpose—at first I guessed it tested your reflexes or your timing or something. Whatever it was, I couldn't do it. A light ran down a strip, and you were supposed to stop it at a specific point. It reminded me of playing the Kicker video game at Al's Supermarket. I wondered if they were testing football players or scoreboard operators. I tried it about 40 times, and I just couldn't stop the light at the specified point. I would not quit, but no matter how hard I tried I couldn't get that damn light to stop at that damn point. I was getting very frustrated.

Then I figured out the purpose of the test. It was a psychological test. It was impossible to do it. I am convinced that they had a hidden switch they could turn on and off. They wanted to see how long a person would work at a task before getting so frustrated he would give it up or lose his temper and bust it or curse it or pick it up and throw it across the room. I am sure that's the objective of this test. More than positive. But I wouldn't give up. I did it 50 times, 60 times before they finally quit on me!

I wanted to keep going but they wouldn't let me.

Instead of performing for the scouts at the Combine, I invited them all to my own workout on the Greentree practice field at the U. A hundred and fifty scouts showed up for my Pro Day. I was working out under my own conditions. I put on my Charles Barkley Phoenix Suns shorts, my tank shirt, my track shoes, and my bouncing shoes so I could do my vertical jump. I opened the workout by putting my cleats on my hands and walking out of the locker room on my hands. A 285-pound man, walking on his hands. That was how I always warmed up when I went out onto the field. If I had really wanted to impress them I would've danced on my hands for them. After all my measurements were taken I bench pressed 225 pounds 16 times. When I stood up Tom Coughlin said to me, "You only did 16 reps?" Then he sort of frowned and added, "Brenden Stai did 39."

Brenden Stai? I had just played against him in the national championship game and totally dominated him. "You mean that guard from Nebraska that switched sides and got his ass whooped? That Brenden Stai? Tell you what, Coach," I told him, "you put on the tape of that

game and then you tell me which player you want on your team."
Nobody had told me that football was played in the weight room. I
lifted for maintenance, to keep everything tight, not to build upper-
body strength. I got my philosophy about lifting from training with
body-building champion Brad Lowe, who told me, "Every morning in
Africa there's a lion that wakes up knowing he must outrun the swift-
est gazelle or he'll starve. And every morning in Africa a gazelle
wakes up knowing he must outrun the fastest lion or he'll perish. The
moral of that story is that when the sun comes up your ass better be
running."

In the fourth quarter strong legs are a lot more important than a
solid top. The strongest player in the league can't do much standing on
wobbling legs, while I was a rock on my foundation. I win. So I told
Coach Coughlin that when they put a bench press on the 50-yard line
and start keeping score I'll start lifting a little more.

I had a good workout. I ran a 4.65 40, did some drills. I did everything they asked me to do. I just blazed through everything. I was in
the locker room after the workout when someone told me the Cleveland Browns' coach Bill Belichick was waiting outside for me. I put on
my shorts and ran outside. "I'm sorry, Coach," I said. "I didn't know
you were waiting on me."

"That's okay," he said. "Go take a shower. I'll wait." We started
talking about my workout and he told me, "Son, I want to draft you so
bad my dick is hard."

"Well then, what's the problem?" I asked.

"Mike Lombardi (the general manager) won't let me." Apparently
they had a report from NFL security that I was a bad guy, that I hung
out with dope dealers and drug fiends. I had heard that report was out
there, but I didn't think anybody who knew me would actually believe
it. I had a good time, I definitely had a good time, but my focus was
always on football, and I never did anything to detract from my practice or performance. I went to the clubs in Miami, just like most col-

lege students, and we all knew there were dope dealers and even prostitutes in those places, but I wasn't part of that at all. All they had to do was talk to my coaches or my teammates, but apparently they didn't bother to do that. They would have found out the truth. But Belichick's explanation didn't bother me; there were a lot of other teams out there. It didn't occur to me that this report would cause me so much trouble. Belichick knew Lombardi was making a mistake, although I suspected the real decision was being made by the owner, Art Modell. I guarantee that had Cleveland drafted me we would have won there. They had the core of a very good team with a great coach; they were just missing a few pieces. I would have had to get used to that cold-ass weather, but we would have won.

As the draft came closer I didn't know which team would pick me at what spot. The fans and media love to play the guessing game. A lot of people thought I would be the first pick, but nobody had me going any lower than fifth. I played this game too. Every player does. Each slot has an approximate salary range, which obviously goes down with each pick. Wherever I went, I knew that for the first time I could afford to eat at IHOP three times a day if I wanted to and still have enough money left over to buy my mother her house.

I tried to figure out where I fit best. The two expansion teams, Carolina and Jacksonville, had the first two picks. While the thought of being the number one selection was exciting, I was hoping Carolina didn't take me with the first pick. I wanted to go to Jacksonville. It was 90 minutes away from home, it was the Florida sunshine, and it wasn't Tampa. It made sense for them too, because I was a Florida boy, which would help generate fan enthusiasm for a new team. But if they passed on me, I figured at worst I would go to the Washington Redskins who had the fourth pick and needed a tackle. I did a lot of interviews. When I was asked how I'd feel about playing for an expansion team in Charlotte, North Carolina, I said confidently, "Whoever picks me I'll have a lot of adjustments to make. I'll have a whole new city to get acquainted with, but I can handle it whether it's an expansion team, the Super Bowl champions, or the lowly Bucs."

Of course I was kidding about the lowly Bucs. They picked seventh and nobody believed I would still be on the board by that time, so I could be nice about it. Tampa Bay was the worst franchise in the history of the world. Growing up I was a huge Dallas Cowboys fan, but on Sundays we got the Bucs games on TV. I could kill CBS right now for exposing us to that torture week after week. It was terrible. San Francisco was playing Oakland, the Battle of the Bay, and we got the Bucs at the Detroit Lions. My Cowboys and the New York Giants were playing for first place and that game was being broadcast to the major markets, but in Florida we got the Bucs and Cincinnati. Oh, I used to pray that lightning would come down and strike the tower so I could see the Cowboys. But it never did, so I had to watch the Bucs, the *Yucks* we called them, losing week after week. The only member of my family who wanted me to be drafted by that sorry-ass franchise was my brother, Hershel. Hershel was a huge Bucs fan. We'd watch the games together and always be arguing. Before the draft he kept saying how great it would be if I got drafted by Tampa Bay. I'd just look at him like, the Yucks? You are out of your mind.

As a courtesy though, I did have lunch with the Bucs' brand-new general manager, Rich McKay. He asked me some pretty direct questions about the rumors that were being spread. I told him the truth, that I wasn't going to look him in the eye and deny that I had ever tested positive for marijuana. There weren't too many college students at that time who could make that claim, I said. But I guaranteed that it would have no effect on my ability to play pro football.

It was like waiting for your birthday. You know the worst thing that's going to happen is that all your presents might not be so great. I was going to be paid millions of dollars to play the game that I loved in the greatest league in the world. I told my mother that her working time was done, but she was cautious about it. Her life had not been overflowing with good things. When the principal at her school asked her to tell him by April 20th if she was coming back to work the next year she asked if he could wait for her answer until the 23rd—the day after the draft. That was the way she was brought up. As it turned out, she had some reason to worry.

I was in my apartment about a month before the draft when I was told that the *New York Times* was reporting that I had tested positive for marijuana and cocaine at the Combine.

Oh. My. Goodness. The phone started ringing and didn't stop for a month. Here is the absolute truth: Before going to the Combine I was in New York City for the Heisman Trophy ceremony. The University of Colorado's Rashaan Salaam had won the Heisman, and the two of us went back to his hotel room. He locked the door and lit up a joint. I'm not going to claim I hadn't smoked marijuana in college—everybody tried weed in college. But when he lit it up I hesitated, "C'mon Dawg," I said. "I'm going to the Combine."

"Me too." Okay. So we took a couple of puffs. It was an exciting night, and it wasn't much different than having a couple of drinks. Well, except that the alcohol clears your system faster than marijuana. When I was tested at the Combine I had 23 nanograms in my blood, and the cut-off line was 20. If I'd woken-up that morning and had a glass of water and taken another piss before being tested I might not have tested positive. Rashaan had less body fat than me, and he didn't test positive. So the truth is I did smoke marijuana.

But I never did cocaine. Never. Cocaine's a dummy drug; it makes you rob from your mama.

This story wasn't just going to hurt my reputation; it was going to directly affect my future. I knew there were teams who wouldn't draft me if they thought I was using drugs. I called my mother and my agent. Drew Rosenhaus told me that the NFL never comments on its drug testing program, and I pointed out to him that this story came from somewhere. We called the NFL, and the next day the league made its first official announcement about the program in 75 years, issuing a statement that the *Times* story, which listed six players who supposedly had tested positive for drugs, was wrong. It said specifically, "The report today that Warren Sapp of the University of Miami tested positive for cocaine at the Scouting Combine in Indianapolis is inaccurate." But the report then said that other players who reportedly had failed the test for marijuana had not failed that test. My name was not included in that list. The meaning of that statement was clear as a referee's whistle in an empty stadium. Thank you, NFL.

The *New York Times* refused to correct the story, claiming they were right and the NFL was wrong about the results of its own test. I spoke with a reporter there and tried to keep my temper. "Dude," I said, "you are talking about my life. You are telling me I snorted cocaine. Don't you think I would know if I did one line of cocaine?" Made no difference to him. It was only my life that got changed. While football fans knew my name and that I was an aggressive player, for a lot of people this was the first time they were learning anything about me, and what they were being told was that I was just another drug-abusing athlete. My reputation was being formed in people's minds, and there wasn't anything I could do to change that. They had heard this type of story about other athletes before, which made it easy to believe. I know that for some people I am forever going to be linked to drug abuse. *Sports Illustrated* got it right when they wrote, "His name wears a stain now, and it won't fade easy." The fact that it wasn't true made no difference.

People were advising me to sue the *New York Times*. I didn't need that; all I wanted was for that reporter to admit he made a mistake. Maybe he just got some bad information. Instead the paper continued to claim they got it right. No, they got it dead wrong. It would be impossible to be more wrong.

I could defend against the best running back in college football, but there was no defense against this. You can't tackle a lie. Instead I volunteered to take a drug test every day, four times every day, if they wanted me to. And I did. We sent out the results to every one of the 32 NFL teams. But the damage had been done. Those teams who didn't want to draft me anyway, like Jacksonville, now had an excuse when their fans complained. We can't take Sapp, he's a druggie. Carolina's general manager Bill Polian, with the number one pick, said, "We don't make any distinction (between marijuana and cocaine) when we determine a player's grade." Art Modell, the owner of the Cleveland Browns, said he was morally uneasy about drafting me. C'mon, you kidding me?

Another scout claimed his team wouldn't draft me because my arms were too short. Although what they probably were saying was that my arms weren't too short to reach the drugs. I couldn't figure out what that man was scouting, but I have a 6'8" wingspan, which doesn't seem too short to me. We can't take Sapp, his arms are too short.

Then, at 11:30 the night before the draft, the NFL security report claiming that while I was in college I had tested positive for marijuana six times and cocaine once, and that I had been going to clubs and hanging out with dope dealers, pimps, hookers, every damn cliché you can think of, was leaked to the media. This came out the night before the draft, while I already was in New York with my whole family. I was getting ready to celebrate one of the greatest days of my life, and it turned into a nightmare. It was devastating. How was I supposed to respond to that? According to the report, not only was I abusing drugs, I was basically a thug. If that was true, I wouldn't even draft me. If it was true, my mother would have put me out on waivers.

I was never tested for drugs seven times at Miami. While I was there I took a total of five drug tests, three of them for the NCAA. If the security department report was accurate, that meant I had failed three NCAA drug tests, and the NCAA hadn't done a thing about it? I was the best defensive player in college football playing in Miami, the dope capital of America, and until 11:30 the night before the draft nobody had known anything about that? But all of a sudden they turned me into David Copperfield. I had created the illusion of being a great football player while I really was a derelict and a drug abuser.

What I did not know was that a man from NFL security had been following me for several weeks. Who knew that the NFL had its own spies? I got to assume they were also following the other top draft choices. The reports were accurate about one thing: Some nights I definitely did go to clubs. And it's true that most every club in Miami had dope dealers, pimps, and prostitutes hanging out, and I was dating two women who worked at one of those clubs. Those are the facts.

When the story came out I called my family to tell them about it. Then we all got together and we prayed. My mother was furious about what they were doing to me. I had to calm her down. "It's okay," I told her. "I'm still gonna get my money." Although probably not as much, in fact maybe several million dollars less. There is a saying that when you ain't got nothing, you got nothing to lose. Usually it's said by people who ain't got nothing. Well, maybe it's true, but I didn't have nothing, and because of these stories, the next day I was going to have two or three million dollars less than I had earned.

After Drew Rosenhaus explained to my family what these allegations meant, he suggested that maybe they shouldn't go to the draft with me. He knew it could be a tough day. My mother stood up and said to him, "This is my baby and we are going to that place. And we are gonna sit there and we are going to be proud."

Here's the biggest fact: As a result of this report leaking, the NFL fired the security director and cleaned out his whole staff. They brought in an entire new security department. Maybe it had nothing to do with me, maybe it was just a big coincidence. The whole damn department, gone.

Those stories shook up the draft. I didn't have any idea where I was going. Drew Rosenhaus said optimistically, "I expect him to go somewhere in the top four. This is the most unpredictable draft I've ever seen."

Most football fans have seen the NFL draft show on ESPN. The top choices sit with their families until the commissioner calls their name. Then they hug and kiss, and the ladies scream, and then they go up to the podium and put on their new team's cap. The NFL invited me to appear on this show. Even before all this started I didn't want to go. I wanted to stay home in Plymouth and have all my friends in my backyard for a big barbecue. This wasn't New York's draft pick; it was a big day for Plymouth, Florida. But the NFL convinced me to come. They gave me and my family a whole floor in the hotel for ourselves. I didn't feel real comfortable about it. I didn't know how I was going to feel or react, but ESPN's producers promised me that they would not have the camera in my face. "We're not gonna make this the Sapp show," were the exact words.

Another lie. That was the last time I ever put my own situation under somebody else's control.

The next morning my family prayed together again and then we went to the draft. Whatever happened, I reminded myself, I still was going to end up with more money than my family had ever seen. But what should have been a glorious day for me had turned out to be very complicated. It was about to get worse. By then my reputation was banged up, so I wasn't surprised when the first three picks went by. But after that one by one the players sitting in that room with me got picked, and they did the hugging and kissing and went onstage, and that room got awfully quiet. People I had played against and domi-nated were getting picked before me. It was like being in a choose-up game and watching the skinny little kid with glasses get picked before you. I knew that some teams needed help at other positions, but I couldn't help comparing myself to people picked before me. Him? You're tak-ing him? You ain't ever going to win with him. What's wrong with you? It was ridiculous. It was then I began to understand how much those false accusations were costing me. I had to sit there surrounded by empty chairs with the camera right on me, and inside I was getting more and more angry each time a team passed on me. With the fourth pick the Washington Redskins, who needed help on defense, took a wide receiver, Michael Westbrook. I shook my head and thought, "You people don't even want to win, do you."

The Philadelphia Eagles had traded up with Tampa Bay for the seventh pick and had a chance to draft me to replace my friend, the late Jerome Brown. Instead they selected defensive end Mike Mamula, who had raised his value by putting up good numbers at the Combine. Okay Philadelphia, I thought, you're gonna win the Combine next year. But if you don't want the best player left on the board, that's okay.

I thought the Jets might take me with the ninth pick. Playing in New York would have been fine, that would have been a fit. The Jet fans at Radio City Music Hall were cheering, "We want Sapp! We want Sapp!" Beautiful, I thought. I look nice in green. Instead the Jets took tight end Kyle Brady. The next day the *New York Daily News* showed those fans holding up a big banner reading "You Sapps!"

By then I was furious inside. I'd been sitting there longer than two hours. This had become the Warren Sapp Drama. That camera couldn't avoid focusing on me; they were running out of people in that waiting room. Even if I had done the things I had been accused of doing it would have been a hard day, but knowing the truth made it even more difficult. After San Francisco took a wideout, J. J. Stokes, with the 10th pick, I leaned over and told my mother, "They can take all the offensive players they want, but if they take one defensive tackle before me, we are all getting up and leaving."

With the 11th pick the Minnesota Vikings took defensive end Derrick Alexander. Angry as I was, Derrick was my homeboy from Florida State, and I wouldn't do anything to take his moment away. So I sat there.

Tampa Bay had gotten the 12th pick from the Eagles. What happens at the draft is that a team calls you before making its selection. I couldn't believe it when my phone started ringing. Oh no, Tampa Bay. Bucs coach Sam Wyche said to me, "How you feeling?"

How am I feeling? How am I feeling? One thing I was smart enough not to do at that moment was tell him how I was feeling. Then he said, "We're thinking about taking you. Think you can handle it?"

Really? I wanted to hang up the phone on him. You're thinking about taking me? I thought, are you fucking kidding me? You are the Tampa Bay Buccaneers, the worst team in football, and you are debating whether or not to take the best player in the draft? Just imagine Bill Belichick on that same phone; he'd have me ready to charge up a hill. "Son, we believe in you. We want you. Are you ready to be a Cleveland Brown?" Not, "We're thinking about taking you." The man was operating on another planet. They knew damn well they were getting a bargain—they were stealing. In fact, before they made the selection official Rich McKay wanted an assurance from Drew that we would not hold out. "This is a controversial pick," he told Drew. "We have new owners and we can't afford a holdout." Drew gave him our word that we would sign a fair contract.

Meeting with reporters after the draft, Wyche told them, "There isn't anything that affected his playing football. There's no addiction indicated in any way." That was some great vote of confidence in his first draft pick: He isn't a drug addict. Everybody always said that Sam Wyche is an offensive genius and that must be true, because he definitely offended me that day. That was the beginning of my short and bad relationship with Sam Wyche.

Commissioner Paul Tagliabue had a big smile on his face as he announced, "With the 12th pick, the Tampa Bay Buccaneers select University of Miami tackle Warren Sapp."

Yeah! Yeah! (That was my brother screaming. I looked at him and wanted to kill him.) He was thrilled. My family was going to be able to come to every home game. And right away my mother found something good, telling me, "You know, Jesus had 12 disciples, just feel like you're one of them."

I didn't feel that way at all. I was numb. I just wanted to get out of there. I told Drew Rosenhaus, "Remember I told you I didn't want to come. Just go ahead and book us the first flight out of here and let's go home." About the only good thing that came out of that day was that the Yucks used the 28th pick to take Florida State's Derrick Brooks. McKay knew what he got that day, saying, "That night I sat outside and we had a beer or two and smoked some cigars. We knew this draft gave us the opportunity to change the losing culture of the franchise. We'd drafted two great players who had been leaders on great college football teams." He definitely wasn't wrong about that. Between the two of us once we got it going we would make 17 straight Pro Bowls, ten for Derrick and seven for me.

A few days later Brooks and I went over to One Buc, the Tampa Bay practice center, for the first time. As we walked into the locker room the first person I saw was the strong safety, John Lynch. I'd seen him play a little on TV, and he had a reputation for being a hitter. "Lookee here, Brooks," I said loudly, "there's that hard-ass white boy that likes to knock people out."

Lynch smiled his big old smile and said, "It's about time they got me some help around here."

I liked that. "Let's go to work," I told him. The defense that eventually was going to dominate the NFL was forming up.

I had to keep reminding myself that football was my job now, and I had no choice where I was going to work. Maybe it was in Tampa, but when I looked it was still in the NFL. Of course, I did have to look toward the bottom of the NFL before I found them. Way, way down at the bottom. When Derrick and I got drafted Tampa Bay had lost double-digit games, meaning at least 10 games, for the past 13 seasons, the worst losing streak in NFL history. When they joined the NFL in 1976 they lost their first 26 games. One time somebody asked the first head coach, John McKay, about the team's execution. He thought about it for a few seconds and then decided, "I think that might be a good idea." After the Bucs beat New Orleans for their very first win, the Saints fired coach Hank Stram. Tampa Bay's tradition was losing. The Bucs were known basically as the place where careers went to die. Rich McKay, the general manager, admitted, "It was a very, very tough place to play because you never had the impression in that building that every day people woke up and worried about winning football games. You always had the impression that winning was a priority, but it might not be in the top five." And that was the general manager speaking.

At that time the only person I ever heard of who was happy to be there was defensive tackle Brad Culpepper, who had spent two years with the Minnesota Vikings backing up John Randle. When Rich McKay picked him up on waivers in 1994 Culpepper called his wife and told her he had good news and bad news: "The bad news is that the Bucs are terrible. The good news is that they're so bad I can play for them!"

Everything about the organization was bad; bad coaching staff, bad practice facility, bad bright-orange team colors, even a bad team logo. Bucco Bruce was the logo. The NFL had lions and giants, cowboys and panthers. We had the sappy pirate. C'mon, how intimidating is that, Bucco Bruce? He was this sad-looking pirate who actually had his earring in the wrong ear. What kind of pirate has an earring in his wrong ear? He was supposed to be sneering, but he actually looked like he was winking. I had just played for the hardest-ass team in college football. We took pride in our arrogance. And I was going to wear Bucco Bruce on my helmet?

The Bucs did have one thing that was even better than the Dallas Cowboys: They had the best cheerleading outfits. Their cheerleaders wore little orange shorts and white blouses. Anybody who thinks professional players being paid a lot of money to focus on football don't notice the cheerleaders would be wrong. Everything counts in pro football; but Daisy Duke shorts probably count twice. That was it, though; that was the only good thing about the Bucs.

When the reporters asked me how I felt about joining a team with a long tradition of losing seasons, I told them, "Maybe, but that was B.S.—before Sapp." Everybody laughed at that, typical big guy coming in with a big ego, with a lot of bravado, except that I meant it. One thing that had never changed about me, I hated losing. I still hate it. I didn't know one single thing about playing in the NFL, I hadn't even put on a uniform, but I knew that I wasn't going to play for a loser.

Drew kept telling me everything was going to be great, and started negotiating my contract. Whatever I signed for, I knew it was going to pay a whole lot more than working in the nursery back home. And I told my mother to inform the school she would not be coming back to work. She was officially retired!

The negotiations actually went smoothly. The NFL has salary guidelines for each draft slot, but Drew did a little better than that rate. He played their game and beat them at it. We agreed to a deal, and the Bucs called a press conference to announce it: $4.4 million for four years, with a $2.2 million guaranteed signing bonus. *Guaranteed* is a big word that they try to make small, because the guaranteed money is the real value of the contract.

With the media waiting outside Drew told the Bucs that we'd thought about it "and I just can't do it at $2.2. I need another $100,000 guaranteed."

Rich McKay told him no way.

"Okay," Drew said. "Listen, I'm going to go get Warren and we're gonna walk out." The Bucs gave up that extra $100,000. I was paid a $2.3 million signing bonus. Drew did not receive any of that money. For all those people who believe the agents are making a fortune, I paid Drew 1 percent of my $400,000 rookie-year salary, or $4,000. Hardly paid for his airfare. It was impossible to estimate how much money the drug lies cost me, but the Eagles gave Mike Mamula $6 million over four years or $1.6 million more than I signed for.

The first check I got was for $1,000,000. One million dollars, with the remaining $1.3 million to be paid in three installments when I passed the league-mandated drug tests. Except it wasn't exactly one million dollars. By the time they got done taking everything out of it, it was actually $667,237.62—with my name written on it. I held it in my hand, and I thought, I can spend a thousand dollars a day, every day, for the next year and still have almost half of it left. For the first time in my life I knew that I could walk into any store, buy pretty much anything I wanted to have, and be able to pay for it.

A check that size changes your life, but not always for the good. For some people it tears loose a cannon and they go right through it. I saw that happen in the NFL more than once. Some people just couldn't hold on to it. It's hard going from nothing to something, especially when you're young and believe you've got a long career and a lot of big checks in front of you. Hey, this is just the first check; I know they'll be more and bigger coming. Hey, this is just my third check, just my fourth, and suddenly they start disappearing faster and faster. Some people have so much fun with that money they forget what it took to earn it. They stop doing those things that got them there. I didn't get the vaccination for that myself. When I signed my second contract with the Bucs that would happen to me too.

That was ironic: Some people got paid so much money that it wound up costing them their career.

One thing that first big check does is bring a family together. My oh my, I did not know how large a family I had until I got that first big check. It was amazing how far my extended family extended. "I'm your mother's third cousin on your aunty's side, three times removed." Good, so I didn't have any problem removing them a fourth time.

When you grow up in Plymouth, Florida, nobody teaches you how to be rich. *Rich* means you got more money in your pocket than you need to pay the bills that month. Nobody ever needed an accountant or a money manager: Investing? Sure, we'll make an investment, we'll invest in eating dinner tonight. Money comes, money goes, more money goes. That's just the way it is. Real money got made under the tree with a pair of aces.

First thing I did was take my mother down to the Mercedes Benz dealership where one of my homeboys worked washing cars and delivering them and bought my mother the first new car she ever had in her life. It was a big beautiful car—that car had a backseat big enough to break dance—and came guaranteed that it wasn't going to overheat in the Florida summer. Then we drove that car over to the affluent side of Orlando where I bought her a brand-new home that was still under construction. We made them change the address because originally it had been *8666*, and my mother was clear about the fact that she was not living in any house with *666* in its address. So it became *8664*. Handing my mother the keys to her new house was one of the proudest moments of my life. If that was the best thing that ever happened to me because of football it would have been enough.

The first NFL game I had ever been to in my life was in 1979, when my aunt Ola Jones took me and my brother to Tampa to see his Bucs win the first playoff game in their history, beating Ron Jaworski's raggedy-ass Philadelphia Eagles, 24–17. We sat in the end zone, and I remember that every time either team attempted a field goal or an extra point they put up a huge screen behind the goal posts to prevent the football from going into the stands. The screen fascinated me; everything about being at a pro football game fascinated me. For a little kid football player, it was like walking into Wonderland. Football and food, two of my favorite things together. I remember knowing that someday I was going to be on a field just like that one—except it would be in Dallas. No part of my dream ever took place in Tampa.

When I reported to training camp they asked me what number I wanted. Picking your number can be a delicate thing; there are some people who take it very seriously. They got to have a certain number or they can't play. They get superstitious about it. They truly believe that it makes a difference, and if they believe it maybe it does. Not for me though. They had numbers *78*, *63*, *97*, and *99* available. Offensive tackle Scott Dill was wearing my Miami number, 76, and some people expected me to pay him to give it to me. The media thought it might be a big story. That was just foolishness. It ain't the number, it's what inside that jersey. My real hero's number is 33, which is what my brother wore, but that was a running back's number so I couldn't wear that. I loved 80, which was worn by the Cowboys' Tony Hill. That was a great number: "When everything got shady, dial 80!" But the number I really wanted from the jump was 99, because that had been Jerome Brown's number in Philadelphia. It fit me like a glove, the fact that it was sitting there waiting for me meant that the Football Gods had determined that was supposed to be my number. Sapp, no. 99. It became my theme: 99 problems I'm providing for your offense on Sunday afternoon.

On my first day of training camp I put on that ugly-ass uniform with *99* on the back and trotted onto the field. When I jogged into the stadium at the University of Tampa about 4,000 fans started cheering for me. I hadn't expected that at all. I was so surprised I looked around to see if maybe Deion Sanders was behind me.

Turned out that was the highlight of my rookie year. After that everything was downhill.

It was the hardest year of my life. People who have played sports have heard the expression, "There's no *I* in team." Well, the people who say that never played in Tampa Bay. That first year there also was no *team* in Tampa. When you go to an NFL game you see the shiny uniforms, the cheerleaders, the tailgaters, the big, bright scoreboard, and the team on the field, but no one sees what goes on behind all that. I had been drafted into a terrible situation. The people there were satisfied with losing. That place was a three-ring circus: The head coach couldn't head coach, an assistant coach who looked to me like he was trying to sabotage the head coach to get his job, and my teammates looked at rookies as a threat to their job security. Rich McKay was continually bringing in new players to try to find people who could play. It was hard to get close to any teammates because they might be gone the next week.

Right away the players who had been there a few years began calling me "Super Rookie," and it wasn't meant as a compliment. "Super Rookie's gonna do it all by himself." "Don't worry about it, Super Rookie will take care of it." It got nasty, and it made for some hard days. There was a great deal of resentment toward me from some of the veteran players. I told one of them one time, "You do know the good teams pick at the bottom of the draft, don't you? If you all was so fucking good, I wouldn't be here." But these were people who couldn't be insulted. They were comfortable about losing. Winning hadn't been a priority, the general manager said.

I kept thinking, is this it? Is this really what the great NFL is all about?

It definitely was not fun and football games, cheering fans, and big paychecks. It was a lot of jealousy, greed, backstabbing, and finger pointing. I had never experienced anything like this. In college we breathed as a team. On Saturday we would go out and handle our business. But that first year at Tampa we had no structure, no standard, no desire.

Sam Wyche and I never did arrive on the same planet. When he was with the Cincinnati Bengals he had a reputation of being a great player's coach, probably a genius, but I always thought that a coach actually had to win some championships before he became a genius. I knew a bunch of the people who played for him in Cincinnati, and they loved the man, they would block walls for him, but the Sam Wyche we got in Tampa was something different. I was fortunate in my career to have played for Tony Dungy and John Gruden, who knew how to motivate their people. Wyche thought you motivated people by making snide comments, by belittling people. One time I remember the team was on the practice field, and he just tore into Bob Wylie, the O-line coach. In front of the whole team he said to him, "Bob, you know why your players are pussies? Because they're coached by a pussy."

A few words, and he destroyed that coach in front of his players. It was embarrassing. There was nothing Wylie could do but take it. If he stood up to him he was done, but if he took it he also was done. His players couldn't respect him after that.

So it wasn't a surprise that his coaching staff was disloyal. We spent the whole season watching Defensive Coordinator Rusty Tillman trying to sabotage Wyche so he could get the head coaching job. He'd say, "He don't need to be here. I can do that job." What the hell? I thought an assistant was supposed to help the head coach, not help bury him.

The problems between us started when I came to camp weighing about 295. Wyche thought I'd be stronger at 270 or 280. Instead of just telling me to lose some weight, he'd make these little snide comments: "You could've made that play if you weren't carrying that extra weight," "You would've got there if you lost a few pounds." He didn't even look at the way I was playing; he was busy reading the scale. We used to call him "a frame guy," the kind of person who admired the frame instead of looking at the picture. Wyche spent too much time focusing on things that didn't make any difference. He was worried about what people ordered from room service when we were on the road, or what time we got to the facility for practice, instead of concentrating on game preparation.

So my weight became a big issue with him right from the beginning of training camp. One afternoon we were on a bus going to Miami to practice with the Dolphins, and Jerry Angelo, the director of player personnel, started lecturing me about how my weight was going to affect my entire career. I'd been in the NFL about two weeks, and he was analyzing my whole future. It surprised me. After looking at hundreds of hours of game films they had made me their first draft pick and guaranteed me more than two million dollars, and now the first thing they were trying to do was change me. Really? I listened politely to every word he said, I knew it was coming directly from Wyche, and when he slowed down I asked him, "Hey, Jerry, who made you a fucking nutritionist?" That whole bus started laughing. In fact, people in cars going by the bus started laughing. C'mon now, at least let me play a little before you start criticizing me.

Every coach has his own way of motivating players. For example, Bill Parcells used fear: People were afraid they were going to lose their position or that he was going to cut their ass from the squad. One time, supposedly, he handed Lawrence Taylor a plane ticket and told him that the Giants were going to get Rickey Jackson from New Orleans to take his position. "I need him up here to play against Jackie Slater. I'll give him your number and tell him not to take his helmet off the whole game, and nobody'll know the difference." Jackie Slater was a beast, and LT got four sacks against him.

Tony Dungy, who eventually would replace Wyche, was the best motivator I ever played for. He made you feel like a man. With him too my weight was always a topic of discussion, but he understood how to make his point about it to me. In 1998 I was watching game films with the defensive coordinator, Monte Kiffin, who was making the point that I was out of shape, when the door in the back of the room opened. Somebody came in and just stood there, but I couldn't tell who it was. After we watched one play Kiffin asked, "Is that all you got?"

"The eye in the sky don't lie," I admitted. "That's all I got."

Then from the back of the room came . . . the Voice of God, which is how we referred to Dungy. "Ninety-nine," he said, "that's not good enough." Then he paused and finished his thought, "For you." Closed the door and left. That was an arrow hitting the center of the target. Not good enough . . . for you. Whew, that's making the point.

In 2000 I came to work weighing 326 pounds, bigger than I was when Dungy was complaining I was already too big. But I was in great condition. I had put in the work that summer and I was ready to play. We opened the season against the Patriots in Foxboro. When I weighed in on Friday at 326 Tony didn't say one word to me, he just turned around and walked away. That said a lot to me. But I went up there and had a monster game. I was all over Drew Bledsoe. I was so close to him the whole game that if the laws had been different then people might have thought we were married.

The next Monday morning the whole team was stretching when Tony Dungy started walking nice and slow toward me. When he got up close all he said was, "326 pounds."

I threw my hands up in the air in frustration and said, "Coach, you watched me coming here every day and doing my work. You saw me doing every drill . . ."

He said to me, "I'll make you a deal. You play like you did Sunday and we don't need to talk." That was the way to handle it. All I asked Sam Wyche was to judge me by what I did on the field, not on the scale. But that was not the way Sam Wyche ran his team.

It wasn't like the whole team embraced me either. I had been drafted to replace Santana Dotson, and they brought Brad Culpepper in from the Vikings to replace Mark Wheeler at the other tackle spot. Brad Culpepper was a Florida boy, and we formed a partnership that first year: We promised each other that this losing attitude was going to end and we were going to turn it around. My man Culpepper and I were just two Florida boys who loved the game and made that commitment to each other. He was a warrior and he was in my foxhole with me. We were almost exactly the same except for the fact that I am black and he's white, and growing up he was an Eagle Scout and I . . . I . . . was not. But other than that we were exactly alike, except that when he wasn't studying his play book he was studying for the law boards and I . . . I . . . was not. What did bring us together was our love for the game and our determination that we were going to change this losing culture. We were gonna dig our way of that hole. We started working together. Every day at the beginning of practice we'd go off by ourselves to the left corner in the back of the end zone to do our stretching. In the games we usually would go in together to give Dotson and Wheeler a blow—except we outplayed them. We'd go in and make a big play, and when Wyche took us out we'd look at each other and laugh, "We fucked up his plans, didn't we?" Our relationship definitely was not politically correct. I called him *Whitey* and he called me *Colored*, "C'mon Whitey, get after it." "After you, Colored."

The first thing we had to do was replace Dotson and Wheeler. You can't blame those two for not liking us. We were trying to take food off their table, but they definitely showed their resentment. There is a tradition in the NFL of taping rookies. I don't mean taping their ankles or recording their conversations, I mean mummy-taping them to the walls, taping them to the goal posts, just wrapping them in tape. Every once in awhile I would walk out onto the field and see some mummy dangling upside down from the crossbar, hanging from a rope made out of tape.

In the NFL every rookie gets taped, but some rookies get taped more than others. Especially first-round picks who aren't too shy to say out loud what needs to be said. The first pick gets the most money, so the most is expected from him. I was a big target; if you listened to Wyche I was about 20 pounds too big a target. But almost every week, right into the season, I got my ass taped to the uprights. One time they taped Culpepper and me back to back in the middle of the floor. And it seemed like it was always the same people doing the taping and enjoying the hell out of it. Taping is not voluntary. There's 40 of them and 12 rookies, and when it's your turn the other 11 ain't going to be rushing to help you. There's always enough extra tape. Fighting back isn't a good option either, because you are not going to win, and the taping is going to be worse. When they came up to me the first time I knew what was happening. "Oh man, right now?"

"Put your hands down," they ordered me. Next thing I knew I was getting real friendly with the goal post. Rookies also get dumped in the cold water. Okay, it's dumb—but it's also funny as hell. One time some players threw buckets of water at rookies. I don't mean they threw water; they threw the whole bucket. Maybe they didn't understand the whole concept, but they literally threw a bucket and hit someone upside the head. It stopped being funny right then for me. I didn't want to see anyone get hurt.

The one time I stopped the hazing was in 1999, when they wanted to tape our rookie kicker Martin Gramatica to the goal posts. I stopped them because he was our only guaranteed points. I told them, "Are you out of your fucking minds? The only way we win games is with this little fucker." I had a rule, you could do anything you wanted to anybody on the team except my head coach, my quarterback, and my kicker. Everybody else is fair game, but these are the only people on the field who actually have to think during the game, and they needed to be left alone.

About the middle of my first season I finally had enough of all that taping. I told them once that I was sick of it. "Okay," they said, "but we're still gonna tape your ass up, Sapp." They left me no choice. I retaliated. Rookies also are responsible for Saturday morning breakfast. It used to be that you just had to bring breakfast for the people who play your position, but it's changed now, and rookies have to provide breakfast for the whole team. That can be expensive. When my turn came I had it catered for $1,100, and they set up a nice table and made omelets and bacon. It saved me a lot of ass whipping. Oh, those people loved those Saturday omelets, so I gave them a choice: Tape me up this week, and I promise you there ain't gonna be no breakfast here Saturday morning. "Go tape Brooks up," I told them. "Brooks don't talk and I can't stop talking."

"Get the tape."

"I've giving you my word here, no breakfast this week. None of them delicious omelets."

"It ain't your turn anyway."

"But it's gonna be. And I ain't feeding you motherfuckers. You tape me and I'm done with it."

That was a tough decision for them, but their stomachs won. That is what finally got the taping stopped.

I started the first five games of the season. I went into the NFL expecting to be a productive player right away. In college I had never played against anyone who could stop me, and I thought the NFL was just stepping up.

I remember running on the field in Philadelphia's Veterans Stadium for my first real NFL game. At the U of Miami coming out of the tunnel through the smoke into the cheer definitely was cool, but it was nothing like this. It made me pause for just a second to take it in with all of my senses. I was there, I was in the NFL, I'd made it.

That was the famous "For who? For what?" game. The Eagles had signed free agent Ricky Watters to a monster contract. He was going deep on a pass play, the ball was there, and Charles Dimry was defending. Instead of going for the ball and thinking he would get laid out by Slim Dim, Watters short-armed it. He pulled back and let the pass fall incomplete. When the reporters asked him about that after the game he said, "And get knocked out? For who? For what?"

For who? For what? For the monster contract you signed, that's for who and for what.

We laughed about that after winning the game 21–6. Slim Dim was as skinny as this page. He wasn't going to put a dent in Watters. There is an old story they tell in the league about confrontations like this: If Slim Dim had hit Ricky Watters, and Ricky found out about it . . . but Ricky backed away from contact. In the league, believe me, people notice that.

I got my first NFL sack in that game. I was going up against the veteran guard Guy McIntyre. Randall Cunningham was the quarterback, and on third down and 6 he dropped back to pass. I took Mc-

Intyre to the house. I ran up his numbers and then slipped underneath; it was just me and Randall and here we go. He took off, and everybody knows he can run, and I was right behind him. As he was on the move he kept looking for a receiver, but we had good coverage. When he got to the sideline I grabbed him and pulled him down and he covered up. It was what we refer to as a dummy sack, meaning it was dumb for him to take it. He easily could have just thrown the ball away. It wasn't a highlight sack for me, but I ran him down and got it done.

I had a solid first game. What surprised me most was the amount of holding that goes on inside on almost every play. I had to learn how to use my hands to knock down my opponent's hands. But overall I had a solid game, and I began to think this league wasn't going to even slow me down.

I learned differently in our seventh game of the season against the Minnesota Vikings, when Chris Hinton taught me that this is a man's game. Hinton was a veteran offensive lineman, 34 years old. The other guard was Randall McDaniel, maybe the best guard ever to play the game of football. Rather than lining up against the guaranteed Hall-of-Famer, I thought, I'll just take that old man Hinton and whoop on him. I'm younger, quicker, and better looking. Time to show him there's a new sheriff in town. No problem with him. First play, Hinton came off the ball, grabbed the front of my jersey with two hands. He picked me up and started shaking me, yelling, "Rrrrrrrrrggggggg! Rrrrrrrrrggggggg," shaking me like a rag doll while bashing me with his helmet. "Lemme go," I was yelling, "lemme go." The play ended, and he just dropped me and walked away. Well, I thought, this isn't good. That was the only time in my entire career that I was scared on the football field. I couldn't believe that I had to go against a man that big and that strong and that mean. It was pretty obvious that Chris Hinton was mad about something, but I didn't care what it was. I went over to the other side. McDaniel may have been the greatest ever, but at least he wasn't crazy.

I couldn't do much with McDaniel. At one point during the game I turned to the official and complained, "Ref, he's holding me."

In college when I told that to an official, next play, there's the flag, "Holding!" In college, I was Warren Sapp, All-American. Thank you very much Mr. Official.

But not in the big-boys league. When I said that, the official gave me one of those, are you kidding, looks, and said, "Grow up." That's when I knew if I was ever going to be any good in the NFL I would have to work for it. I wasn't going to float by on my talent and pleasing personality.

I struggled that first season. The team got off to a good start, and after seven games Wyche walked around telling everybody, "Five-dash-two," but there was no structure at all to his strategy. And it seemed like every week we were installing a different defensive scheme, making it up as we went along. We played with a five-man front line, a four-man front, a three-man front. It basically was whatever he thought of that week. The same thing was true on offense. If he called six straight plays, it would be six different formations, with six different sets of personnel. Each formation had its own name, so players would know when they were supposed to be in the game. The coaches would call out zebra personnel or cheetah personnel; we had jaguar personnel, tiger personnel. The names had no relation to the formation: What's the difference between a tiger, cheetah, and jaguar? It made no sense at all. Maybe running all these different formations made it difficult for the other teams to prepare to play us, but it also made it difficult for us to prepare to play. We didn't have one bread-and-butter formation; we had no signature scheme that we could depend on. Instead of lining up and saying, this is who we are, this is what we do, and we are going to bust your ass doing it, he would try to reinvent the game. He would trick you, slick you, and stick you. Everything was new every week. Without bread and butter you can't have a full meal.

What also surprised me was the total lack of teaching that took place. I was a talented kid who wanted to get better. I had the natural ability but not the experience or the knowledge. And no one on that coaching staff worked with me.

The situation got really bad the fifth week when the team bus to the stadium left the hotel without me. We were playing Carolina at Clemson, and the bus was scheduled to depart at 10:15. I didn't go to the team breakfast because I didn't like the food they served, and it wasn't mandatory. At 10 o'clock Sam jumped up and yelled, "We're leaving!" They piled on the buses and took off. I came down a few minutes later, and the lobby was deserted. A woman told me, "They left about two minutes ago."

The team doctor came downstairs and started shaking his head, "That son of a bitch didn't leave, did he?" That son of a bitch did exactly that. There is no way of describing the way I felt. I was angry, betrayed, frustrated, puzzled. I had never been abandoned by an entire team before. Pro football definitely was tougher than I anticipated.

I raced to the stadium and got there just after the team. When the D-line coach asked me if I'd missed the bus, I asked him, "How could you tell somebody who wasn't there that the bus was leaving early? How was I supposed to know?"

We won the game, but on Monday Wyche told me I was fined $2,400, "but if you pay it within 24 hours I'll cut it in half."

I told him that I wasn't paying any fine at all.

And he told me I was no longer starting because "a starter would be on the job on time."

It got bad. I pointed out that most coaches would make damn sure he's got his 22 starting players on the bus before it leaves, especially if it's leaving early. At that point we were "three-dash-two" so I think he felt that we all replaceable parts. The man was sabotaging himself. I was good enough to start in the three games we'd won, but I missed a bus so I lost my job? No. You lose your job on the field, and you lose it to someone playing better than you. Not someone who got on the bus before you. He was trying to teach me a bus schedule at the expense of the whole team. He was a damn fool.

When the reporters asked me about it I didn't try to bury him. "It's no big deal," I said. "A decision was made. You don't worry about things you can't control. I believe I've played all right. I mean, I haven't looked at myself on film and thrown up."

For each of the next three weeks I was in the game for 13 plays and spent the rest of the time standing on the sideline next to Brad. Even my mother had nothing to cheer about, and my mother would cheer the hot dog man. I was a player, not a watcher, and I didn't know how to deal with it. Me and Brad just said, "Let 'em go. That's the way they want it, let 'em go." It tore me up, just tore me up.

I felt myself falling into the don't-give-a-damn Tampa Bay Buccaneer mentality. I knew that no matter whether I played or not I was still going to get my same check. So if they thought I wasn't good enough, that was their choice. Our two D-line coaches, Tom Pratt and Kenny Clarke, pulled me aside for a conversation. "You know Warren, you've only played . . ." they started to tell me.

I finished it for them, "13, 13, and 13 plays the last three weeks."

"So what's going on?"

My coaches were asking me why I wasn't playing. What's wrong with this picture? "You tell me. Aren't we supposed to have a rotation going on?"

Coach Pratt said, "I thought there was a rotation, but I'm looking up and you're not playing."

"Well, someone decided to start Santana and Mark Wheeler and put me and Brad on the sideline, and one thing I know for sure, it wasn't me and Brad made that decision." It was surprising to me that my D-line coaches didn't know why I wasn't playing.

For the first time in my life my attitude got bad. I had never been late for a practice in my life. All of a sudden I would oversleep and be late to work. I didn't even have an alarm clock, instead I would have a wake-up call. But I was sleeping with five pillows, and during the night I'd throw a pillow off the bed and knock the phone off the hook. That wake-up call just went to hell. I was fined several times, but the worst thing about it was that I stopped caring. A couple grand here, a couple grand there, it didn't matter. That was awful; football had always been my passion, my identity. Instead of blood cells, I used to bleed little tiny footballs. I knew how to play football; I didn't know how not to play football. Every night after practice I would stop by the ABC on the way home and grab a bottle of Remy. I'd sit in front of the TV and drink a whole liter of Remy and wake up there the next morning. I had never been so disgusted in my life.

Occasionally I'd look at the stories in the newspaper, and too often they were about how I wasn't playing to my potential. No kidding. I wasn't playing to my potential because I wasn't playing. Doesn't take Al Einstein to figure that one out.

I never had one conversation about this with Wyche. He tried to patronize me by putting me on offense, blocking for Errict Rhett, before we played Atlanta. He named the formation with me in the backfield to block "rhino." I figured that one out; it was "rhino" because I was a big, powerful player.

I hadn't played on offense since high school, we were five-dash-two, and Coach Genius was still making unnecessary changes. For the first time since high school, I played both ways. But to show how screwed up that situation was, I scored the first touchdown of my NFL career in that game—on defense. In the first quarter we had the Falcons down on their own 5-yard line. Our defensive end, Eric Curry, didn't have a single sack, and I wanted to get him going, so we played a game. The Falcon's quarterback, Jeff George, saw Curry coming right up in his face. Curry was pretty raw, so Jeff kind of hopped to the side and flipped the ball toward running back Ironhead Heyward. I just stepped in front of Heyward, caught the ball with one hand, and ran it in. Touchdown! Touchdown Sapp! It was like we were playing back on the Dust Bowl. Oh my goodness! I had never scored a touchdown in college. Curry jumped on my back, Hardy Nickerson jumped on his back, and I carried them into the end zone. Laughing. There was no way to describe the thrill. It was like having a child—except you get six points for it. I was so surprised I didn't even have an end zone dance.

Wyche put me in on offense in the third quarter. I don't know that we fooled the Falcons, but it definitely confused the hell out of my mother. She was coming to every game with my aunt Ola, and when she saw me running out there to play with the offense she had no idea what was going on. We were on their 2-yard line, and Wyche called a handoff to Rhett, with me clearing a path for him. I told Errict Rhett in the huddle, "Don't be eating lunch back there." I put a block on a lineman to break him open, and he walked in for a touchdown—but we still lost the game 24–21.

When Wyche had first told me he wanted me to play on offense I said, "I really don't care to do this, but if you think I'm the best fullback on this team I'll do it. But just one thing, don't throw the ball to me."

He said, "Why not? I know you can catch."

"I'm definitely going to catch it if you put it near me, but that's not the point," I said. Then I repeated, "Just don't throw the ball to me." He wouldn't listen to me, though, and in our 12th game he called that pass play. We were playing the Packers at Lambeau Field and our quarterback, Trent Dilfer, tried to throw one of those dinky little passes to me. It got picked off, like I was afraid it was going to. It was the type of pass I had picked off three weeks before. After the game I told Wyche, "Dilfer can't throw that pass; that's why I didn't want you trying to throw it to me."

Wyche also had me playing special teams. Special Teams Coach Big George Stewart said a little bit apologetically, "You're gonna have to cover kickoffs. I don't want to do this, but he's making a point."

I said, "Fine. Doesn't matter, it's fine by me. I can do it, no problem." I'd been the up man on the punting team at Miami, meaning I protected the punter, but I'd never covered kickoffs. That's where they put the pain in pro football. Whoa. The way it worked was that the receiving team built a wedge, a five-man wall, in front of the ball carrier, and the defense had to break through that wall. There wasn't much finesse, unless you consider hitting people with a sledgehammer finesse. We kicked off, and I sprinted 30 yards and started rattling around like a pinball, knocking down as many people as I could as fast as possible. *Bam! Bam! Bam!* And you got to keeping looking all around because in that situation you are both the ball and the pin. Many people as you want to hit, want to hit you first. When we finally made the tackle I got up and started running off the field—man was I glad that was done. *Tweet! Tweet!* Oh my goodness. Flag goes up in the air, "Offside, number 93." Oh Demetrius, how could you do that to me? Demetrius DuBose was offside. We had to do the whole thing again. I wanted to kill the man.

After that experience I came to believe that it should be mandatory that every rookie in the NFL cover a kickoff. That would give them a better appreciation for what the grunts of the team do, the people who are never going to be stars, who will never get any notice unless they miss a block, clip somebody and get penalized, or make one of those wince-on-your-couch killer blocks that they show to death on *SportsCenter*. The grunts are the players who get a lot of pain and a little glory. And no matter who you are, playing special teams will make you appreciate how fortunate you are to be playing in the league. But what it does most of all is make you want to work harder and get better so you don't have to play special teams anymore.

I did it that one time. I'm glad I did it. But I knew that if they asked me to do it again I would tell them to go to hell. That was not my job.

That five-dash-two pretty quick became six-dash-ten. Nobody was surprised that the Bucs had another losing season—that's the only thing we led the league in. The Bucs set the NFL record for consecutive losing seasons. The worst thing about it was that nobody seemed to be too upset about it. The Bucs losing was like paint drying; you wait long enough and it was going to happen.

By the end of the season I knew I couldn't play for Sam Wyche. I decided I was not going to be part of that circus. So I went to see General Manager Rich McKay to tell him that. He knew why I wanted to see him; he knew he had to make a choice. I walked into his office and before I even opened my rather large mouth he put up a hand to stop me. "Don't say anything Big Dawg; we're gonna get a new coach, and we're gonna move this thing forward."

I said, "Thank you very much," turned around, and walked out.

We had a lot of the pieces we needed to win. The core of the defense, Brooks, Culpepper, Lynch, linebacker Hardy Nickerson, and I were all there, and all of us were desperate to win. We just needed someone who could impose his vision on our talent. Sam Wyche was not that guy and thank goodness Rich McKay knew it.

I went down to the Super Bowl, and there were rumblings that Tampa was going to hire Tony Dungy. Dungy had never been a head coach. He'd been an assistant at Pittsburgh, Kansas City, and Minnesota, so he had put his print on some of the best defenses in the league. I saw Derrick Thomas, Neil Smith, and Johnny Randle, and they didn't hold back, "Man, you get Tony Dungy you are going to love him to bits."

Least nobody called him a genius.

But that wasn't quite the end of that season of my life. My brother Arnell had developed a serious blood condition working for public maintenance for the city of Houston, Texas. Apparently he'd been breathing bad air without a ventilator. He was taking blood thinners, but they didn't seem to be helping him. He went into the hospital in the spring and I went to see him. He was really excited about the coming season, really excited about Dungy.

I got the call from my mother at four o'clock on a Monday morning. I'd been working out on Sunday and I was exhausted. And then she told me my brother had passed. That didn't make sense to me. He was 36 years old; the doctors were taking care of him. I don't remember putting down the phone, getting dressed, or driving 80 miles on I-4 to Orlando. I remember sitting in the driveway of her new home and looking at my watch. It was 5:30. I didn't know how I possibly could have gotten there so quickly, but that morning nothing made sense to me.

I walked into the house and broke down right in her arms. I finally went into the kitchen, and I was standing there, and she asked, "You want to see him?"

See him? I thought that there had to be some protocol for this situation, the police, coroner, somebody. Didn't you have to call an ambulance? I walked into his bedroom and Arnell was sitting up in his bed. I stood there staring at him, shaking my head in complete disbelief, tears running down my face onto my shirt. At his funeral my mother whispered to me, "Are you all right?"

"No," I said. And I wasn't. He'd died of a blood clot. For the whole next week I sat in a corner by the pool. Just sat there. I would get up, go to the bathroom, get something small to eat, and go back to that corner. At the end of the week I went home, but believe me, I left a part of me in that house.

FOUR

A reporter once asked me what I thought about Tony Dungy. I told him, "I would take a bullet for that man. Long as it didn't kill me, of course." That's compared to Sam Wyche; for him I wouldn't have even taken a paper cut.

I am a believer in the Football Gods. I've seen proof of their existence too many times to doubt they are real. I know that if you respect the game and play it the way it is supposed to be played they will reward you, but if you cheat yourself or the game, if you give less than a full effort, the Football Gods will find you and make you eat humble pie. If I had gone to them and asked them to give me a coach who will teach me the skills I need to play the game at the highest level as well as encourage me to grow as a man, they would have sent me Tony Dungy.

And if they had asked for a sacrifice I might have had someone in mind.

Tony Dungy was not management's first choice. In fact, he wasn't even one of their first five choices. He was way down on their list. Like broccoli on a shopping list, you only pick it up if they're out of green beans. Dungy had never been a head coach and wasn't widely known outside the league. He was soft-spoken and confident; he definitely wasn't a flamboyant self-promoter. But at least two big-name coaches they wanted to hire weren't interested in the job. McKay finally real-

ized that Dungy was the ultimate overachiever, that he'd been successful in every situation, and offered him the job. It was a pretty brave
decision. Tony Dungy wasn't the NFL's first black coach—Al Davis
had hired Art Shell in Oakland—but he was the first black coach in a
predominately white city who didn't have a history with that team. I
didn't know too much about him. He had been Minnesota's defensive
coordinator, which meant he was the man who had cut Culpepper. But
even Culpepper was thrilled when Dungy was hired. Said he was a
great coach who would look you in the eye and talk to you about anything in the world, not just football. That was the first time I'd ever
heard anybody praise his executioner for doing such a good job.

My life, not just my playing career, changed the day I met Tony
Dungy. Soon as I got back from the Super Bowl I went over to One
Buc, our training facility, to meet him. I wanted to know what we were
getting. We ran into each other in the locker room and went back to his
office. The first day I met him I had a longer conversation with him
than I'd had with Wyche in a whole year. He told me, "I'm gonna take
your chains off. I've been watching the tape of the way they have you
playing. That's not your game. I want you to play like you did in college, get off the ball fast, take off up the field, and create as much havoc
as you want."

I heard harps playing in the background. I thought, I must be in
heaven. "What?"

"I'm going to let you go," he said flatly. "Same as I did with John
Randle." He told me we were going to play a 4–3, four men on the line,
every play, and he was committed to making it work. No more experimenting, no more fancy foolish formations, 4–3 every down. He was
going to install a system and stick with it. "I don't care what's gone on
here the last few years. We're going to find the players that fit our system and we're going to win with it." Then he looked at me and added,
"And I'm asking you to lead."

"That's not a problem," I said, but warned him, "We got some people in here who ain't gonna agree with this." The only way to make a defense like that work is to do it repeatedly and then repeat it again. Good football requires the simple repetition of tedious movements over and over and over. It's about as fancy as a hammer; it's just being better at what you do than your opponent is at stopping it. I told Dungy, "Trust me, I've only been here for one year, but there are some people here . . ."

He shook his head. "Don't worry. They won't be here. But that's what we're going to do."

From the first day of practice Dungy set out to change the culture. No more Yucks. "The opponent here is expectations," he told the media. "There never have been any." He walked into the job and told us to tuck our shirts in when we practiced. Some people complained about that, wondering what difference it made. He told them, "On Sunday you have to tuck your shirt in." Those people who challenged him on things like that soon went away. "They won't be here," he'd told me, and then he started weeding them out. Guys who didn't show up for conditioning in the off-season went away. Guys who refused to do the work in practice went away. On the third day of practice we were doing a four-bag drill. We did it over and over and over. Defensive end Eric Curry asked our D-line coach, Rod Marinelli, "We gonna do this same thing every day?"

Marinelli said, "Yes, sir," and I knew that Eric was not going to be there.

Dungy had a way of making his feelings known with very few words. We lost our second game of the season in Detroit, 21–6. On the flight home somebody plugged in a jukebox so we were playing some music, drinking a little bit, talking loud—maybe it got a little raucous. We left a lot of empty bottles on that airplane. The next morning Dungy said evenly, "On the ride home I couldn't tell if we'd won or lost. In fact, from what I saw on that plane I would have thought we'd won the game. I never want to have that experience again." No yelling, no threats, but we got the message.

After he'd left that room I stood up. As far as I remember this was the only time I specifically addressed the fact that we were playing for a black coach. I said, "We got to do better than that. We got a black man leading this team and a whole bunch of black players. We are representing him and everything he is about. We can't be known as a bunch of hoodlums, 'cause you know he ain't all that. We got to be better." Dungy never had to deal with us on that subject again.

He treated his players like men and demanded they act like men. He didn't set a lot of rules; he let us police our own locker room. It was directly the opposite of Wyche. Every person had to take responsibility for doing his job. No excuses, no explanations. You have one job to do in this system—get it done. You're supposed to block the end, block the end. It's not that hard: If you cut up a pie in nine pieces it doesn't take much to eat one slice. Anybody can eat their one slice. But eating the whole pie is a task. That was the philosophy he taught us: It takes all the pieces coming together, not just one superstar. Tony liked to say that he didn't want the 53 best players. Talent alone will not get it done. He wanted the 53 players who worked together to give us the best chance to win. He taught the game in its simplest form. He clearly and simply defined the job he expected you to do, and in practice we went over it and over it. He emphasized the fundamentals of football. He demanded we execute the same way every time, that we do it at a high level of excellence. Get it right, now do it again, now do it better.

Every Monday morning he brought the whole team together to watch what we called the dummy reel. This was tape of all the mistakes that we'd made during a game, many of them being mental errors rather than a physical breakdown. Tony Dungy never yelled, just asked. Did you dot your *I*'s and cross your *T*'s? Trust me, you did not want to star on Tony Dungy's dummy reel. After every play he would stop the tape and calmly ask the person who'd made the mistake, "Why did you do that? What were you thinking of right there?" That was always his question, *why?*

That answer had better not be, "My sainted mother."

It took a little while, but gradually it became clear to everyone that Dungy knew what he was talking about. The evidence was right there on that reel. The eye in the sky did not lie. When someone made a mistake, when they were not in the gap where they were supposed to be, if they were lollygagging or going rogue, that football would find that hole. It was an amazing thing to see. It was like a magnet, drawn right to the mistake. Damn, those Football Gods are tough! But when we did what we were taught to do, when we were in our assigned spot, the defense worked. We could see that right there on the film. So when the same people began showing up on that reel every Monday, making the same mistakes, we knew we weren't going to have to worry about them much longer. "Eric, what gap you got right there?"

"The C-gap."

Wrong answer. We knew we weren't going to have to worry about that next season. Eric was not going to be there.

Eventually we all showed up on the dummy reel. That was inevitable. Seventh game of the season we lost to Arizona 13–9, mostly because we still were undisciplined. Early in the second quarter I got drawn offside. Oh man, I hated making mental mistakes on the field. I looked at Brooks and he was shaking his head, "Sapp . . ."

I told Brooks, "Don't worry, you don't ever have to worry about this fat bastard doing that again." I did not have another offside penalty for six years. Monday morning we were all on that dummy reel—me, Brooks, John Lynch—and we looked at each other right then and decided that was it. That was the last time we were going to be in the moving pictures. Dungy preached discipline—discipline, discipline, discipline—and we were his choir. He kept showing that reel and people kept disappearing. It took some time, but Dungy weeded out those people not willing to do the work his way.

Dungy even changed the team colors from that putrid orange that made us all look like overgrown Creamsicles to a respectable red and pewter. Instead of Bucco Bruce our logo became a flag with a skull and crossed cutlasses. A shiver-your-timbers logo, rather than that silly Disneyland pirate. All of a sudden we were able to look in the mirror and feel good about ourselves.

He also brought in a new coaching staff. Listen to this defensive staff: Lovie Smith, Monte Kiffin, Herm Edwards, and Rod Marinelli. Maybe the best defensive staff in pro football history. After four years of college and one year in pro football, I was still playing my Walter Peoples Special, just doing what comes naturally. I had no technique at all. For my last two years in college and my rookie year in the NFL I had very little coaching. It was mostly, Go get him big boy, you can do it, nice job. Now go do it again.

This was the year I began learning how to play the game of football. They gave me my education. They taught me down and distance, projections, formations, everything I know now I learned from that group. My natural ability, my speed and power, had enabled me to get to that point; coaching took me the rest of the way.

Rod Marinelli was the D-line coach. Marinelli was a no-nonsense Vietnam marine combat vet. A little bald guy with eyes that could pierce steel and a big attitude. Soon as he walked into a room he owned the place. His first words to us were, "You don't know who I am. My name is Rod Marinelli, and you are going to be the best fucking defensive line in the NFL. If you're not interested in becoming a better player don't waste my time; just go grab your lemonade and sit down. But if you want to be in this boat, grab a fucking oar and start pulling. You do it my way, and I promise you you're going to have more sacks, more tackles, more pressures, more everything than any other D-line in this league."

Lead the league in sacks? We looked at each other like, this dude is in the wrong room. Where does he think he is, Green Bay?

He told us that we were going to work harder, longer, and be smarter than any team in the league. Then he gave us the plan to do it.

He taught us techniques, he taught us work patterns, and he gave us the knowledge we needed to get that edge. We all bought into what Rod was selling. The key for him, just like Dungy, was simplicity: Work on your fundamentals. There are only a few ways a lineman can block you: He can reach you, cut you, scoop, double-team, and pass protect. We worked on those five different blocks practically every day. Over and over and over. Our fundamentals were so good that one time when we were playing the Redskins Culpepper got hit in the head and must have had a mild concussion, because he lost his peripheral vision. Concussions just weren't a big issue in the league at that time. Nobody understood how dangerous they were. The trainer came out, held up three fingers, and asked Brad, "How many fingers?"

Brad's estimate was pretty damn close. Fortunately, they were grading on a curve. That's good enough Whitey, you're still breathing, you can play. Brad couldn't see at all, he barely knew where he was, he was playing on instinct—but his fundamentals were so strong he had 10 tackles and a sack.

We spent a lot of time at practice watching film. Most teams watch film of their next opponent to understand their tendencies, and we certainly did a lot of that, but we spent as much as 90 percent of our time watching film of our own practices and games. Everything we did right or wrong was up on that screen. We'd watch ourselves, and we'd analyze and evaluate our performance and then go out to improve. For Rod Marinelli it wasn't what our opponent was going to do, it was what we could do to get better. How did we do on that block last game? What can we do to handle it better? It was all about us, not about them. We didn't try to trick anybody, we didn't have any of that zebra, cheetah, rhino crap, we just played smash-mouth full-speed-ahead football. We heard the same words from him every day: After they kick it off it's about fundamentals and will. When we executed our fundamentals we won the battle in the trenches.

Marinelli also emphasized taking responsibility. If we hadn't played well on Sunday, first thing Monday morning he would apologize to us. "I didn't have you prepared to play this week. It's my fault. But I promise you I'll have you prepared to play next week." Uh-oh. Maybe it was his fault, but we definitely paid for it. That was a kiss of death. We knew we would be practicing long and hard that week. I guarantee, playing in a game was easier than Rod Marinelli's drills in practice.

He was a motivator, a teacher, a cheerleader, and a drill sergeant. Even when I was making the All-Pro team every year he was still pushing me hard to try new moves, to explore, be creative. That was his thing, try on a new pair of shoes, don't limit yourself to the fastball. Do more, do better. He used to tell me all the time, try a spin move; you can spin if you want to spin.

I didn't want to spin. I wasn't going to spin. I told him, "I never turn my back on the quarterback."

Even with that new coaching staff we started off that 1996 season 2–8. We were 0–5 and beat the 5–1 Minnesota Vikings, 24–13, when I just took the ball right out of Warren Moon's hand. He didn't see me coming. Warren, gimme my ball. It'd been so long since we'd won a game that when we went to dump the Gatorade over Dungy—we almost missed him. He was standing still and we still just about missed him. How do you miss a coach with the Gatorade? We just nicked him on the shoulder.

But after that we lost three more games in a row. We were doing everything the coaching staff told us to do. We were working hard in practice, we were completing our assignments, and we still were 2–8. Every week Tony kept talking to us about turning the corner, but we couldn't even reach the corner. Honestly, we were beginning to wonder. Maybe Dungy's way wasn't the right way.

Playing on a losing team can take your desire away. It's hard to give a total effort every week when you're getting beat game after game. In the streets people look at you with pity. I'd stop my car at a traffic light, and the squeegee man would offer me a quarter. When I walked into a restaurant people pretended they don't notice me—and I am too big to miss. It's like living in the dark. I hated it, just hated it.

The game that made all the difference was our 11th game of the season, against the San Diego Chargers, who at that time were one of the best teams in the league. This was the game that transformed that franchise. We were playing them out on the West Coast, where the Bucs never won. On Thursday night the whole D-line decided that we were going to get together and just have a good time with each other. We hadn't been playing that well, and we knew we had to step it up. So to release some of the pressure we had a little party on Brad Culpepper's deck overlooking Tampa Bay. In retrospect, no one ever admitted inviting all those lovely girls, but as Brad's wife will confirm, they definitely were there. I don't remember too much about that night. I remember there was that chair that busted under Chidi Ahanotu, and from what I remember Friday's practice was pretty damn ragged.

That Sunday morning I was lying in my bed in the hotel in San Diego watching Chris Berman on ESPN. Usually on Sunday morning I'm at work so I never got a chance to watch the game previews. But California was three hours behind Tampa time, and I was up early enough to see this. We'd won the last week and had played well, so I was waiting for Berman to say something about the cool young Bucs getting better every day. Instead, that man came on my TV and said, "The San Diego Chargers are playing the Tampa Bay Yucks." What? Did I hear him right? The Yucks? He was calling my team a joke. The Yucks. And then he proceeded to criticize my quarterback Trent Dilfer. Now, I do not allow anyone to criticize my head coach, my quarterback, and my kicker. That was my job.

Chris Berman probably is going to take credit for what happened. I was furious. I told Brooks, "You hear that? This shit stops right here. Today. I don't want to hear that one more time."

At the pregame meal I got up in front of the team and told them word-for-word what Berman had called them. "You got to be fucking kidding me," I said. "If it don't boil your blood to be called the fucking Yucks then you don't belong here. This bullshit stops right here, right now. This is the last time we get disrespected in front of the nation." This probably was the most passionate speech I made in my entire career. I'd had it with losing; I'd had it with being called a joke.

I don't even think we finished breakfast. We got on the bus and went to the stadium. You have never seen a team more riled up and ready to play. We were going to kick Charger ass that day. We were primed, we were ready, and we were losing 14–0 before we could even break a sweat.

Unbelievable. First quarter, San Diego quarterbark Stan Humphries completes a 63-yard touchdown pass to Charlie Jones, 7–0. Then we fumble deep in our territory, and Leonard Russell runs it in 14 yards, 14–0. But then something happened. We didn't panic. We didn't quit. We went to the fundamentals we'd been practicing. Dilfer completed 30 of 40 passes, I got two sacks, and we came back to win that game 25–17. We got on the plane that night and partied all the way back to Tampa. Coach Dungy never seemed to notice.

We absolutely knew we had turned that corner. We became a team that afternoon. From that day on we knew we could be very good. Anybody who beat us was going to have to look us right in the eyes and punch us in the mouth. We were building. We used to call it chopping wood. When you look at a forest you know you can't chop down the whole thing, but if you start chopping one tree at a time suddenly you look up and half that forest is gone. That was our attitude: Chop this one, chop that one, come back tomorrow, and chop some more. Chopping wood, baby, every single day.

After that win the D-unit began getting together every Thursday night. Every week we all met up somewhere. One week we'd drag Whitey and Lynch to an all-black club; the next week they would take us to a rave at a white club in Ybor City. Nobody was afraid to step out of their element and try something new. One time Marcus Jones's mom cooked us all chitlins and hog balls. It didn't matter where we ended up, we partied as a unit. We were tough and proud and smart enough to stay out of the newspapers—and block by block we were building the best D-unit in the NFL. We finished the season the happiest 6–10 team in history, and we did not have another losing season until the year after we won the Super Bowl. It turned out Marinelli knew what he was talking about: Over the next five years we got more sacks than any defense in the National Football League.

Okay, thank you Chris Berman. Without your mouth getting us angry it's possible America never would have heard those magic words spoken on *Hollywood Squares*, "Warren Sapp to block."

That game not only turned us around, it also transformed San Diego. It was like the Football Gods decided to play this tremendous joke. Somebody up there got their wires crossed. Beginning with that game we became a league power. And after losing to us, the Chargers, who were a respected team, suffered through seven consecutive losing seasons, becoming the second-worst team in football.

In Tony Dungy's system everything started with the D-line. On Sunday afternoon everybody is watching the pretty people, and the broadcasters are giving them a lot of love, but a football game is won or lost in the trenches. The fans are all cheering for that big handsome quarterback, watching him throw that beautiful spiral, and they don't even glance at that fat guy grabbing at his feet who made him throw it two-tenths of a second quicker than he intended. So rather than it being a completion, it clips the receiver's fingertips and drops incomplete. Most people simply do not appreciate the D-line; most times they don't even remember we're there until somebody gets noticed for a penalty. Brooks used to say that I played the game four feet and down, while his game was from four feet to six feet, which definitely is an interesting way of looking at football.

D-line play has evolved tremendously. In the early years of the

NFL, offensive linemen used to block by raising their arms and elbows to a flat plane about level with their shoulders—hands touching and pushing forward. Their hands had to be touching. Deacon Jones made them change all that. He used his hands as weapons, slapping O-linemen upside the head to move them out of his way. He was like Godzilla knocking buildings out of his way until he got to the quarterback. Except that he was tougher and meaner. The league finally figured out that D-linemen were more athletic and better looking than O-linemen, so they changed the rules to permit O-linemen to extend their arms and grab hold of D-lineman within the framework of their shoulders. They'd grab and hold on, trying to move the D-linemen in whatever direction they wanted him to go. To prevent that from happening D-linemen had to learn how to fight them off. Basically every play consists of, get your big ugly hands off me. A great D-lineman absolutely has to have quick hands; he has to be able to prevent any O-linemen from grabbing hold of his jersey and hanging on for the ride. To be successful you have got to prevent the offensive lineman from getting a grip on you.

The fans don't understand or appreciate the violence that takes place on the line. The TV cameras rarely isolate these one-on-one, or usually in my case one-on-two, confrontations. And that's a shame because so much takes place so quickly. A lot of people think it's like two bull elephants bumping heads in a mosh pit—just mindless crashing, kicking, grabbing, punching, shoving, gouging, head-butting—but in addition to that there is a lot of skill involved. Playing on the line is like sumo wrestling; the planned application of speed, strength, balance, and intelligence.

But in the trenches every down is hand-to-hand fist fighting, ultimate, challenge all-out combat. Every play. Marinelli used to call it *Jab-o-Lay*! It is a mano-a-mano fight, or sometimes with me it was mano-a-two-mano fight, 60 or sometimes 70 times a game. Like my mama always told me, to get some ass you got to bring some. An O-lineman would come at me with his hands up, and I'd have to chop and push and punch to get away from him. And with Tony it wasn't just every game, it was every practice. By the end of a game or practice my hands would be badly bruised and all swollen up.

It really was a version of martial arts. Linebacker Hardy Nickerson used to keep fighting sticks in his room, and we would practice over and over with them to improve our hand speed. *Thukthukthukthuk.* One time we were playing New England, and the Patriots O-lineman Max Lane was playing with a broken hand. It was all wrapped up, making him look like a human Q-tip. On the first play of the game I walked up to the line of scrimmage and suggested to him, "You might want to stick that up your ass 'cause you can't touch me with it."

An O-lineman without the use of his hands is like a green flag at the Indianapolis 500. There is no way Max could stop me. He could use that hand as a club, but he couldn't grab and hold. First time I got hold of Drew Bledsoe I informed him, "You do know he's gonna get you killed today." I went over him and around Max all afternoon.

There are different defensive formations, but Rod Marinelli liked to play the standard 4–3. That's the way the Football Gods intended the game to be played—4–3. That meant our four D-linemen against their five offensive linemen. Our four on their five, that was a fight. Three on five ain't a fair fight. The way Marinelli described it was, "If you're gonna play a 4–3, then those four horses better pull that damn carriage, because there ain't no carriage before the horse." The D-line was his horses. Tony Dungy created the famed Tampa 2 defense, which consisted of four D-linemen, three linebackers, two cornerbacks, and two safeties. The weakness of the Tampa 2 was that in a 4–3 alignment you're just a little bit thin in the defensive backfield, so if the D-line doesn't penetrate, if we can't pressure the quarterback into making him throw the football a little bit quicker, it will be a long afternoon indeed. For the Tampa 2 to work the front four has to create havoc; we had to pressure the quarterback. The rush has to force the quarterback to release the ball quick. In this system the nose tackle is the horse that gets the carriage moving.

Most football fans don't really appreciate the importance of timing in the game of football. Plays are timed not just to the second, but to the tenth of a second. If a receiver gets to the place he wants to get to when he wants to be there, the defense has failed. Basically, the job of the D-line is to take that stopwatch and smash it to pieces. Mess up that timing. My objective was to disrupt the timing of the offense by building a camp three yards deep in their backfield. Penetrate, attack, disrupt. If you try to run an off-tackle play, whoops, welcome home, son. If it's a passing play, I'm making the quarterback uncomfortable in the pocket, chasing his ass out of there, and I've done my job. And while I'm busy doing that our cornerbacks are jamming their receivers at the line of scrimmage to disrupt the timing of their pass routes.

Down there in the trenches every play is a four- or five- second battle for supremacy in which you use every weapon you have to dictate your will. Everything you have learned, all the training you've had, the thousand hours you've spent practicing, plus every bit of your natural ability is tested in those few seconds. No thinking takes place in the trenches; there's no time or need for it. Once the ball was snapped, I was gone. I knew instinctively where I wanted to go and how I was going to get there. Instinct and ten thousand reps in practice. Thinking isn't going to help, it's all reaction. And your reaction is dictated by your experience and preparation. Usually by the time a thought takes shape the play is already done.

I used to tell people that I did my job in a phone booth. That was about the amount of space in which I had to do my work. Every play two men entered that phone booth, but only one of them was coming out. To get out of that phone booth you had to be quicker and smarter than the other guy. I always said that all the great D-linemen had two things in common, a loose screw and a motor from hell. That loose screw was the thing that made offensive players pause and wonder, do I really want a piece of that? Am I ready for what he is bringing? Do I really want to fight right now? That motor meant you could go all day without slowing down. Play after play without slowing down.

I was good at a lot of things on a football field, but the skill I truly mastered was rushing the quarterback. Most of the time I had two men on me. I never minded that, unless they were hiding a 12th man that made the offensive line just a little bit weaker someplace else. When they lined up two men on me I could hear John Lynch behind me start salivating. If they tried to play me one on one, trust me, 75 percent of the time I was taking you home. Your quarterback was going to get hit in the mouth. It wasn't that I was bigger or stronger than those people on the O-line; I had my own technique.

For a lineman, footwork is the foundation. My philosophy of football was simple: Five steps to the quarterback. I had my route planned. I always tried to take exactly the same-length step every play, a six-inch step. I would practice that endlessly. Six inches. Exactly. That was the right distance to allow me to keep moving while maintaining my balance. How many football fans know that D-linemen try to take the same measured step every single down? Those people who were surprised that I was able to keep pace with the lovely Miss Kym Johnson on *Dancing with the Stars* obviously did not understand that I'd spent my entire pro football career working on footwork, balance, and rhythm.

More than anything else, footwork and balance is what I always look for in a young player. His feet have to be in harmony with his movements. If your footwork is in balance then I can't push you over, and if I can't push you over you can get down low and play the game. But once a player crosses his feet, or keeps them too close together like he's walking a rail, he's off-balance, and then I got him. Against me, it was like playing chicken with a 16-wheeler. Everything else can be taught. If his stance is too wide, or too close together, I can push him any way I want. And I will. But if his feet are in the right position, he has a solid foundation to do whatever it is he wants to do.

My greatest asset was my initial push, the speed with which I came off the line when the ball was snapped. I tried to get on the offensive lineman before he could get out of his stance and get his feet set. Oh my, the D-line practiced that every single day. We used to compete with each other to see who could get off the line the fastest. Other teams would watch films of our games and think that the projector must have accidently been put on fast-forward because we were so quick off the line of scrimmage. The instant the ball was snapped I was already moving, usually laterally right into the gap between the guard and the tackle before either one of them could react. What I wanted to do was make them start turning, so I could use my momentum to turn one of them into a revolving door.

The D-lineman always has the advantage. I know what I want to do. The offensive lineman basically has to guess my intent. How am I going to get by him? Am I going to rush straight up his numbers? Am I going to try to go inside? Or maybe I'll give him a little fake inside and go outside. As I'm moving forward I'll be faking, shaking, jamming, and juking, trying to get him to commit. And once he commits, I got him. He's mine. I had a very low center of gravity, so soon as I got underneath, once I got my body inside his body, I had control and I could move him.

Some O-linemen were totally predictable. They moved in a rhythm: Stand up, left foot, right foot, left foot, right foot, crunch. Stick out their hands and start punching. I'd dance right along with them, right foot, no left foot, right foot, and when they punched I'd push them aside and go right past them. Best move I ever put on an O-lineman without touching the quarterback was in 2000, against Jamie Nails of the Buffalo Bills. I was rushing quarterback Rob Johnson. Jamie Nails was backing up to protect him. I dropped a shoulder to the right, juked left, gave him a little bit of zigzag, and he crossed his feet and fell right over. Fell right back with his arms straight up in the air. He looked like he was fainting. I never even touched him. Kept going right at Rob. Basically, I was going to kill him, but he threw the ball away. When I got back to our huddle Brooks was looking at me in awe. "Dawg," he said, "you just made a 300-pound man fall over without touching him." Still, that was my greatest move ever.

The D-lineman is also responsible for protecting his gap on a running play. A gap is the area between two offensive lineman, and your job is to make damn sure no running back comes busting through your gap. It's like being the sheriff heading off the outlaws so they can't escape through the pass. One of the most important changes Tony Dungy made on the defense was going from a 2-gap system to a 1-gap system. When I got to Tampa Bay Wyche was using a 2-gap system. In a 2-gap system a defensive lineman is responsible for both sides of the blocker, so you have to make contact with him and then find the ball carrier. In the 1-gap system you're responsible for only one side of the blocker so there is no hesitation at all. You have to move with the gap, wherever it goes on the field. If that gap moves 20 yards because the offense is running to the left the responsibility doesn't change. If the ball carrier is in your gap he is your man. There is always a temptation to leave your gap and go toward the ball, but as soon as you do that the Football Gods will call an audible and send the play through the gap you abandoned. The 1-gap system was innovative and it fit my skills perfectly. I took ownership of my gap. It was mine, and you ain't coming through it. It got to a point that they didn't even try. Dungy's system fit me like a bikini on Stacey Dash. It allowed me to flourish. The third game of the 1997 season we were playing in Minnesota, and I put a move on the great Randall McDaniel and sacked Brad Johnson. Whitey smacked me on the helmet and told me, "Buddy you have arrived. You just whipped the best! You're there!"

By putting in the 4–3, Tony Dungy, Monte Kiffin, and Rod Marinelli transformed our defense. If there was a message game that announced to the league that we were no longer the same old Yucks, that when you were playing Tampa Bay you'd better bring your A-game and a large medical staff because we were going to take it to you, it was the opening game of the 1997 season against San Francisco. That was also the game in which I began making my reputation, personally taking out practically a whole future wing of the Football Hall of Fame. I always call this my revenge game, in which I was finally avenging the 49ers–Dallas Cowboys NFC Championship Game played on January 10, 1982. That was the game that Joe Montana beat my Cowboys with "the Catch." I was nine years old, sitting on my couch crying my eyes out and having to listen to my brother ridiculing me for being a big crybaby. A loyal fan never forgets or forgives, and this was my chance to get even.

Dungy always told us that the only way to be the best was to beat the best, so this was our test. It was Steve Mariucci's first game as head coach of the 49ers. On the fifth play Steve Young ran a bootleg. I read it and caught up with him from behind. I reached out with my too-short arms and grabbed the back of his shirt and started pulling him down. As Young was going down his helmet collided with Hardy Nickerson's knee. That actually was the play that caused the NFL to ban knee-to-helmet hits. Young went down cold and laid there still. I looked at him, and his eyes were rolled back in his head. I looked at Brooks and shook my head. "He's dead," I told him.

Mariucci had to bring in his backup, Jeff Brown. In the second quarter we cracked Brown's sternum. There is a rule in the NFL that if you put a third quarterback in the game before the fourth quarter you can't bring back the starter. That meant that Young would not be able to return. Mariucci felt he had no choice, and he put Young back in the game. That was a shame. We didn't know very much about the dangers of concussions then, but Young should not have been playing. He couldn't even call a play. They called two consecutive timeouts to help him get his head clear. I said to him, "Steve, you all right?"

He smiled at me, "Yo man, I like you."

"Well I like you too, but you're dinner tonight."

In the second quarter Jerry Rice was running a reverse. This was the 49ers' signature play, they'd been running it for about 10 years, and I'd seen it often enough on film to recognize it. Rice was getting away when I reached out with my right arm to grab his jersey, but instead my pinkie caught the bottom edge of his face-mask grill. Twisted my knuckle so badly that my pinkie still goes off in its own direction. But as I yanked him down he blew his anterior cruciate ligament. It was totally unintentional. I just went to put him on the ground, and he blew out his knee, but the official threw a flag on me for grabbing him by the face mask. "Oh come on, ref," I said. "That wasn't intentional." Five yards!

Rice was down on the ground. I said to him, "Jerry, you all right?" I was waiting for him to give me a thumbs-up that he was okay.

He ignored me completely. He wouldn't look at me and he didn't say a word.

"Fuck you, too," I said and then turned around and went back to the huddle. I had to get ready for the next play.

Maybe the greatest player ever to put on pads had to be carried off the field and did not play for three months. Without Rice and with Young staggered we upset them 13–6. The 49ers went on to win their next 11 games. We'd beat the best, and then we started beating the rest. I found out later that season that Jerry Rice was upset that I hadn't called him in the hospital to apologize. Apologize? You don't apologize for a clean hit. I had absolutely nothing to apologize for, but I was very sorry he was hurt.

That is the only play of my 13-year career I wish I could change. At the Pro Bowl a couple of years later Jerry Rice walked up to me at the pool bar. It is tradition at the Pro Bowl that first-time selections are responsible for a two-hour window at the bar. That tab can add up pretty quick, so you do find yourself reminding people about the evils of drink. This was the first time Rice had ever spoken to me, and he said, "My wife would like to talk to you."

"Your wife wants to talk to me?"

He pointed to a lovely woman and said, "She's right over there." I walked over and introduced myself to Jackie Rice, who told me, "I want you to know there are no hard feelings in my house about what happened. You are good with the Rices."

But after we beat the 49ers in that game people were forced to pay attention to the Bucs. And to me. Taking out two Hall-of-Famers in two quarters was the foundation of my reputation. It wasn't all good though. Everybody knew I played tough and strong, but there were people who also believed I set out to intentionally hurt people. Sapp the wild man! Sapp the thug.

That wasn't right. I played very hard, but I never played dirty. My check was not going to change because I knocked somebody out. My basic philosophy was let's go out and play 60 minutes of football. I'm going to give you everything I've got, and you'll give me everything you got, and there will be nothing in that ballgame that will stop me from having a drink with you later. Maybe my Twitter address was *QBKilla*, but I have no regrets about the way I played the game of football. Nada. Football is a violent game, and I brought violence to my job. Actually, that was the job requirement. And the violence also has always been a major part of the appeal of the game. Violence sells, that's no secret. In fact, the TV program that helped make football the most popular game in America was called *The Violent World of Sam Huff.* Sam Huff was a Giants linebacker who wore a mike during a game in 1960. It was a big deal back then. In *Time* magazine they quoted him saying, "We try to hurt everybody. We hit each other hard as we can. This is a man's game."

That hasn't changed; it's just that the players got bigger and the hits got harder. The NFL and all the media have glorified the violence. TV celebrates football's greatest hits, from Chuck Bednarik clotheslining Frank Gifford and knocking him out cold to the most spectacular hits of the week. *SportsCenter* isn't showing the week's best handshakes; it's showing the most violent collisions. Textbook tackles don't make the highlight shows, but if you hit somebody so hard you knock off his helmet that's going to be shown over and over. It's nothing new; that's the way it was back in the aspirin and ice era and that's the way it is now. They've been showing Bednarik hitting Gifford on TV for 50 years. Let's be honest, fans love the violence. I have never seen anybody turn off a football game because the players were hitting too hard. Remember, it's the fans who give a standing ovation to a player when he gets carried off the field. Sure, easy for them, he's on a stretcher and they're standing. The league has taken steps to try to improve safety, but football is a contact sport, and if you don't make contact you aren't going to be playing.

I love and respect the game of football and every person who has played it, especially those very few people capable of playing it on the professional level. But I have to admit that there were three times during my entire career when I had mean intentions. First, during a game against the Cleveland Browns in 2002 I sacked quarterback Tim Couch and he really got angry. I never did find out what was so different about this hit. It was a clean hit, a hard hit, but clean. I was just doing my job, but all of a sudden he threw the ball right at me, hitting me in the face mask. Really? You sure about that? I tried to do the right thing, asking the official, "You saw that? You ain't gonna throw a flag?" The official turned and trotted away, so I looked at Couch. "Don't worry," I warned him, "you'll pay for that."

Got him big later in the game. Oh, did I hit that man. I came in on him from behind, slapped my arms around him, picked him up, and slammed him down so nasty that the whole stadium shook. Instead of a sack, the broadcasters should have called it a Sappquake. I know he felt it because three years later a lovely young woman approached me and said she had been Couch's fiancée at that time, and, "He used to have nightmares about you," she said. "He'd wake up calling your name."

"No."

"Yes." And she didn't look crazy either.

Second time I got angry was after I sacked Cincinnati quarterback Akili Smith and the man made the mistake of calling me a name no Florida boy wants to hear. I was standing on the defensive line talking to my man Simeon Rice while the Bengals were getting set, and I used a term that is acceptable between friends, but only between friends. There is a lot of personal history that goes into making it acceptable. But Smith heard it and bounced it back at me. We had no personal history. You do not say that to me, no you do not. It has a different meaning. I admit this, I bludgeoned him. I know how to get blood out of a 180-pound quarterback, believe me I do. I grabbed Smith from behind and held his arms as we went down. I opened him up and dropped him down. The helmet hit the bridge of his nose and smashed it, and he started bleeding like a hog.

The third person was Detroit Lions' quarterback Joey Harrington. "Joey Sunshine," the fans called him, but when they did they were being sarcastic. The man was the third pick of the 2002 draft. The first time I watched him play I said to Brooks, "You got to be kidding me. How do they even allow that kid on the field?" But to listen to him talk he was the greatest thing for football since pigskin. I believed he needed the education that I was able to provide for him.

I think he might have known how I felt, because one time he came to the line of scrimmage, and I saw fear in his eyes. As we lined up I looked at him, and there definitely was something going on. I told Simeon, "This is going to get ugly." He called signals in an unusually high-pitched voice. Didn't sound right at all. The word that Simeon used to describe it was *pimping*. The Lions went three-and-out, and the next set of downs the second-team QB came in.

A Detroit lineman asked me, "What did you two do to him?"

"Nothing," I said. "We didn't get the chance. Where's he at?"

Gone, was what the man told us.

Gone? What's *gone*? We're playing a football game here. What does that mean, gone?

"His heart rate was way up. His heart was about to jump out of his chest."

I said, "You are a liar." We talked about it for the next three series. Harrington had gotten so nervous he'd had to leave the game. True or not, that's what they told me.

Now, there also were times on the field when I simply lost my temper during a play and maybe got a little carried away. Football is a tough game played by tough people with a lot at stake. During our run to the Super Bowl in 2002 we were playing the Ravens in Baltimore, and Chester Taylor came through the line and I wrapped him up. It was a plain running play, nothing special—I had him in my grasp. He wasn't going anywhere, but his legs kept moving like he was going to run over me. Really? Okay. I snapped. One quick moment of football insanity. I picked him up in the air and I slammed him down. He laid there on the ground trying to figure out what had happened. *Sapp* happened Chester, that's what happened. I knew what I'd done. Even before the officials threw the flag I turned around and waved to my teammates. "C'mon, ya all," I said and started walking back the 15 yards I knew I was going to be penalized.

I was fined $10,000 by the league for that hit. I think the official explanation for the fine was "illegal slamming of a running back on his head."

I always hit hard and almost always hit clean. In fact, I think fans will be surprised to learn that there really isn't a lot of dirty play in the league. It's not the rules that prevent it, the players police it. The dirty players get weeded out real fast. Careers are short enough, and there are enough injuries without adding a risk factor. Players know that if they intentionally take a cheap shot at another player it's going to come back at them big time. The whole damn posse is coming after them. And there have been times when even their own teammates don't give a maximum effort to protect them. One time, I remember, I got hit late and low in my legs. I looked at the man who did it and asked him calmly, "Is that how we're playing today for four quarters? Just lemme know. I can do it that way."

He put up his hands, "Oh no. My bad, Dawg. I tripped, that's all." We had no problem after that.

There was a time when some offensive linemen were cutting on the back of D-linemen's legs. The league didn't care; we were just fat dumb linemen down there in the trenches. It was only after we started taking care of each other, we definitely had our ways of taking care of it, that the league changed the rule. Now your head has to be out in front when you block someone; you can't cut him from behind. The result has been many fewer injuries and knee operations.

There are some things you just don't do in the NFL, rules or no rules. The league wanted to encourage wide-open offense. Great for TV, but bad for the defense. So receivers began believing they could run across our zone defense without being hit. They were running everywhere, like little roaches when the lights come on. That wasn't going to happen to our defense. If a receiver ran across our zone John Lynch would knock his ass out—and we would all split the fine. We told all our D-backs, don't you even think about not hitting his ass. "Hit his damn ass, Lynch."

"You got me no. 99?"

"I got you, baby. I'll help with that fine."

Trust me, any receiver looking at that film was going to know that there was a price for coming across the middle of the Tampa Bay defense.

It would end up costing us $25,000 a year in fines, but we sent the message that if you came across we were going to knock you the hell out.

Tony Dungy, Monte Kiffin, and Rod Marinelli built a defense that hit as hard as any in the NFL. We were relentless. Relentless. We were coming at you from all corners. Me and Brooks, John Lynch, Whitey, Ronde Barber, Brian Kelly, Hardy Nickerson, we just weren't going to allow anyone to disrespect the Bucs. Eventually we turned around the culture. I remember telling Dungy at the beginning of one season, "Give me 17 points and we'll win a championship." I knew we were that good. That's all we needed from the offense: seventeen points—two touchdowns and a field goal. Not even that. The defense was setting up 10 points a game; so we just needed the offense to drive for one touchdown. The six years from the time Tony Dungy came in till we won a championship, that was 96 NFL games, we gave up an average of 16.02 points per game.

By Dungy's second year, 1997, it was obvious we were building something special. We'd replaced those sorry Creamsicle uniforms with the powerful pewter and red, we moved into brand-new Raymond James Stadium, and we buried Bucco Bruce. There was just a whole different attitude. That was our learning year. We finished that season 10–6, our first winning record in 15 years. Then we beat the Lions 20–10 in our first playoff game.

The defense came together as a unit that year. We learned to trust each other. We were tough on each other, but there was a level of respect there that we hadn't had before. We knew we were good and we were going to get better. We expected to win. In our seventh game that season we lost 27–9 to Detroit when Barry Sanders broke two 80-yard touchdown runs. We stood on the sideline watching the replays, and both times it was obvious that John Lynch had blown his assignment. Two years earlier we might have been ripping at his throat. But we all knew how hard he played, how much ability he had, and how tough he was on himself. There wasn't anything we could say to him that was tougher than what he was thinking himself. He was sitting all alone on the bench, his head bowed, and I went over by him to try and pick him up. He wasn't going to do us any good sitting there moping. The worst thing any football player can do is let the last play influence the next play. "Listen 47," I told him. "That's not the last time he's gonna break off a big one on somebody. There's nobody else but you I'd want in that situation. So you missed Barry Sanders, big fucking deal. Welcome to the long list. And I promise you this: You ain't gonna be the last name on it."

Lynch still likes to say that this was the game that got him on television. Because whenever they show one of Barry Sanders's car commercials you always see Lynch running a few steps behind him.

By 1998 people were expecting us to win. We had blown the door-mat off that damn door. We felt like we had turned a third-world country into a resort destination. One of the last barriers we had to break was the myth that we couldn't play in cold weather. We actually had lost 28 straight games when the temperature was below 40 degrees. Who kept track of that kind of statistic? Our last game of the season we played the Bengals in Cincinnati, and it was 39 degrees at kickoff. It was . . . under 40 degrees. There is a wonderful photograph of me and Brooks standing on the sideline looking at puffs of our breath. But after we won that game 35–0 some reporter found out that we had never won a game when the temperature was under 38 degrees. After that whenever we won a game below a certain temperature the media went lower. Eventually it was like, the Bucs haven't won a game when the temperature is below minus 15 in more than 100 years. It made a good story.

My relationship with Tony Dungy got stronger the longer we were together. Tony was a quiet leader. He wasn't a rah-rah coach, but when he said something he meant it, and it was wise to pay attention. He never shouted to make a point, and he rarely lost his temper. One time Rod Marinelli was running a new drill, and we were sloppy and slow;

people just weren't putting in their best effort. The next day Tony told him, "I watched the tape of you walking through that new drill. Maybe you want to run it at full speed today." Ooo, that hurt. Then he just walked away.

The one time I saw him get mad was at practice before we played Green Bay in the 1997 Division Playoffs. Playoff money was a bonus, and everybody in the organization shared in it, including the secretaries, the equipment people, everybody. I think we figured that for this game it came to about $15,000 per person. When the stakes are the highest the money is the lowest. But for some of the people on that list, that extra money made a big difference. We were running an O-line D-line pass rushing drill, going one-on-one and all of a sudden a fight broke out. It wasn't a real fight. People were just trying a make a point; we certainly didn't want anybody to get hurt before a playoff game. I was over on the side and wasn't involved. Tony came running clear across the whole field. I had never seen him get angry before. While he was still on the run he started screaming, "What does this have to do with winning? Somebody tell me does this have anything to do with winning?" We were all standing there quietly because we knew the answer. The answer was no, it does not. Then he shouted, "Do you people have any idea what you're doing? You're playing with people's money."

Whoa! The ground shook. We never forgot that day. If the Tampa Bay Buccaneers had a rallying call, that was it. You're playing with people's money. That was all that man had to say on that day.

Eventually Tony and I became very close, so close that after I was married we lived a few houses away from each other. Sometimes his daughter, Tia, would babysit for us on Friday nights. Growing up I never had a father-son relationship, but I think it would be something like we had, a person you could talk with about anything. Tony's world was much bigger than football. Whatever was in the news, whatever was going on at home, he always had time to stop and speak with me, and I valued his advice. Never once did he tell me don't do that, don't go there. Instead he was supportive, even if on occasion he probably thought I'd gone a little far. He was the coach who made you want to be a better player and a better person. Once he told me, "You got enough natural talent to make it in this league without extra effort, but if you're willing to work to the limit you have the opportunity to be great."

Where do I sign up? It was under Tony Dungy's leadership that I first became an All-Pro. Actually there are a lot of players who could make that same statement. He put people in a position to succeed, gave them the support they needed, and let them play. He did that for me, and in 1999 I was named the NFL's Defensive Player of the Year.

The D-line led the team, which was unusual in the NFL. But we just were never a strong offensive team. Tony took us as far as the defense could go. The defense and the offense are actually smaller and very different units within the larger team. It's like welding the front end of a Cadillac to the rear of a Chevy. We got to know each other, but I'll be honest, those offensive people always seemed a little strange. We spent all of our time practicing to stop what they were practicing to do. We went up against each other in practice every day. It is a proven fact that people who play on the defense are smarter, braver, better looking, and nicer to their mama.

Our offense was almost entirely dependent on the defense handing them a short field. Our offense was that legendary three yards and a cloud of dust, punt and play great defense, although sometimes our offense got more dust than yards. Trent Dilfer, our quarterback, basically was an interception just waiting to happen. There were times when we practically pleaded with him, we know you're not going to score a touchdown, but please, just don't turn it over. We need some time on the sideline to catch our breath. Just get us one first down and we'll get you set up. We'll put it on the doorstep for you. You can ring the bell, can't you?

No one on the defense ever complained about it though. Tony

would never allow that to happen. We knew we weren't an offensive juggernaut. The offense was doing all it could, so what would have been the point of criticizing them? This is how bad it got: In October, 1998, we lost to the Saints in New Orleans 9–3. The defense held them to 52 rushing yards. Tony came into the team meeting, and the first thing he did was compliment the offense, telling them, "You guys did a great job controlling the clock. Nice going." Then he looked at the defense, shook his head sadly, and said, "You guys have got to do better than that."

Tony Dungy came within one terrible call of having a dynasty in Tampa. We played Kurt Warner's St. Louis Rams in the 1999 NFC Championship Game. "The Greatest Show on Turf," they were called. Their offense was so great some people advised us not to even bother showing up for the game, there must be some more useful things you could do to fill an afternoon. We decided to go anyway, and we decided we were going to drag them into a war. I was criticized for predicting, "It's gonna be a street fight, and we'll see how they like it." But that's what it was, our shutdown defense against their freewheeling offense. Our game plan was to contain Marshall Faulk, probably the greatest running back in pro football history; their game plan was to keep me out of their backfield. At halftime they were winning, 5–3. Five–3? What kind of football score is that?

We kicked a field goal in the third quarter to go ahead 6–5. We did take the battle to them. Both teams were hitting, knocking, banging. If you love smash-mouth football, oh my God, you had to love this game. We shut down that offense. We held them to five points and we handed them two of those points with a safety. Ain't got no gas in that car. We were all too tired to waste any energy thinking about how tired we were. But this was our first championship game, and we dug deep. Tony Dungy's three-yards-and-punt offense had put us in a position to win.

But with less than five minutes in the game they intercepted a pass and moved into our territory. Kurt Warner moved them down to our

30. When you're on the field looking at the scoreboard and the clock, all types of calculations go on in your head. I figured if we stopped them from scoring a touchdown, even if they kicked a field goal and went ahead 8–6, we had plenty of time to go down the field and kick a game-winning field goal.

They were on our 30 with 4:44 remaining. Four minutes forty-four seconds from the Super Bowl and one of the greatest turnarounds in NFL history. I think it was third and 12, and our defensive coordinator, Monte Kiffin, called a blitz. Oh man. Kiffin was a blitz-happy coach; as much as he loved to blitz was how much I hated it. Kiffin and I had different football philosophies. Nothing made him happier than watching Ronde Barber come storming in—and then he could take the credit for calling the game. There was a reason that Ronde Barber is the only defensive back in the history of the game with 25 picks and 40 sacks—because Kiffin would send him in at times he should not have sent him. We would argue all the time about blitzing. I told him, "I'm here to rush the passer, Babe. It's bad enough I got to take on a double-team every damn down. Now you're telling me I don't get to rush the quarterback on third down?" No thank you. They did not need me to play that game.

When we first got together Monte would take me out of the game on third down and let Ronde blitz. I'd stand there on the sideline scratching my head, thinking, I definitely can't sack the quarterback from the sideline. Finally I went to Rod and told him, "Listen, I need third down. If Kiffin wants to blitz, let him blitz on first down. I got no problem with that. It kills the run, it's secure because I got the contain, and Ronde'll get first-down sacks. But third down has to be mine. I'm not coming out on third down. That can't be."

I went to Dungy and said the same thing: "Tony, I'm asking you to give me third down. I'll stay home first and second down, that keeps Derrick Brooks free to do his thing, and Ronde can go ahead and blitz, but third down has to be a rush down. You got to let us go after the quarterback on third down. Just give us a chance. If it don't work, then I'll let him blitz, but I promise you, we will get there." Tony finally agreed—and we set an NFL defensive record by recording a sack in 69 straight games.

I always believed Kiffin called it so much because he wanted the glory; it made him look like a great defensive coordinator. I hated it because when we blitzed I had to stay home; it robbed me of all my effectiveness. A blitz effectively takes the D-line out of the action. I remember during a timeout in the middle of a football game they showed a Dodge commercial featuring Kiffin on the Jumbotron. And in that commercial Kiffin was diagramming our blitz. In the middle of the game there he was on the Jumbotron drawing up our blitz. My, oh my!

So it did not surprise me that Monte called a blitz on third and 12. Apparently, it didn't surprise anybody. Kurt Warner came up to the line, looked at the way we were lined up, and called a timeout. I knew right away he sniffed it out. I was absolutely certain he'd seen our free safety coming down. I told Brooks, "Tell Monte he saw the blitz, that's why he called the timeout. So we got to get out of it." I figured we would go cover two and be able to make a tackle before they gained 12 yards.

I walked into our huddle, and dammed if Kiffin hadn't called it again. A blitz leaves the secondary a little short, and you get more one-on-one coverage. I could not believe he didn't change his call. Okay, I thought, nothing I can do about it. The ball was snapped, and wide receiver Ricky Proehl took off up the sideline. Warner sight adjusted and threw it up. Brian Kelly was in an almost perfect position, but a perfect throw beats a slightly-less-than-perfectly positioned defender. Brian was all over him. If Brian makes that play, we win the game and go to the Super Bowl, Dungy gets the credit, and history is changed. One catch. Instead, Proehl caught it in the crook of his elbow, bobbled it, and the officials said he had control for the touchdown.

Our rookie quarterback Shaun King, who had replaced Trent Dilfer after he was sacked by Seattle's Phillip Daniels and broke his collarbone in our 10th game, did a nice job bringing us downfield. In that situation I was just a fan; there was nothing I could do to help. I'm not very superstitious, but just like other people watching the game, I kind of looked for a lucky way to stand. Like any other fan, I know that there is absolutely no connection between standing or sitting a certain way and the outcome of the play. It's ridiculous—but sometimes we all just do it anyway. You never know when the Football Gods are paying attention, and if they catch me with my left leg over my right leg instead of my right leg over my left leg they will make my team pay. With 47 seconds left Bert Emanuel came across the middle and caught an 11-yard pass. He had control of it, but as he was tackled the bottom of the football made contact with the ground. The officials ruled it incomplete. ESPN listed that as one of the worst calls in the history of sports—and it was probably worse than that. Emanuel had complete control of the ball the whole time, nobody questioned that, it was just that the nose of the ball touched the ground. It would have been first down on the Rams 22, and I know we would have rolled in from there. We'd done a similar thing to beat the Redskins the previous week. Instead King threw a couple of Hail Marys, and we lost the game, 11–6. I was sick, absolutely sick. If Kiffin had listened to us and called off the blitz they never would have scored. We would have won the game. Two weeks later the Rams won the Super Bowl—just as we would have, and it would have guaranteed a long extension as head coach for Dungy.

Instead, at the end of the 2001 season he was fired. The reporters were writing that he just couldn't win big games. His job came down to a game against the Eagles. Newspaper stories said if we lost that game he was gone. We got whupped, 31–9. I have never been so angry in a locker room. As we got on the bus I sat down right behind Dungy and asked if everything was all right. He was grim but nodded, "I think so." Then he added, "I'll be here." He'd spoken with the Glazers, who owned the team, he told me, and they'd assured him that he was not going to be fired. Except that as soon as we got home they asked him to meet with them over at Rich McKay's house. They believed that Tony just couldn't get the offense going, and they had to make a change. Tony had taken over a terrible team and put it in a position to compete for the Super Bowl—and then he was being fired for not winning that Super Bowl. Really? Rich McKay told me that was one of the toughest meetings he'd ever been in. "We were sitting in the living room talking with Tony. My sons were upstairs crying, my wife was in the hallway crying. I was sitting there with the Glazers, and the only person whose eyes were dry was Tony, who was handling it better than anybody. He was trying to make us feel better."

I always knew football was a business, but it never hit harder than that day. It was like my father had been fired: Okay Dad, you're out of the family. Made me want to quit the family too. I remember having a conversation with Rod Marinelli who said it was going to be very hard to work for these people because they'd broken their word.

When I heard the news I went over to Tony's house. He took it a lot better than I did. "Warren," he said. "Get yourself together, go back to the team, and lead them. Whoever they give you as head coach, you're gonna have to be the leader. I'll be fine, and you'll be fine, and both of us are going to get our championships."

As it turned out, he was hired by Indianapolis before the Bucs named his replacement. He wanted to bring his defensive coaching staff with him, but the Bucs refused to allow them to leave. Tony Dungy went on to become the first head coach in history with 10 consecutive playoff appearances and won the 2007 Super Bowl. Of course, he won that Super Bowl with Peyton Manning on the other side of the ball. To replace Tony, Tampa Bay's owner Malcolm Glazer paid Oakland $8 million and four draft picks for Jon Gruden. All I knew about Gruden was that his dirty-ass Raiders had beaten us 45–0 on my birthday, and his defense liked to hit people late. Gruden was a California blond, good-looking dude, so I thought of him mostly as a little Chucky doll from out West.

I admit that I began to appreciate him a little more after a reporter asked him how he expected to get along with me, and he answered, "Warren Sapp is Warren Sapp. He is a great football player. I want to be part of his playmaking. The only way we would trade him is if somebody forked up a small continent."

Oh, *that* Jon Gruden. I knew I was going to like the man. From the get-go his personality was almost exactly the opposite of Tony Dungy's. Tony was quiet and stern; when he said something everyone heard him. The message was strong. Coach Gruden might be sending a similar message, but he would do it in much louder, much more emotional and direct way. Dungy never overreacted; the speeches he gave were about perception versus reality. He was a mountain of a man, always standing there in front of you, always dependable. Gruden was a volcano; he was always bubbling over, always talking, funny as hell. From Gruden's very first practice we knew things were going to be different. As we were walking out to the practice field he warned Lynch, "First play, I'm buzzing a slant right by your right ear, and you ain't gonna know what to do . . ."

It was hard to believe; our coach was trash-talking us. But that's who he was. Before practice he'd walk through the locker room challenging the defense, laughing as he told us, "You poor guys, short yardage today, and we're going to dominate you guys. Fucking dommin-ate!" Dungy showed us clips of the work we were doing. Gruden always slipped something funny into the films; guys in college messing up, guys at the Combine, anything to catch our attention.

The biggest advantage Gruden had when he came in was that Dungy had been there before him. Together they made the perfect coach. Dungy took a bunch of kids and turned us into a football team by making discipline and a strong work ethic an essential part of our culture. When Gruden came in we were a smart, veteran team. For example, with Dungy we practiced in pads and all our gear. That's what worked for the 1970 Pittsburgh Steelers, and that's what we did. We didn't get to take off the pads until maybe Week 14. And even then we only took off our bottom pads and wore shorts. With Gruden we never put on our pads. We practiced without pads and we practiced fast. The drive that Dungy had instilled in us paid off for Gruden. Whatever we had to do, we did it, and we did it without complaint. If we'd had those two coaches in the reverse order it would not have worked, but this was perfect. I always said that Tony Dungy put the damn cake in the oven, and then Jon Gruden came in and put the icing on it. Of course, Sam Wyche couldn't even get the mix out of the box.

First thing Gruden did was make the offense accountable. He drove them hard, and he was relentless. When he came in everybody was calling him an offensive guru. His offense was going to score points; we were going to be tough on both sides of the ball. We opened the season at home, losing to a poor New Orleans team in overtime. Second week we beat the Ravens 25–0—without scoring one touchdown. Not one. Brooks ran back an interception 97 yards, special teams returned a punt 56 yards, we got a safety, and Martin Gramatica kicked three field goals. People were thinking, hell, Dungy's offense could have scored no touchdowns. Easy.

Gruden just kept at it; the man never slowed down. Word was that he came to work every morning at 3:15. That made a great story, but let's be real about this: Who's gonna know? Who is really going to check to see if that's true? Okay, go ahead, guess.

Damn right I did. One morning, on my way home, I decided to see for myself if it was true. My wife and I had a rule: My key had to be in the door by 2:30. After that time there ain't nothing open but IHOP and legs. I called my wife, JaMiko, and told her I was going to see if Jon Gruden really showed up for work at 3:15.

Naturally, she believed me. I think her exact words were, "You're lying." When I met JaMiko Vaughn she was working at the CIA in Washington, D.C. Her father, James Vaughn, was a career military officer. Trust me, you do not lie to JaMiko.

"No, I got you, Baby," I said. "I just want to see if this guy is for real." She finally agreed, and I drove on over to One Buc and pulled my car right into the spot that read "Reserved for Coach Gruden." I put on some music and I waited.

At 3:16 he turned the corner and pulled up beside me. "What are you doing in my spot?" he asked.

If I'd been thinking a little quicker I would've told him, "JaMiko wants your autograph." Instead I told him, "I just wanted to check on the myth."

He smiled at that. "Well, I'm here."

"You are," I agreed. "But it's 3:18." He asked me if I wanted to come in, but I told him I had to go home to go to sleep. I don't sleep much, ever, and I was back in his office by 7:00 a.m. After that I used to show up in his office at that time pretty much every morning, and the two of us would just sit there for an hour or so, talking more about life than football.

He'd be sitting in front of his computer in a dark room. The first time I walked in I turned on the lights—and he told me right away to turn them off. I told him once, "I figured you were hiding a couple of bodies in here." We really bonded over the fact that our kids had the same nickname. He asked me about my kids, and I told him, "Deuce came down the stairs this morning . . ."

He looked up. "What'd you call him?"

My son's name is Warren Sapp II, but we have always called him Deuce. "Deuce. Warren Sapp II. So we call him Deuce."

He smiled, "Yeah, that's what we call my son too."

I had learned the art of defense from Dungy. I wanted to learn how the offense works from Gruden. He wanted his offense to tear your heart out and beat it into the ground. I used to sit in the quarterback meetings to try to understand his thinking. We didn't have any super-stars on that offense, just some very solid players. Brad Johnson was the quarterback. Mike Alstott, the A-Train, was our featured running back. Roman Oben was the left tackle. Wide receiver Keyshawn John-son was the biggest name, but I had my own feelings about that.

Little Chucky Doll was always boasting about his great offense, telling everybody, "I want to win that championship because we scored 40 points." The man wasn't no fool; he knew that wasn't going to hap-pen. He knew that on this team we buttered our bread with a sledge-hammer. In fact, at one of the first defense meetings he challenged us, saying, "This defense is supposed to be so damn bad. You have been dominant but let's see how good you really can be. Let's see if you can score on defense. I want nine touchdowns out of the defense."

Nine touchdowns on defense? Didn't the man understand the game? We looked at each other, thinking, wow, shouldn't he be working on the offense scoring touchdowns?

That offense was never great, but he instilled a real swagger in them; he made them believe they were better than they really were. And once we started winning they began to believe in themselves. The greatest thing about that offense was still our defense. When we needed to score points in the playoffs, we scored points. Unbelievably, when Dwight Smith intercepted Rich Gannon for his second pick-six of the 2002 Super Bowl, that was our ninth defensive touchdown.

When it came to his offense, the man was an unbelievable opti-mist. The next-to-last game of the 2002 season we were playing the Steelers at Raymond James Stadium. A win would nail down the num-ber two seed in the playoffs and guarantee at least one home game, but Brad Johnson was hurt so Shaun King started at quarterback. We were down 17–0 in the second quarter when Martin Gramatica kicked a 50-yard field goal. Three points wasn't much, but it got us on the board before halftime and cut their lead to two scores. As our offense ran off the field the officials threw a flag. They called a penalty on the Steelers that would have resulted in a first down for us on their 28-yard line. I couldn't believe it when Gruden decided to accept the penalty. On a good day our offense would struggle to score three times, and King was not having a good day. Take the points and we only had to score twice. But that was the depth of the confidence Gruden had in our offense. As soon as I saw what he was doing I ran right up to him and demanded, "What the hell are you doing?"

He looked at me like he was General Patton. "I'm scoring a damn touchdown!"

I could not believe it. "You seeing the same game I'm seeing?" I asked him. "You can't take the points off the board. Don't you understand, you cannot tempt the Football Gods. Take the points. Our quarterback's on the bench, just take the damn points. You don't want to piss them off."

He shook his head. "You and your damn Football Gods."

"Damn right," I said. "Just honor them, and they will bestow a championship on us. We play a game where an inch can make the whole difference in the game. Why would you want to take the chance of screwing with them? You do not take points off the board."

He insisted. Four plays later Mike Alstott, our most reliable running back, fumbled on the 7-yard line, and the Steelers recovered. We ended up losing that game 17–7. The Gods had spoken.

With Gruden it was all about having fun; the man could be a clown with a plan. Very early one morning in 2003, I walked into his office and turned on the light, and he immediately went into his vampire mode, covering his eyes and ducking away. "Turn it off! Turn it off!"

"What up, Baby," I said. We were playing Atlanta that Sunday. I always loved playing there because it is one of the few cities in the NFL where you look up in the stands on the 50-yard line and see a lot of black faces.

He blinked his eyes. "You're killing me with that shit this early in the morning."

I sat down. "Well, when you hear me coming to the door put on your shades."

"I hear you okay. I hear you when you pull up with that fucking-ass music you're blasting every morning."

Chucky Boy didn't like my music? I explained, "Listen, I need that music. I got to wake myself up on my way to the job, because I want to be fully awake when I get here. So what's up? What you got going?"

He looked at me and had this big smile on his face. "This week I'm going to grow the legend."

"What? What are you talking about? What legend?"

"The legend of Warren Sapp."

What the hell was he babbling about this time? "It ain't like it's a weed in your damn garden that needs to be watered."

Then he said flatly, "I'm going to throw you a touchdown."

I'd been there before and wanted no part of that. "Oh no you ain't," I said, waving him off. "We got enough trouble right now with this damn offense to start jacking around. There's no need for it. The last thing Keyshawn wants to see is me catching a touchdown pass. It's really gonna piss him off."

Actually the last thing Keyshawn Johnson wanted to see was anybody except himself catching a pass. The fact that I was a defensive tackle catching a touchdown pass would only make that worse. Gruden had this big mischievous grin on his face. "I don't give a damn what Keyshawn wants to see. We are going to do this. All I'm asking from you is don't drop the ball. Deal?"

I did try to talk him out of it. I did. I remembered when the Bears used the Fridge on offense. It was sort of a joke, and everybody knew when he went into the game he would be getting the ball. I told Gruden that I'd play offense for him, but I wanted him to run the ball so I could block somebody.

Gruden named my play, Y Hurricane. That had meaning. *Y* is the designation for the tight end, and *Hurricane* was me, because I was a Miami Hurricane. Y Hurricane. None of that cheetah, rhino, elephant junk. It was a goal line play in which I came out of the backfield, went about five yards into the end zone, and caught a little flip pass. In practice that whole week I ran with the offense against my very own defense. Oh my goodness did they express their opinions. "Fucking traitor! Son of a . . ."

I said, "Stop. Gentlemen, please remember that we are all a team here."

One thing I had to remember when I went into the game was that I had to tell the official, "Number 99 reporting eligible." In football, numbers relate to positions, and supposedly no. 99 is not a receiver's number. But by reporting I became an eligible receiver. It is done that way to prevent sneak plays. Right, the other team isn't going to notice me, a 300-pound defensive lineman in the backfield? Gruden made me do it in practice so I wouldn't forget it. He made me run right over to him and say it in his face. The first time I did that he clicked on his little microphone and announced, "This big motherfucker is reporting into the game as an eligible receiver. Now why do you think he's doing that?"

The team loved Y Hurricane. Well, the offense loved Y Hurricane. When we ran it in practice the defense really did try to stop me. They did not want me to score on them. So the first time I scored I treated my D with great deference—I rubbed it right in their faces. You kidding me? Think I wasn't going to remind them about my superior athletic skills? This was the birth of my touchdown dance, the Beyoncé. Once I got into the end zone I started shaking my booty, just booty popping; hopping and popping. Bad, like a girl. Oh, did I rub it in. The O-line was going crazy celebrating. The D-line was falling down on the turf laughing. Gruden was laughing so hard he could barely talk, which was a pretty amazing thing in itself.

The rest of the week the defense fought hard to prevent me from scoring. But on Friday I got them again, and damn if I didn't do the Beyoncè. Even bigger. Then they started ragging on me, "No way you're going to do that dance in Atlanta if you score."

"Oh yeah. I catch the ball, I'm doing my dance."

"Oh no. You wouldn't dare."

We will see. This wasn't an end-of-the-game gimmick play. We were winning 7–3 when Gruden grabbed me as I came off the field after we forced the Falcons to punt. "If we get into the red zone don't be screwing around on the bench."

"What are you talking about?"

"It's time," he said. "Let's light this fucking place up." I was ready. And when the offense got downfield Gruden did it. "Gimme Y Hurricane," he shouted. I trotted over to the referee and said, "I'm reporting eligible, 99 reporting eligible." He clicked on his belt microphone and announced to the whole damn stadium, "99 is reporting eligible." Our whole squad knew what was coming and was standing up along the sideline. Gruden was holding people back, trying to hide his smile behind his clipboard.

In the huddle Brad Johnson, who'd taken over at quarterback a year earlier, called my play. The right guard, Cosey Coleman, more told me than asked me, "You *are* going to do the dance, right?"

"Shut up," I told him. In my entire career I'd never been nervous on a football field. I knew what I was doing. This time I was nervous. My stomach was churning. This was my opportunity to be one of those pretty people—but what if I dropped the ball? For years I'd been telling my teammates about my great hands. If I dropped the ball I'd never hear the end of it. So I told myself, just don't drop the damn ball, Sapp.

When we lined up I looked at the safety, who was the only player with a chance to cover me. The ball was snapped, and that safety just shot across in front of me and was gone. I was wide open, and I took off for the corner of the end zone, screaming, "Brad! Brad!" Johnson didn't even have to fake because I was so free. He rolled out to his left, but instead of sticking it in my gut, he lofted a little floater in front of me. He pulled the string on it. I had to reach down and put my elbows together. I caught it facing our bench. Touchdown! Touchdown Sapp! The Sapp attack lives! The first player to reach me was Cosey, who was telling me, "Do the dance! Do the dance!" I looked up, and Brooks was coming down the sideline running at me full speed. I thought, it's now or never.

It was time to do . . . the dance.

I looked over at the sideline, and I swear one-half of the team was screaming at me: Do it! Do it! The other half, basically the entire defense, was also screaming at me: You'd better do that fucker. You better not cheat us.

There was no way I could do the full Beyoncé, the dance I'd done in practice, on television. It would've put the commissioner in the hospital. Just imagine him watching the game and seeing me shaking my booty: Oh my God, what is Sapp doing this time? So instead I did the R-rated version. And I will give credit to Jon Gruden: He was right, he grew the legend. Fans loved the Beyoncé. Months later even Beyoncé asked me to do the Beyoncé for her. And later, somebody did a video of it and posted it on YouTube. Check out Sapp Dance at http://www .youtube.com/watch?v=SZ8QsfqAa2k.

It was an amazing season. After losing our opener to New Orleans we won five in a row, and then we went up to Philadelphia. In every season there's usually one game that makes the difference; it sets you on the path up or down. For us, this was that game. We'd lost to the Eagles the last three times we'd played them, including two games played in Veterans Stadium. This time we went in there confident we would win—but we lost 20–10. We hated losing to that team. We lost to them year after year after year. It definitely does get inside your head. What do we have to do to beat these suckers? After the loss we got on that bus and we were fuming. Burning. I was sitting next to Brooks when Gruden sat down right in front of us and sort of twisted around in his seat. Then he said, "I got them."

"What you talking about?" I asked. "You got what?"

"I'm telling you," Gruden said totally confident. "I got 'em."

"You heard that, Brooks," I said. Then I promised Gruden, "Okay, you are going to get that trip back; we are coming back here to this same damn stadium. It's going to be a whole lot colder, and the stakes are going to be a lot higher, and I'm gonna make you prove that statement to me. I promise you that. And I never lie."

In January we walked back into that stadium for the NFC Championship Game. We'd never won a playoff game on the road. We'd lost two playoff games at that stadium without even scoring a single touchdown. The Eagles were big favorites. This was the last game that was ever going to be played in that stadium, and the temperature was below 32 degrees. We had never won a game played in temperatures below 32 degrees. I never wanted to win one game more in my whole life.

In preparation for this game Jon Gruden gave the single best motivational speech I've ever heard. In reality, most coaches' speeches aren't like in the movies, where the coach builds up and up the momentum until the team charges hell-bent onto the field ready to rip down the entire stadium. If a coach does give that type of speech it's usually Saturday night. The Sunday speech is the matter-of-fact review of what we need to do to win the game. All business. Gruden gave this speech at the beginning of the week. He stood up in front of us and explained that there were 10 things we needed to do to beat the Eagles. Ten things! He went down the list one by one, blah blah blah, blah blah blah, we'd heard it all. But then he got to the number one thing we needed to do, and he started talking about their kick returner Brian Mitchell. "I want Brian Mitchell's ass on a plate," he said. "And once we finish with the Philadelphia Eagles we are going to go to San Diego for the Super Bowl . . ." he paused, grinned, and concluded, "where the coach is gonna get *two* hotel rooms for all my bitches!"

That room erupted. Exploded. That was it, that was the greatest motivational speech ever. There isn't even a second place. "The coach is gonna get *two* hotel rooms for all my bitches!"

I said to Gruden, "Yes, you are one sick fuck! Let's go get this done."

We opened up the game by kicking off to Brian Mitchell and then took off after his ass. Which we intended to deliver to Gruden on a platter. Mitchell returned the kickoff 70 yards. First offensive play of the game Donovan McNabb hands it off to Duce Staley, who ran it in for a touchdown. One play, 7–0. The Vet was rocking. Here we go again. Same old Bucs.

Not this time. I gathered the defense around me and I shouted at them, "You know who we are, right! We are the Tampa Bay Buccaneers. Trust me, that touchdown is not gonna beat us today, so nobody even flinch. Just forget it, it's nothing."

I went to the offense, and I told them straight up, "You get me some points. Just move the damn ball." Martin Gramatica kicked a 48-yard field goal, 7–3. We locked the Eagles down on D; that weak-ass offense was not going anywhere against us. We are playing the game. When we got the ball back we gained eight yards on the first two downs, so we had a third and 2 on our own 24-yard line. Before the play I said to Brooks, "Look, here comes the damn blitz again." Brad Johnson picked it up too. He gave a little fake and then put that ball right on the money for Joe Jurevicius. Joe was going through a really rough time. His little baby boy had been born premature and was fighting for his life, and we all were rooting hard, so this was perfect. He caught the pass running across the middle and took it 71 yards. We were on the goal line, and I heard Chucky Doll screaming, "Y Hurricane, Y Hurricane." I'm here Coach, I am definitely here. It didn't surprise me; my man Gruden had told the media the day before that as far as he was concerned I was the best-blocking tight end in the league.

I went right over to the official and said softly, like I was telling him a secret, "99 reporting eligible." He clicked on his microphone, "99 REPORTING ELIGIBLE." The whole damn stadium started booing. The stadium? More like the whole city of Philadelphia, the entire state of Pennsylvania, started booing.

My mother stood up and told them what she thought about that. She'd made a sign and held it up high as she could—and an Eagles fan came running up and stole it. Didn't bother her at all—she just reached down and grabbed the backup sign she'd made just in case.

I didn't care either. I told Johnson, "Call that run play right behind me." I went up to the line of scrimmage and put my hand down. I looked right at the Eagles' defensive end, N. D. Kalu, and remembered what Rod Marinelli had once said. "Whoo! N.D.," I said, quoting Rod, "If I tell you a duck can pull a truck, hook his ass up." An instant later the ball was snapped. I came off the line of scrimmage, grabbed N. D. Kalu's ass, lifted him up, and turned him around. I sealed the whole right side of the defense. Mike Alstott took a handoff and got right behind me, running it in. It was 10–7 and the rout was on.

All of a sudden that big stadium wasn't so loud. Close it down!

Oh, I wanted to win that game so bad. In the second quarter I got poked above the eye and started bleeding. I ran over to the sideline to get stitched. Our team doctor, Joe Diaco, was a smoker. He had this habit that whenever someone got hurt, he would smoke a cigarette before working on them. One time I ripped open my hand and a bone was poking out of it. It was so ugly that he had to smoke *two* cigarettes before he pushed it back in. This time, as I ran over to him I shouted, "Doc, light that cigarette right now!"

"Got you," he said, putting a cigarette in his mouth. We took off running for the locker room. It took seven stitches to close that wound.

At halftime Johnny Lynch kept walking around telling everybody, "Just 30 more minutes, 30 more minutes." My eye was almost shut by that point, but no way I was coming out of that game. On the Eagles' first series of the second half Ronde Barber hit McNabb and forced a fumble. Ronde was playing this game for his pride. He'd had a great season and was pissed that he hadn't been picked for the Pro Bowl, so he was taking it out on the Eagles. With under four minutes left in the game we were up 20–10, but the Eagles were driving. Ronde baited them on a blitz, faking that he was coming, and then dropped back and picked off McNabb's pass. Dwight Smith and I escorted him 92 yards for the touchdown. Ronde came running right up to my face and shouted to me, "Fuck the Pro Bowl! We are going to San Diego!"

When our plane landed that night thousands of people were there to greet us. Looking at them, I just couldn't help but think about how far we had come. In the old days we'd come back after getting whupped, and there would be five or 10 people out there to welcome us. And I'd look at them and think, you people have lost your mind. But this time the highway was lined with people from the airport all the way to One Buc. Both sides.

The Yucks were going to the Super Bowl.

FIVE

Before every single game John Lynch and I would meet in a corner of the end zone, bang our helmets together, and lock in for the game. That was our tradition. The Super Bowl wasn't any different—except for one little thing: I was so psyched up for this game that I forgot to put on my helmet. That didn't stop me. This was the Super Bowl; nothing was going to stop me. Just like always Lynch and I met in the corner, banged helmets, and . . . Oh. My. Goodness. I was staggered. Lynch looked at me and shook his head in total disbelief, telling me, "You're a fool."

"It's on today, Johnny," I screamed at him. "It is on today!"

The Raiders were a four-point favorite, they had the most productive offense in the NFL, and there were a lot of experts who predicted they were going to blow us out. But there was no way we were losing this game. No team in the whole history of the Super Bowl has ever had a greater advantage than we did that Sunday. Our opponent was the Oakland Raiders—and Jon Gruden had been their head coach for the previous four seasons. The Raiders were still running the offense he had put in. He knew every play in their playbook—because he had written the playbook. In fact, in practice during the week before the game he played quarterback for our scout team. He was pretend–Rich Gannon, calling audibles, huddling guys up, running to the line of scrimmage. But what really surprised us during the game was that they were still using Gruden's audibles. They might just as well have told us, "Um, listen Warren, we're gonna run an option-pass on this play."

There was nothing the Raiders could run that would surprise us. We were well prepared for their offense, but the fact is that the Raiders also knew what we were going to try to do. They knew it because they had seen us doing it all season. This was the only Super Bowl ever in which the best offense in the NFL, led by Rich Gannon, went up against the number one defense. We were going to finally answer the complex question, is a good offense the best defense or is it a good defense that is the best offense? When we lined up in a certain formation they knew we were running cover 2; the whole damn stadium knew it. That was our strength, and we weren't moving away from what we did most often and best. Football fans may not believe it, but there aren't that many surprises that take place during a pro football game. Winning always comes down to execution, to which team is better in doing what they want to do, which team is better at doing their own thing than their opponent's ability to stop it.

We had been building toward this game for eight seasons. We had no curfew Monday night so most everybody stayed out late. It was either really late or very early. Our first meeting was scheduled for Tuesday morning at 9:00 a.m. I got up about 4:30 a.m. and opened my door. All of a sudden Brooks's door opens, two doors down Lynch's door opens, and then Ronde's and Dwight Smith's. By 5:30 that morning we were sitting in a small room looking at film of Oakland. A little while later the door opens, and Monte Kiffin, our defensive coordinator, turned on the lights. He looked surprised to find us there. "What the hell is going on here?" he asked.

"It looks like we're watching a little film," I said. "Now turn off the damn light, c'mon in, and sit down and be quiet."

That whole week running up to the game was almost surreal. There's nothing that it can be compared to, and there is no way to prepare for it. If I sneezed the media wanted a full medical report. By the Thursday before the game the media had run out of stories so they started writing stories about the fact that there were no more stories. One reporter asked Brooks, "How about Sapp? Have you seen any big changes in him?"

Brooks said, "Oh yeah." They pushed the microphone closer to his mouth, and he revealed, "He was wearing sunglasses!" That was a big story: Sapp goes Hollywood! Usually I never wore sunglasses, but I had put them on to cover my stitches—until someone asked me why I was wearing sunglasses. Soon as they asked that I took them off.

I tried as much as possible to keep to my regular game-week routine. I've always believed the bigger the stage, the more normal you wanted everything to be. But when you've finally made it to the Super Bowl that was very difficult. For example, normally I didn't bring two magnums of Cristal to the stadium with me. In our locker room before the game I reminded my people, "Anybody who leaves this game without winning a championship and says it doesn't bother them, they lying. They lying to themselves, and they are lying to you. This is what it's all about. The money is going to come and go, but once you got that ring they can never take it away from you. That ring'll last in your family for centuries, and no one can ever take it away. Hundred years from now they can look back at you and say, you were a champion and here is the proof.

"Let's get this done one snap at a time. Let's get out there and do what we do, lay it all out there. I love all of you."

But as Celine Dion sang "God Bless America" the magnitude of the event hit me harder than I had thought possible. My eyes teared up, and later some people thought I was being emotional about the game, but at that moment I was actually thinking about my brother. I was standing there because he had taught me discipline and pointed me toward success. Discipline, discipline, discipline—make something of yourself. He would have been so proud of me standing there that day.

Maybe I was wearing Air Jordan in fourth grade, but I really rooted for Charles Barkley. *(Courtesy of Annie Roberts)*

That's me with my mother at Apopka Homecoming (above). *(Courtesy of Annie Roberts)*

My mother making things bloom, as always. *(Courtesy of Annie Roberts)*

My first hero, my older brother Parnell.
(Courtesy of Annie Roberts)

The quarterback giveth and I receiveth at Apopka.
(Courtesy of Annie Roberts)

The form that earned me exactly one college basketball scholarship offer.
(Courtesy of Annie Roberts)

Most Flirtatious

Warren Sapp received the most votes for Most Flirtatious male. Although Warren is often seen flirting and joking with many different girls, he has an ideal woman in mind. In fact, his ideal woman attends Apopka High School.

I have always strived to be the best at whatever is important to me.
(Courtesy of Annie Roberts)

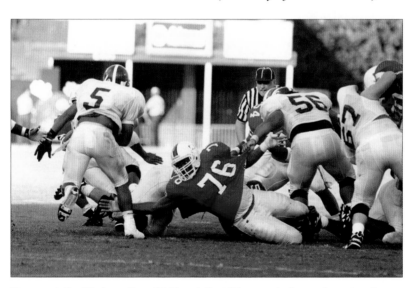

It was at the University of Miami that I began to learn how to play the great game of football. *(Courtesy of UMiami)*

Maybe the Lombardi Trophy isn't the most beautiful, but to me it was the most meaningful. *(Courtesy of UMiami)*

Showing my joy at being drafted by the Bucs. That's Bucco Bruce on that helmet. *(Courtesy of the Tampa Bay Buccaneers)*

Me and my close friend Bret Favre, getting even closer. *(Courtesy of the Tampa Bay Buccaneers)*

Another day at the office: Me as a Lion tamer. *(Courtesy of the Tampa Bay Buccaneers)*

The Lombardi Trophy doesn't weigh much—but only people who have won it know how much heavy lifting it takes to get to hold it up high. *(Courtesy of the Tampa Bay Buccaneers)*

The *Dancing with the Stars* spotlight shining on myself and Kym Johnson.
(Photofest)

My NFL Network *GameDay* teammates (from left: Rich Eisen, Steve Mariucci, Marshall Faulk, Kurt Warner, me, and Michael Irving). *(Ben Liebenberg/NFL)*

At the 2011 Super Bowl with the *Inside the NFL* team: (from left) Cris Collinsworth, me, Phil Simms, James Brown, and the owner of the Cowboys, Jerry Jones. *(Courtesy of Elinor Fukuda)*

The Captain and Deuce actually believed I was going to ride the zip line above the forest with them in Costa Rica (above), while I much preferred to go dolphin petting with them (below). *(Courtesy of JaMiko Vaughn)*

Here I am discussing strategy with three-month-old Mercedes, and with her mother, JaMiko. *(Courtesy of JaMiko Vaughn)*

The Most Happy Fella. *(Courtesy of the Tampa Bay Buccaneers)*

There were a lot of people I loved in Qualcomm Stadium that day, but without him it just wasn't complete. I knew who I was carrying in my heart.

The game did not start well. On the third play of the game Charles Woodson intercepted Brad Johnson and returned it 12 yards to our 36-yard line. On Oakland's very first offensive play Rich Gannon threw an incomplete pass. It was right then, John Lynch told me later, that he knew we were going to win this game. One play. Our D-backs had spent countless hours watching films of Gannon. He was a great quarterback, but on passing plays he'd drop back into the pocket and pump fake once and then pump again before he threw. He was very good at it. Those fakes were realistic and made it very difficult for defensive backs. If Gannon had enough time to get settled in the pocket it was going to be a long afternoon. But on that first play after the interception he dropped back, pumped once, turned, and . . . and he got smacked in the mouth. *Boom*! We got him and Lynch realized Gannon wasn't going to have time he needed to do all his faking. We can do our business better than they can do their business. Lynch stood still for just a second and thought, after the first play, we just won this game.

Our D stopped them on that first set of downs, but they kicked a field goal, 3–0. I wish Lynch had told me then that we had won the game, because there were a few moments when I got a little nervous. Oakland kicked off, and Aaron Stecker looked like he fumbled—man, what is going on here? As they were reviewing the play I reminded my people, "If you weren't the Bucs we wouldn't have to earn this thing. We got to earn it." Then the officials reversed the call.

The defense was playing great, just great. The Raiders couldn't move the ball with a backhoe. Dexter Jackson intercepted two passes in the first half. One time they did start moving. On a third and 6 Tim Brown ran an out pattern, and Rich Gannon put it right there for him—and he just dropped it. Dwight Smith looked at Brown and said, "You telling me you waited 15 years to get to the Super Bowl to do *that*?"

The greatest receiver in the history of the world, Jerry Rice, didn't make his first reception until the middle of the third quarter. Naturally, when he did, I was right there to congratulate him, telling him, "Welcome to the Super Bowl." He gave me a questioning look, like what was I talking about? "That's your first catch," I reminded him. "Welcome."

We grabbed Oakland by the neck and stomped on them. At halftime we were winning 20–3. Halftime can get pretty emotional. I've been in a lot of locker rooms at halftime: In Tampa Bay Monte Kiffin would scream at us and throw grease pencils against the wall to make his point. Back at Miami U Tommy Tuberville loved to break things—he once put a fist through the grease board. A few years later, when I was playing in Oakland and Rob Ryan was our defensive coordinator, we would practice halftime ducking, because he would go berserk, absolutely berserk, screaming, cursing—he loved to throw his clipboard. The Super Bowl halftime is an extra 15 minutes long, which gives coaches that much longer to prepare their team for the rest of the game. But we were so confident at halftime that I put a towel over my face, laid down, and went to sleep.

I did do one thing at halftime though—I stole a football. Got me my Super Bowl souvenir. Most people believe the footballs used in NFL games are brand new. They're not; most game balls are beat-up balls. Only K balls, the balls used by the kickers, are new. A brand-new NFL football is slick and slippery and very difficult to throw. So equipment managers spend all week rubbing down game balls with brushes until they are black. Black. Quarterbacks tell their receivers, after scoring a touchdown do not take that football; hand it back to the referee so we can keep it in play. At halftime I kind of casually picked up a Super Bowl game ball and put it in my locker.

Gruden was on cruise control. Nothing fazed the man. He actually was going to throw me a pass in the Super Bowl. In the second half we had the ball on Oakland's 1-yard line. Suddenly I heard Gruden yelling, "Where's Sapp?"

"I'm right here," I yelled to him. "What do you need?"

"Come over here," he said. "Look, if we don't score on this play, I'm gonna throw it to you."

I went and grabbed my helmet. Brooks gave me a look like, do you believe this guy? "What?" I said and got ready to go in. Johnson threw a short incomplete pass. I got ready to go in . . . and the official blew his whistle. Kenyatta Walker got called for illegal hands to the face right at the end of the play. Ten-yard penalty, moved the ball back to the 11. Too far for the old Y Hurricane. Just imagine that: If Kenyatta did not stick his hand in that dude's face Gruden was going to run that play in the Super Bowl. Life is sweet.

About the only unpleasant thing that happened that whole day was that my family almost got into a fight in the stands. My aunt Ola was sitting with some of my other relatives. Fortunately I hadn't been able to get enough tickets in one section for my whole family so my mother was sitting somewhere else. I felt bad about that, they loved to sit together, but there wasn't anything I could do about it. My family cheered loudly for me, which apparently irritated a drunken Oakland fan who threatened them, cursed them, and finally started throwing cushions and food at them. Every time I made a play he got angrier. They ignored him. It was only when he wrapped his Rolex around his knuckles and drew back his arm like he was going to hit someone that the police got involved and escorted him out of the stadium. Ola May told me how thankful she was, saying, "There's a reason God does the right thing at the right time. If you had gotten us all tickets together your mother would have been sitting there, and we would have either ended up at the hospital or the police station!"

With 1:18 left in the fourth quarter Derrick Brooks intercepted Gannon and ran it in to put us ahead 41–21. At the end of the game before I left the field I went right up to Oakland's great wide receiver Tim Brown and asked him, "Can I have your helmet?"

He said, "What?"

"I'll give you mine," I told him. I wasn't only a player; I have always been a passionate football fan. I collected the helmets of players I admired. At that time I had about 14 helmets in my collection at home. Tim Brown was one of the greatest receivers in history, having caught more than one thousand passes. There are only four men in history with 1,000 receptions, and I already had collected helmets from the other three.

"All right," he said, shrugging. He snatched his mouthpiece off his helmet and handed the helmet to me.

"Thank you," I said. "Good game."

I caught up with Brooks, who was crying for joy, and we hugged. We didn't say too much to each other—we didn't need to. We knew what we had accomplished. We had shared so much since the day we were both drafted, and together we had helped turn this franchise around. I found Lynch and wrapped him up. Brian Kelly had his kid in his arms. John Lynch was walking around with his kid on his shoulders. I got my little girl and put her up on my shoulders and carried her around. Even in the middle of that celebration I was aware how special it was. I knew that I would never experience the same level of excitement and satisfaction again. We had done it. We had taken that franchise from worst to first, and we had done it the right way. I never wanted to leave that field. Finally though, I went into the locker room and got ready to pop open my magnums of Cristal. There were two security guards standing over my cooler. It looked like the Men in Black had invaded our locker room. "Don't even think about it," one of them said.

Turned out the NFL does not permit players to celebrate in the locker room with alcoholic beverages. So when you see that postgame celebration, that is not champagne being sprayed around. It didn't matter to me.

The best player in the Super Bowl gets to go to Disney World to be greeted personally by Mickey Mouse. I didn't quite make that; instead

I got to meet Jimmy Kimmel! That night was Jimmy Kimmel's very first show, and I had been invited to represent the Super Bowl champion Tampa Bay Buccaneers. Oh, that sounded so good—the Super Bowl champion Tampa Bay Buccaneers. Me and Snoop and Coldplay and that actor, George Clooney, were on that first show. Of course, I was there only because we had won the game. There was someone sitting in the Oakland locker room probably feeling totally despondent; not only did he lose the Super Bowl, he also didn't get to go on the first *Jimmy Kimmel Live!* show. So I quickly put on my world champions T-shirt, world champions hat, regular old jeans, Jordan shoes, and took off. I had a police escort to a helicopter and flew directly to Los Angeles. When I got to the Kimmel show they gave me a bottle of Cristal and a Double-Double In-N-Out burger with no onions and fries. Now, I admit that this isn't the most interesting story about winning the Super Bowl—but it damn well better get me an invitation to *Jimmy Kimmel Live!* to promote this book!

After the Kimmel show I flew right back to San Diego to catch up with my boys. When I got back down there we were in the full-fledged party mode, but the team party was winding down. I grabbed a couple of my teammates, two other friends, and we went in search of a party. We heard there was a party going on at the top of the W Hotel. Okay, that'll do. We walked into that party feeling about as good as it was possible to feel, ready to pop some more Cristal, and I suddenly noticed all these people just staring at us. Not saying anything, just staring. It was then one of my friends said to me softly, "Uh Warren, I think this is a Raiders party." Every person there was dressed in Raiders black and silver.

"How y'all!" I said loudly, smiling as friendly as I could. They had booked the room to celebrate the victory that hadn't happened. It didn't look like they were too happy about that, either. We actually stayed there for a few minutes, and except for those people who looked at us like they wanted to kill us, it was very nice. Uncomfortable, but nice.

When we got back to Tampa on Monday 65,000 people were waiting to greet us at Raymond James Stadium. On Tuesday 100,000 people lined the streets for our victory parade. After the parade we all went back to One Buc. As I got ready to leave to go home I just happened to notice the Vince Lombardi Super Bowl trophy sitting there. Just sitting there with nobody paying too much attention to it. We were all getting ready to meet for our own private celebration. Why not, I thought. In hockey doesn't everybody on the championship team get to bring home the Stanley Cup? So I picked it up. It wasn't no secret; I didn't try to slip it under my shirt or anything. I had taken only a couple of steps when I heard Rich McKay telling me, "C'mon, give it to me, Dawg." What? "C'mon Warren, hand me that trophy."

Okay, so maybe I was getting a little carried away. I put it down, telling him, "I would've brought it back." And I would have. Probably.

My phone was ringing as I walked into the house. The first thing I heard was Shaquille O'Neal asking, "Can I speak to the world champion please?" Oh, those words sounded good. At Miami we'd come close to a national championship, but this time I'd made it to the promised land. I'd made it all the way from the Dust Bowl to the Super Bowl. Finally. Finally I knew what it felt like to be a champion.

It felt good. Oh, it felt good. It felt so good I couldn't wait to receive the official team ring, so I designed my own and went out and had it made. I never took it off. When we finally did get our rings I looked it over and decided mine was much better than theirs.

At the victory parade Jon Gruden told the fans, "There's a storm warning out there. We got a heck of a football team, and we're just getting started." Well, he was definitely correct about those storm warnings. The situation in Tampa fell apart the next season. Winning covers a lot of internal problems, and we stopped winning. There is a cliché that a football team is a family. That's not accurate; if a family is walking down the street and the little baby lags behind, everybody will stop and be concerned and wait. In football, nobody will wait for you. In fact, if that little baby falls behind he's going to get cut from the family. Toe the line, do your own job, or good-bye. Rod Marinelli used to call a football team "a brotherhood of men." Brad Culpepper described a team as a salad, "Some players are grapes, some players are apples." But the thing that Brad forgot to add is that some of them are nuts.

The public has absolutely no idea what is really going on inside the locker room. Only occasionally, like in 2011 when the Jets basically threw Santonio Holmes out of their huddle during the game, do fans learn about personality conflicts that exist on every team. A football team is a temporary alliance between as many as 100 people, where individual personalities are voluntarily surrendered for the good of the team. You have to exclude *self* in a team environment, with the belief that if the team wins—and if I do my job making that happen—some of the glory will trickle down to me. But when you have that many people competing, with a large pile of money at stake, there are obviously going to be conflicts. I have never been on a team where every person liked every other person. There have always been rivalries, feuds, conflicts, finger-pointing—sometimes it even bursts out into fights. These are the best people in the world at what they do, and there is a tremendous amount of pride and some big egos in every NFL locker room. Sometimes the most difficult thing a coach has to do is keep players apart.

I was no different than anybody else. I know, I know, it's hard to believe, but even a lovable hunk of kindness like me was not universally beloved in the locker room. There were some teammates who did not like me. I was involved in my share of fights. For example, D-lineman Chidi Ahanotu and I just did not get along. We played alongside each other, but we didn't get along. Seemed like we were always nipping at each other. Now don't go telling my mama, but I have to admit that sometimes it was my fault. Chidi was a good player; he was known for putting pressure on quarterbacks but not getting the sacks. He owned a nice jazz bar named Sacks. On one of our Thursday nights we all went there and had a nice time. A few weeks later we were making our plans to get together, and Chidi stood up and suggested we all go back to his restaurant, Sacks.

I couldn't resist. See, this is where I get myself into trouble. I stood up and said, "I got one thing to add. Everything Chidi just said is right except for one little thing. They changed the name of his restaurant from *Sacks* to *Pressures*." Ohhh, did that man get angry. He did not think that I was funny. He wanted to fight me right there. That time I walked away.

But that was not the only time. Late in 2000 I had 15½ sacks, and he might have had one-half of a sack. We were sitting in a D-line meeting watching a sack reel to get motivated. As we watched, Rod was riffing on everybody—it was a lot of fun. Suddenly Chidi said, "Stop it for a second. Go back. I think I beat Sapp off the ball there."

Really? I took great pride in my quickness. There was a reason I usually got there first. So I agreed, "Yeah, run that shit back. Let's see who's putting in some work." We watched, and on that play it did look like Chidi got the jump. "Oh boy," I said, "you're going fast. Let's give you two points for being the first one off the ball. Now what the fuck does that get you? I take this personally. I've got 15½ sacks and you're calling me out? You didn't even come here to work out all off-season, and they give you a $30 million contract, and now you got half a sack and you're talking shit to me?" This type of conversation is not at all unusual in NFL locker rooms. We didn't get our mean up on Sundays by being sweet the rest of the week. This is who we are. We lived on the edge, week after week throughout the whole season.

Chidi said something back to me, and I wouldn't let it go. "So you're digging through the trash and you find a little piece of meat, and I guess you're going to put your mouth on it."

Neither one of us would back down, especially in front of our teammates. The situation continued escalating until Rod Marinelli threw both of us out of the meeting. Now we had 600 pounds of anger stomping around the facility. I walked into the locker room in time to hear him talking some garbage. I confronted him, asking him, "You got something you want to say to me? Go ahead, get it off your chest." Then I reminded him of a phone call he'd made to me a few days earlier, asking me to help him with something, repeating what he said.

He didn't like that at all. At. All. I don't remember who threw the first punch—for real I don't remember—but I do remember hitting him with a quick left. About six guys jumped between us. I wanted to fight him. He picked up his helmet and I challenged him, "Please, go ahead and hit me with your helmet. Please do it so I can kill your motherfucking ass. Hit me with it."

These aren't stories I'm proud of, but this is part of my career too. I was raised to be prideful; it is one of the elements of my character that made me drive myself to perform at a high level as long as I was physically able. And while the media rarely report it, this type of locker room confrontation is not unusual in the NFL. Sometimes the anger just keeps growing and growing till it reaches the bursting point.

I guess he thought about it. Chidi did not want to fight me, but my switch had been turned to full power. We went out to the practice field and I was on fire. I was 1,000 degrees hot. I told him, "As soon as we are done with practice I am going to whip your ass on the 50-yard line. You best be there." We were going through practice, and they had to take me out because they couldn't get anything done. Any play I was in was over before it got started. The O-linemen saw that look on my face and didn't even think about getting in my way.

Finally Rod came over to me and said, "I need to talk to you. For the betterment of the team, stop. Just let it go. Please, don't fight with him because if you do it will follow you. It'll follow you and engulf you. All the sacks you have now will be a side story to what you did to a teammate because I know what you're going to do. I see it in your eyes."

I was ready to fight, but I knew he was right. I knew it wasn't worth it.

Chidi and I eventually reached an uneasy truce. And there were other players and coaches in my career that I didn't get along with. Brian Kelly, for example, and I never did see eye-to-eye off the field, but on Sunday we all went to work together. Me and Chidi and Kelly and every other Buc. Maybe we didn't hang together Monday to Saturday, but on Sunday they were my people. On Sunday we bonded. On Sunday I would have fought to protect Chidi so I could beat his ass on Monday. I was taught correctly that my obligation as a professional football player was to show up on time and prepared to play and do my job as best I could. I always said that they paid me to practice, that was my job. I would have played on Sundays for free, that was my passion.

Among the very biggest problems we had on that 2003 team was Keyshawn Johnson. Obviously the fact that we finished the season 7–9 after winning the Super Bowl a year earlier wasn't only his fault, but he sure didn't help. He was fighting with the coaches and players so much that after 10 games basically he was thrown off the team.

Nobody ever doubted Keyshawn Johnson's ability to catch the football. No question he could do that. The Bucs got Keyshawn from the Jets in 2000 for two first-round draft picks, a 12th and a 27th. Our offense was desperate for that missing piece who could help us move the chains, and General Manager Rich McKay gave him an eight-year $56 million contract, making him the highest paid wide receiver in the league. I welcomed him to the team, had him over to my house for a home-cooked meal, and our wives became best friends. My very public problems with Keyshawn Johnson were based on his play on the field and his refusal to accept responsibility for his own failures.

Most of the time the fan doesn't truly understand what they are watching on the field. They see what happens, but they don't really know why it happened. Here's what they see: Center snaps the ball, the quarterback fades to pass and his O-line gives him decent protection, he looks downfield, there is a receiver who looks wide open, but the quarterback throws the ball way over his head or worse, right into the hands of a defensive back. Boo that quarterback. What the hell was he doing! Who taught that guy to play football? Organize the posse, let's run him out of town. No, no, no, definitely not. In fact, it wasn't even the quarterback's fault.

What? What are you talking about, Dawg? You saw that raggedy-ass pass he threw. Maybe, but what the fans didn't see was why. Key-shawn Johnson, for example, had a nasty habit of shorting his routes, which meant he started his diagonal cut early instead of going to the place he was supposed to be. Quarterbacks throw to a spot on the field, rather than to a player. The QB takes the snap, and as he is backing up he's counting one, two, three, and then he turns and throws to the pre-determined spot. The receiver gets to that spot, he's counting too, and on six he turns and the ball is right there. Teamwork is a play of beauty. Teamwork and timing equals a reception.

But when a receiver shorts his route, the quarterback turns to throw and the receiver is not where he is supposed to be. Suddenly the quarterback has to start looking for second and third options. The quarterback does not want to search for options because the entire D is coming after him, the pocket is collapsing, and time is running out for him. At the last tenth of a second to save his own sweet life he unloads. He gets rid of the ball rather than being sacked. Half a ton of defense unloads on him, smacking him good, making him feel it. And the crowd starts booing the quarterback.

A receiver shorts his routes because it makes it easier for him to get open. Literally he is cutting the corner too soon. The problem with Keyshawn was that he did it all the time, and he wouldn't listen to anybody about it. Fortunately we had Keenan McCardell and Joe Ju-revicius, who ran their routes to the proper depth. We won because Keenan would run the primary route the way it had been designed, and Gruden had the guts to put him in Keyshawn's spot. That's an-other reason I love Gruden; he didn't back down to any individual for the good of the team.

I remember Keyshawn explaining to Gruden, "I need to be going left to right, left to right." I thought, you are out of your mind. You can't run right to left? Really? What difference does it make? It's the same damn ball in the air, just catch the thing. Other team scouts must have been pretty damn lame not to pick up on the fact he only ran left to right. It ain't that damn hard, but Keyshawn always had some kind of excuse. It wasn't a big secret that Keyshawn didn't fit into our locker room; he came to us from a different football culture and he never could make the adjustment. Everything was always about him. His ego barely fit in any locker room, but the first practice we had in 2003, the first practice we had after winning the Super Bowl, was the day I officially stopped speaking to him.

We had drafted quarterback Chris Simms, Phil Simms's son. He was a big left-handed kid who could throw the ball. I mean, throw it. Me and Brooks were standing on the sideline calling each other *champ*, "How you doing, champ?" "Pretty good, champ," when Chris Simms dropped back and threw a perfect spiral to Keyshawn—who dropped it. Okay, dropping a pass in practice is not a big deal. It always takes a receiver time to get used to working with a new quarterback. But Keyshawn looked back at Simms and shouted, "Your ball spins funny."

Your ball spins funny? It spins funny? Simms was left-handed so his passes did have an opposite spin. But this was the kid's first professional practice, he wanted so badly to start earning respect and prove himself, and Keyshawn dropped a pass and turned around and blamed *him*. My goodness. Right at that moment I'd had enough with him. I shook my head and said to Brooks, "I swear to God I will never say another word to him. He is too stupid and too arrogant to know when he's wrong." Oh, I was getting into it, all my frustrations with him were rolling out. "He's been here three years, and if you can tell me one time he said 'my bad' I'll talk to him again. One time, Brooks, just tell me one time. All those times he ran the wrong route, all those times he didn't know what the hell he was doing, never one time did he say 'my bad.'"

Brooks had no answer for me. He couldn't. I never did speak to Keyshawn again. What was worse than his own lack of effort, of course, was that his attitude rubbed off on some of the younger players and, I believe, eventually put a dent in their careers. Playing professional football is a very hard job—and anything less than giving a total effort in every practice—it's easy to play hard in a game—will eventually make a difference. Keyshawn skipped team meetings, twice he missed the curfew the night before a game, and when we went to San Francisco he missed the plane coming back without telling anyone where he was. And I saw some people following his lead.

We finally had to deal with the Keyshawn situation in midseason. Once we started losing, some people began looking out for themselves. So after a team meeting one morning I was walking into Gruden's office, and Keyshawn came out of the office and walked right past me. We didn't say anything to each other. The lights were on in Gruden's office, and he had this totally mystified look on his face. I asked, "You all right?"

He sat back in his chair and asked, "What the fuck did I do?"

"What are you talking about?"

"Can you believe this fucker Keyshawn comes into my office and tells me he don't like me, he don't like my offense, and he'd rather retire than play for me next season. He wants out of here."

That was all I needed to hear. "Just hold on," I said. "Don't go nowhere." I got our other five captains and brought them back into Gruden's office with me. Johnny wears his emotions on his face, and it was obvious this was really bothering him. "Tell them," I said.

Gruden repeated what he'd told me, and we sat there and voted Keyshawn off the team. Six–zero, there wasn't one of us who was interested in keeping him. We didn't believe we needed him either. It was Keenan, not Keyshawn, who'd caught two touchdowns in the Super Bowl. McKay deactivated his ass for the last six games of the season; he wasn't even allowed back inside One Buc.

"It's a shock," Keyshawn said, and we all thought the most shocking thing about that was that he was shocked. "Why would you do that when you're trying to win a championship? You're talking about your best offensive player . . ." Our best offensive player? He did not have a clue.

That wasn't the last time I spoke about him, though. One Sunday morning many years later, on Showtime's *Inside the NFL*, I was asked if Dallas quarterback Brad Johnson would be able to get along with Terrell Owens. What is it about wide receivers? Keyshawn, Santonio Holmes, Terrell Owens? Of course, I said, "Brad Johnson has played with worse malcontents than T.O. He played with Keyshawn. Keyshawn was kicked off the team to get him away from us. Terrell Owens is a choirboy compared to Keyshawn."

If I'd shut my mouth right there that would have been fine. But then I wouldn't be me. A few weeks later I was asked on our show if I would watch a new reality show Keyshawn was doing about interior design. "Me?" I said, trying to be clever. "Watch Keyshawn on an interior decorating show? Keyshawn, I knew you were a bitch. And thanks for making it all clear."

Ohhh. My bad. My very, very bad. I never should have said that; it didn't come out at all like I intended. I knew that for sure when my mother called me that afternoon and told me that. She'd met Keyshawn, but she'd also met his wife, so she did not like what I said. She tore into me, reminding me that I had not been brought up to make hurtful comments like that, whether I was on national television or in my own living room. So on the following week's program I apologized to Keyshawn for saying something ridiculous like that, explaining, "A week ago I took a shot at an old teammate of mine, and I really thought I crossed a line because my mother was watching this show, and afterward she gave me a buzz and said, 'You know what, that's wrong . . . You got to apologize.' I said, 'You're right, I am so wrong for crossing that line with Keyshawn and I apologize . . . and good luck to you on your show.'"

Even if you were a troubl . . . whoops. Old habits do die slow.

As it turned out, 2003 also was my last season in Tampa. That's when I learned that being a free spirit in the NFL can be very expensive. The sixth week of the season I was fined $50,000 for supposedly bumping into an official, and I responded to that by calling the NFL "a slave system."

Maybe that was a little bit of an exaggeration; the fact is that we were the best paid slaves in history. But that was another distraction the team certainly didn't need. We finished that season 7–9, and after it was over I became a free agent. I'd gone to Tampa Bay kicking and screaming, but I'd spent nine years there and helped transform the Bucs into a respected NFL power. My relationship with the city wasn't always smooth, but there was still a lot of love in my heart for that place. I would have been happy staying there. In fact, there only was one other place I wanted to play. If I'd gotten an offer from the Dallas Cowboys I would have signed right away. A chance to wear that silver helmet with the big star on it? Whoo-ee. I would have thought I'd died and gone to Cowboys heaven. That would have been my dream come true. I was a big man, but I still had enough of that little boy inside me to want to make my old dream come true. Dallas didn't even make an offer. The definition of *old* is nine years in the NFL. I was only 31, but in football years, figure that's about 124 years old. The fact that I'd been selected for seven consecutive Pro Bowls didn't seem to matter—I was football old. When the Cowboys didn't make me an offer, staying in Tampa became a matter of dollars, and as that turned out it made no sense.

When I went to my very first training camp after being drafted my roommate was the veteran linebacker Hardy Nickerson. Practically the day we met he slammed down the whole collective bargaining agreement in front of my face and insisted that I read it from beginning to end. I told him, "You're crazy."

"You better know what's in it," he told me, tapping it. "That's your future right there." Hardy made me do two things that training camp: Bring a TV set for our room and read that collective bargaining agreement. That agreement established free agency, which changed the financial structure of pro football. It made a lot of players very comfortable, and Hardy Nickerson was one of the people who'd led the fight for it. He explained to me how negotiations had worked before it was signed. After starting at linebacker for the Steelers for three or four seasons, he was negotiating his new contract. He did the calculations and figured out that the average salary of all the starting linebackers in the NFL was $350,000. To be fair, he decided to ask Mr. Art Rooney, the Steelers owner, for $250,000, or $100,000 less than the average. Okay. He was going to give him a break. At their negotiation meeting Hardy wrote down his *$250,000* on a slip of paper and slid it across the desk to Mr. Rooney. Mr. Rooney looked at it, wrote *$125,000*, and slid it back to him. That was how contract negotiations worked before the new agreement was signed in 1993.

In 1997, the four-year $4.4 million rookie contract I had signed with the Bucs was expiring. At the beginning of that season Rich McKay offered me a new deal, five years for $15 million. Everybody knew that the league was negotiating a new multibillion dollar television contract, which meant that the salary cap was going to rise, which would mean much larger contracts. I also knew that the best defensive tackles in the game—John Randle, Dana Stubblefield, Sean Gilbert—were all up for new contracts, and before I signed a new deal I wanted to see how much they got. So I turned down the Bucs' offer.

McKay raised it to $18 million. A lot of money. But one of the few advantages of coming from nothing is that you're not afraid of it. My agent, Drew Rosenhaus, wanted me to accept it, reminding me that a big chunk of it was guaranteed—meaning I got it even if I was injured and never played another game. "Don't say another word," I told him. Drew kept talking, but finally I said to him, "We'll talk about my new contract when we're in Hawaii celebrating my first Pro Bowl. Until then I don't want to make no deal." Negotiating a new contract without making the Pro Bowl is like having your wedding without a bride. It's a nice celebration, but at the end of the day you ain't getting nothing. "Let's just let it roll."

Derrick Brooks's contract also was expiring, and they made him about the same offer I'd turned down. We had discussed going into free agency together, knowing they could not possibly afford to lose both of us. At least one of us would have received a substantial offer from another team, which would have established a real market value for the other one. I found out later that the Bucs were terrified we were going to do that so they really wanted to sign at least one of us. One morning I showed up at the job and there were cable wires on the floor going down the hallway, and I could see they were setting up for a press conference. Oh no! I got ahold of Derrick and told him, "I'm looking at the cables on the floor. I know it ain't my contract so it's got to be yours. Do not tell me you signed for that $15 million."

"I did," he said.

Never in my life could I have anticipated being angry with my close friend for signing a $15 million contract. "How could you do that, man?" I said.

He explained that his agent had told him the new TV contract would be less than a billion dollars, so he was better off signing before it was negotiated.

I had majored in criminology at the U so I knew when a crime was being committed. "That's ridiculous," I told him. "CBS wants back in. TNT wants some of it. Drew says it's going to be at least $4 billion." I stopped. "You know what, I'm sorry. I shouldn't be talking about your money." Then I walked away.

Brooks and I both had great seasons in 1998. Tampa Bay had

made the playoffs for the first time in about 150 years, and we'd both been selected to go to Hawaii for the Pro Bowl. My first morning there I opened the hotel room door and the *USA Today* is lying on the floor. On the front page is a cartoon showing a man holding the NFL logo under his arm kicking a dollar bill sign. The NFL had signed a $17.6 billion TV deal. I ran downstairs and found Brooks in the coffee shop. I slapped the paper down in front of him and said, "You ought to fire your agent right now. Look at that number. Look at that." Brooks is an honorable man. He played the next three years under that contract, making him one of the most underpaid players in the NFL.

But I hadn't signed. Thank you for that, Lord. After the season Drew came to Tampa to lock down my contract with Rich McKay. I handed him the keys to my house in Tampa and told him I was going to Miami while he negotiated the deal. I said, "If you think I want to sit here and listen to you tell me everything the Bucs are saying you are out of your mind. I don't want to know. They're going to try to knock me down, and if I hear about that I'll have feelings that won't go away so quick. You just go in there and come out with the best deal possible, because that's what I'm paying you for."

Meanwhile, while we were negotiating with the Bucs, the Washington Redskins signed the 49ers' Dana Stubblefield for six years at $36 million, the Vikings gave John Randle $32.5 million over five years to stay in Minnesota, Buffalo paid Ted Washington $27.3 million for five years, and Arizona signed Eric Swann for five years at $25 million. Now I knew my market value. Mama, raise your boy to be a defensive tackle. When he sits down there at the dinner table, give him some extra potatoes. Thirty-six million is a big number. I could've lived in Big Al's grocery store playing Kicker for five years, and I wouldn't have reached 36 million points. And I could play that game. When I read that they had signed, I put down the newspaper and took a real deep breath.

Drew called to tell me McKay had offered $28 million for five years, Ted Washington numbers. I told him, "Those numbers don't even go together." The Bucs came back with six years at $33.3 million, John Randle numbers. "Closer," I said. Finally he came back. "I got the number," he said. "I got the largest contract ever given to a defensive player." Warren Sapp numbers. It was $36 million and fifty thousand dollars. "How do you say that?" I asked him.

"Thirty-six-point-oh-five million dollars." Later I found out he'd told the Bucs that I had to beat Stubblefield, that's where the $50,000 came from.

I said, "Well, there it is." Those were my exact words: "There it is." During the press conference I said something like, "Now I know I can afford for my kids to go to college."

To which Tony Dungy had responded, "With that contract Warren could afford to buy his kids a college."

I had the contract, now all I had to do was earn it. Football is not like baseball or basketball where you get every dollar you sign for. Only about $8 million of my contract was guaranteed. Only $8 million, Warren? C'mon. Only $8 million? That was a lot of money, but it meant $28 million was sitting on the table just waiting for me to pick it up. A chunk of that money was due each season, so the team could cut my ass and not pay whatever was left on that table if they made that decision. Eventually that's what they did to Brooks when they cut him in 2009.

There are a lot of people who believe that signing a contract that guarantees an athlete security for a lifetime affects his performance, and it may actually be detrimental to his performance. And I can say without any hesitation that in my case those people would be absolutely correct. My whole life changed that year: In addition to my new contract, I'd gotten married, moved into a new house, and we'd had a baby.

JaMiko Vaughn was my teammate Alvin Harper's sister-in-law. She was visiting Tampa for a baby shower for Monica Culpepper. I knocked on the door of Alvin's house and she answered it. I took one look at her. Really? "Is Hop here?" I asked, which is what I called Alvin.

"I'll go get him," she said and closed the door in my face. She went and told her sister, "There's this big guy at the door."

"Oh, that's Warren," her sister said. "He's safe. You can let him in." Slammed the door in my face, that's how we met. She was a beautiful, smart, independent young woman, the type of confident person who would fit equally well both under the tree in Apopka and in the nicest restaurant in New York. She was going to George Mason University and working part time at the Gap when we met. Our first date was on a Saturday afternoon. We had a home game the next day, and the team always spent the night before a home game in a hotel. We went to an African arts festival, and I told her I had to be at the hotel by six o'clock. She was very considerate—she thought I worked the night shift at the hotel. She had no idea I was a football player. In fact, those first few weeks she was probably the only person in Tampa who didn't know who I was.

As it turned out, I didn't know exactly what she did either. All I knew was that she was living in Washington, D.C. And while she continued working occasionally at the Gap so she could keep her employee discount, her real job was in the contracts division at the CIA.

I called her work number one day expecting to find her at the store. Instead someone answered the phone, "Contracts division." Contracts division? Eventually JaMiko explained, "It's the contracts division of the CIA."

The CIA? My girlfriend was a spy? I had no idea what she did in the contracts division, but I did find out she was the youngest contract officer in the history of "the agency," as we called it. But from that point on, I began every phone conversation we had by stating clearly, "Just in case someone is listening, this is just one man stating his own personal opinion."

We were in Puerto Rico when I asked her to marry me. It was a beautiful starry night, and we had taken a long walk along the beach. We were sitting by the pool, and I got up all my nerve and went down on one knee. She looked at me lovingly and said, "What are you doing down there, Warren? You're never going to be able to get back up."

I asked her to please be quiet just for one moment, and then I proposed.

I will never forget her incredibly romantic answer. She shouted at me, "Holy crap! Are you serious?"

We got married at the Pro Bowl in Hawaii. We didn't do a lot of planning, so at the very last minute all my men had to run around the island searching for size-50 tuxedos. Several months later our first child, Mercedes, "Captain," I call her, had been born. We had moved into a new house. Everything about my life was new and different. I had a new wife, a baby, a new house—and a new contract that paid me enough money to live happily for a long time. So I took my foot off the accelerator.

I had real difficulty that off-season with the honey-do's: Honey let's do this, honey let's do that. I found every excuse not to do my work. I had always gone to the job four, five, six days a week doing what I needed to do to prepare. I told myself it was acceptable to do a little less, promising that whatever I didn't do today I would make it up tomorrow. And then the next tomorrow. I spent a lot of time being a daddy, watching my little girl wiggling. I learned how to change a diaper. A lot of diapers actually. Instead of going to work and then coming home and playing with my kid, too often I skipped the going-to-work part of that equation. And when I did go to the job I worked out with less commitment than I'd had before. All of a sudden eight of the 16 off-season weeks of conditioning were gone. I was too far behind to catch up. I had done exactly what I promised myself I would never do: When I signed my big contract I stopped working as hard as I had worked to earn that big contract. That was a shame on me.

As a result, when the season started I was a little overweight and a little undermotivated. My play was just a little bit less. I'd lost that split-second that made all the difference in my game. I wasn't quick anymore. I could still beat the O-line off the ball, but I couldn't beat them clean enough to get the sack. I had not sharpened my knife; I'd let my knife get dull. And I knew it on the first day of practice. Oh it was frustrating. On the field you can't wave your big paycheck at someone and tell him to get out of your way. It don't work like that. Even the worst players in the game are among the best players at that position in the entire world. If you come to the field not ready to play they will find you out, and they are good enough to exploit it.

In my football life nothing had frustrated me more than a player with great talent who would not do the necessary work to develop it. At Miami Pat Riley played right next to me. He was a beast—6'6", 275 pounds—and ran a 4.5 40. He blew his knee out the final year of school and still was the 52nd pick of the draft. He had one knee and still went only 42 picks after me, that's how much talent he had. But he just didn't want it enough. Not only did he not love playing the game, I used to wonder if he even liked it. I used to ask him, "Why are you playing?" He didn't understand what I was talking about, but it seemed obvious to me that he didn't care. And in 1998, for the first time in my life, I'd put myself in that position. There were games that season that I got beat like a drum. I was embarrassed, and I had never been em-barrassed on a football field in my life. You know something is defi-nitely wrong when you find yourself recognizing a trap, telling yourself you are not going to get trapped, and meanwhile, you are already in the trap. It was like a car wreck that just kept happening. Every play. I couldn't get out of it. My mind would tell my body what it had to do, and my body would respond, "Really? Where were you in July when I needed to be working? You keep this up you're going to get us killed." My man Whitey led the team in sacks that season with eight. I loved that man, but he should never have led the team in sacks. That was my job and I did not do it.

When I read an article in the paper claiming that Gary Walker was a better defensive tackle than me, I'd had it. Gary Walker? Gary Walker was a nice player, but please. I knew what I'd done. I'd taken the team's money and given less than my best effort in return. But Gary Walker? C'mon. That hurt my pride. I promised myself that would never happen again. As a result I rededicated myself to the game of football. That next off-season I worked hard and often, and every time I thought about not doing my work I remembered those different games when I'd run out of fuel or gave less than a full effort. It wasn't about the money, the money was in my pocket, it was about respect. That's a big meaningful word for me.

In 1999 I set out to earn that respect. I got 12.5 sacks, and at the end of the season the NFL voted me the Defensive Player of the Year.

I had earned every single dollar of that $36 million contract, and when it expired at the end of 2003 I was a free agent. The Bucs had to make a choice between signing me or "Booger" McFarland. While Rod Marinelli wanted to sign me, Jon Gruden told me later that Defensive Coordinator Monte Kiffin made the call. Monte Kiffin believed at that time in our careers that the younger Anthony McFarland was a better player than me. I can't blame him for that. In the same situation I might have taken the younger player who looked a little like me on tape; of course the difference was on the field. I had no illusions. I would hear some people claim that in football loyalty was a one-way street. I told them they were fools—in the NFL loyalty was simply a dead end. There is no real loyalty in the NFL, and that's from both the viewpoint of the team and the player. I saw that from both sides after we'd lost the 1999 championship game to the Rams. During my career in Tampa Bay I'd seen players leave for a bigger contract, but none of them had been our key players. On the plane going home after we'd lost the 1999 championship game to the Rams we were already talking about how we were going to take the next step to the Super Bowl next season when linebacker Hardy Nickerson, who made five Pro Bowls and eventually was going to make the All-Decade team, told us flatfoot he was leaving. What do you mean leaving, Hardy? Where you going? We just came out of the championship game. We were the clichéd well-oiled machine, and he was throwing a wrench in the gears.

I'll never forget his words: "I got to go where the money is, man."

That was the moment when it really hit me that we were just hired hands. I know, I know, I was the highest paid defensive player in the game, but it had flowed easy to me. I was young and talented, and I had been insulated from the reality that this game was a tough business. I had negotiated; I really hadn't had to fight for the last dollar. With the money I had earned, I could afford not to be concerned about the money.

That wasn't true for Hardy Nickerson; he had been on the front lines of the labor dispute. He'd experienced the nastiness of the owners and had been hardened by it to the point where it was all about the money for him. I totally understood that his loyalty had to be to his family.

Worked the other way too. At the end of training camp that next year the Bucs cut my man Culpepper to open up a position for McFarland. I couldn't believe it when I heard about it. Cutting Whitey? Why? He was still a productive player. He'd started every game for us in the '99 season and had six sacks. We'd gotten down and dirty in the trenches together. With him next to me I'd won the Defensive Player of the Year. Why would they want to throw a change-up when the fastball was working? It made no sense. He was the only man I let into my territory during pregame warm-ups. I was furious. I tried to figure out if there was something I could do about it, but this was their organization. That was a hard lesson. Mark Dominik, the assistant general manager, told Whitey this was the hardest call he ever had to make, but they made it. I was not happy; they were taking away my playmate. I went to Marinelli, and I warned him, "Listen here, this dude better be ready to play. If he can't play I'm going to have his ass because you just took my partner away from me. I won the Defensive Player of the Year with him beside me, and you took him away from me."

Three years later the Bucs wanted to sign McFarland to an extension rather than sign me to a new contract, but he was holding out. He told them if he didn't have a new deal before the end of training camp he wasn't going to continue negotiating during the season. I took him aside and told him, "Son, don't be a fool, get your money. Are you telling me you're going to cut off negotiations with people who want to give you $30 million bucks? Have you lost your fucking mind? You'd better take their money, because if you don't I will, and I don't think they want to give it to me."

In 2004 I became a free agent for the first time. Jon Gruden asked me right before free agency started that to call him immediately when I got an offer. Maybe the Bucs were waiting for another team to establish the market; maybe they were hoping they could get me back cheaply. I didn't know, but I told him I would do that.

The thing about being a free agent is that somebody had better want you. There is nobody more free than a free agent with no offers. It's no fun being able to sign with anybody if nobody wants to sign you. I wasn't really concerned about that, just aware of it. Really, really aware of it. Drew Rosenhaus told me not to be concerned, as four or five teams were going to come after me. Easy for him to say, he was only 2 percent as concerned as I was. There had been some preliminary interest. The Giants had asked trainer Todd Toriscelli for my physical reports, and he told them that other than an old rotator cuff injury and that sometimes my ankles bothered me, I was ready to roll. Oh, the New York Giants. I could see it: The Big Sapple. I liked that thought.

First thing the first morning I officially became a free agent Drew called and told me excitedly that the Bengals' head coach Marvin Lewis had called and wanted me to sign with Cincinnati. I had been a free agent for one minute, and I already had an offer. The problem was it came from Cincinnati. I thought, are you kidding me? A king like me in the Queen City? It's not that I didn't like Cincinnati, but that summer they were having some serious racial problems there, and I wasn't sure it was the best place for me. I thought, of all the teams in the NFL, that is the one team I would not have expected to make me an offer. Cincinnati offered $16 million for four years. We never heard from the Giants.

Soon as I got that offer I called up Gruden like I'd promised. "Jon, you know today is the first day of free agency. You told me to call you when I got an offer. I got one: $16 million, four years from the Cincinnati Bengals."

"I will call you back in an hour."

I told JaMiko, "If the Bucs meet that offer I'm going to take it and end my career right here in Tampa. We're here, the babies are in school, we won't have to go anywhere. The house is paid for and we're fine."

While I was waiting to hear from the Bucs, Cincinnati upped its offer to $20 million, but the Bengals' general manager Mike Brown told Drew we had one hour to accept it. I had no choice at that point; those people were putting $20 million on the table. The Bengals' offensive tackle Willie Anderson called to tell me that Cincinnati was a good place to play, that they had a good coach, some talent, and we could win there. I told him, "I'm going to accept their offer, I'm coming." But I waited, and I hoped.

Drew called me every 15 minutes. After 55 minutes I told him, "Somebody has to get me out of Cincinnati." But nobody else called. I stared at that phone. The thought of leaving Tampa was a lot different from the reality. I wasn't a fool. I had known that this was a situation that I would face someday. I just didn't think it was going to come at nine o'clock in the morning on my first day of free agency. I wanted that phone to ring. I waited 57 minutes. It was obvious the Bucs weren't going to match that offer. So I drove over to One Buc to start packing up my belongings. I knew I would never put on the pewter and red again.

I was at peace with it. I would never fault a player for leaving a team for money, so I certainly couldn't get mad at the team for not wanting to spend its money on a player—even when that player was me. I'd had a great run there. We won a championship, and I made $40 million and so many friends. I couldn't be mad at those people.

I walked into that building knowing I would never be there again. I'd never walk down that hallway and see all those pictures of my team-mates and our accomplishments. I sat down and started cleaning out my locker when Todd Toriscelli saw me and asked, "What are you doing?"

"What does it look like?"

He was stunned. We'd been together since the U. "Are you kidding me? We're not going to get to 10 years?"

"Nine years. That's it."

I told him what happened, that Gruden hadn't called me back, and he said, "So why don't you just go around the corner and say something?"

"You don't think he knows I'm in the building? These walls ain't that thick."

I was leaving a lot of memories in my rearview mirror. As I walked out of the building Jill Hobbs, Rich McKay's secretary, hugged me and started to cry. Another assistant, Nancy Hasselback, came over and started hugging me. "C'mon," I said, "do not do me like this. I love you all to death, but do not do me like this." Then I went home.

Drew phoned Mike Brown to accept the offer, but Brown had somehow figured out that he had been bidding against himself and re-scinded. Maybe he figured he should wait for Sapp to go on sale, so he could get me cheaper. The good news was that I was not going to Cin-cinnati; the bad news was I had no other offers.

I kept reading about all the teams that were going to make me an offer, but that phone did not ring. It was such a strange feeling. I'd had a good season, I'd been selected for my seventh consecutive Pro Bowl, but there was no strong demand for my skills. Maybe the most difficult thing for an athlete to deal with is the reality that he is growing older and maybe a little slower. I knew that happened. I had seen that happen to other people; I just didn't believe it was going to happen to me. And I refused to accept it. I knew I could still play at a Pro Bowl level.

Drew kept reassuring me to sit tight. I told him I didn't want to sit tight. I would rather be situated than having to worry about where I am going to play. Early the next morning Drew called again to tell me Oakland Raiders owner Al Davis was on the phone with him. "And he said he isn't getting off the phone until you're an Oakland Raider."

Oh my goodness. The perfect combination: Sapp and the tough, mean, take-no-prisoners black and silver Oakland Raiders. I fit their image perfectly: The bad-ass intimidators. It seemed like a match made by the Football Gods. But I was so excited I forgot that those Gods have a sense of humor. Officially Oakland's offer was $36.6 million for seven years, but really it was the same $20 million for four years as Cincinnati. I told Drew, "Make it like I'm going to college. I'm gonna play four more years, then I'm done. Tell Al Davis in four years I'm gone."

When I spoke with Al Davis on the phone he told me flatly, "You will die a Raider."

Die a Raider? I thought, but not too soon, I hope. Whoo, this guy is serious about his football team. I was excited about playing there. When I flew out there to sign my contract the plane was about to land, we'd put away our tray tables and our seats were upright, when a flight attendant came over to me and said, "Welcome to the Raider Nation." Sent chills down my spine.

There have always been rumors that Al Davis's contracts included some type of secret clause that people are not allowed to reveal, and if my contract had one, it remained a secret to me. Davis's contracts were unusual: He gave out only one-, three-, five- or, seven-year deals because that put you at odd years for being a free agent. Three years is a year before unrestricted free agency, meaning your rights still belong to the Raiders. A five-year deal puts you one year after free agency, which means you have lost it. The contract also has an insubordination clause that allows Davis to fire employees for being disloyal and terminate future pay.

When I signed my seven-year, $36.6 million contract with Oakland the situation there was not good. Two years earlier the Raiders had lost to the Bucs in the Super Bowl, but the last season they had won only four games. Four and 12. When the reporters asked me what type of impact I thought I could make I told them straight out, "I guarantee we are going to win more than four games."

And I was absolutely right. We won five games.

Every day at Raiders practices was like a Hall of Fame meeting. I'd look over at the sideline and Willie Brown would be standing there. Or Jim Otto. Ted Hendricks would drop by. Fred Biletnikoff would be there. And Al Davis would be there every day. Other great players like Jack Tatum, Lester Hayes, and George Atkins would come around. For someone like me, who loves football history, it was like being a kid in the toughest toy store in the world. The problem was that they were all on the sideline, while we really needed them on the field. Tradition can't block.

We had some talent there. After splitting our first two games of the season we played the Bucs. My Bucs. My homecoming. Before the game I got my face and my whole uniform painted Raiders black for the cover of the *Sporting News*. In that getup I looked a little like a cute Darth Vader. It was like playing against my family—these were all my people—except this family was trying to bludgeon me. During the game Bucs' running back Charlie Garner caught a little swing pass and broke loose. He was going to take it to the house. I took off running after him. I tracked his ass down and dived and just clipped his heels, bringing him down. Saved a touchdown. As I'm lying there on the ground I looked up, and there was Brooks down looking at me. I smiled. "The old boy still got it in him," I said.

He shook his head. "How'd you get that one?"

"What?" I said. "I wasn't supposed to get him?" The rest of my boys just turned their backs on me and went back to the huddle.

We won the game 30–20, but Brooks had his game too. He showed me who could still play. Early in the game our quarterback, Rich Gannon, tried a little QB sneak at the Bucs' 5-yard line, and Brooks came up and hit him helmet to helmet. *Boom*! A good, clean hit. But Brooks hits hard. Gannon walked out of the game. Nobody knew it at the time, but he had broken a vertebra in his neck, and that was the very last play of his career. Never played another down. It also basically was the end of our season. Rich Gannon was a football player. The man had been the Most Valuable Player in the Pro Bowl two years running and the MVP in the whole league in 2002, when he threw for 26 touchdowns and 4,600 yards. He was the screw that held that rickety offense together. Without him, we just had a pile of pieces. After he was injured we lost eight of our next 10 games.

But as I learned, the real problem in Oakland wasn't on the field; it was up there in the office. I loved Al Davis. I loved the man—he was an absolute legend. Did I say I loved him? I did. But the problem was that he totally ran that franchise, and everybody was afraid of him. He ran that place like Capone ran Chicago. Professional sports is not a democracy; it's one man, all the votes, and Al Davis was the one man. In the four years I was there we had three different head coaches. I swear, when Al Davis walked around the building I was the only person who would stop and talk to him; everybody else ran from him. They ran and hid. It was like they could smell him coming. He's coming! He's coming! The word would spread and everybody would break out running. When people had to go upstairs near his office the rule was to keep your head down because if he sees you he'll want to chop it off. Al Davis and I would sit in his office for hours and talk. The man always had a great story: "Mike Tyson used to live in my neighborhood, but when I was there he couldn't walk the streets. We kicked his ass." In his stories he was always kicking somebody's ass. If a reporter wrote something he didn't like, he'd say in his kind-of-raspy voice, "If I was 20 years younger I'd kick his motherfucking ass."

The problem was that the game had gone past him, and everybody was afraid to tell him that. He was still planning as if Cliff Branch was outside and Jim Plunkett was dropping back to throw it 80 yards downfield. Every day it was the same thing: "Deep ball. Deep ball. That's what I want, deep ball." The organization was dysfunctional. He insisted on approving the game plan every week, but he was never around. The coaches wouldn't film practices because if there was film he would look at it and call up the coaches in the middle of the night demanding some explanation. We'd work on a game plan all week and then come in on Saturday, and it would be completely revised. The whole organization was crumbling around him, and everybody was afraid if they said something he'd fire them.

At times during the game he would call down plays from the press box. During our second preseason game somebody came up to me and said, "Watch this, we're going deep right here, Dawg."

I asked, "How do you know that?"

He said, "The phone just rang."

It was a damn shame. The team was completely undisciplined. There was no accountability. Nobody cared. They genuinely didn't give a damn when they lost a game. They were more concerned about where they were going that night than the fact that they had lost a football game. The players didn't even like each other. They talked about how much money other people earned and why they should be making more than that player. It was all backbiting, bickering, and bullshit—although everybody smiled for the reporters and the fans still turned out every Sunday and cheered.

I had never been in a situation like that before, and it just sucked the life out of me. I couldn't believe it: This is the Oakland Raiders? This was supposed to be the great franchise that had brought a new kind of toughness and arrogance to football. I was signing up to join the "win baby, just win" people—but by the time I got there that was gone. Gone, goodbye. All that was left was the pretense of a first-class front. The whole situation disgusted me. I had learned in Tampa what it took to build a winning atmosphere, and I knew one thing: What I saw in Oakland wasn't it.

The year before I got there Raiders coach Bill Callahan had admitted, "We've got to be the dumbest team in America in terms of playing the game . . . It's embarrassing, and I . . . apologize for that. If that's the best we can do, it's a sad product." Al Davis fired his ass.

But it didn't take me long to see what he was talking about. When I talked about this with cornerback Charles Woodson he said, "C'mon Dawg, that's not right."

I challenged him, "Can you honestly say that when you come to work you feel good about what we're doing day in and day out?" Eventually Woodson left Oakland and signed with Green Bay, and that's when people began to talk about how hard he worked and described him as a leader. Not in Oakland, no sir. I couldn't get him out there to work. There was no coach able to push him, and there was no penalty for not working hard. Oakland definitely made me appreciate the way Tony Dungy had pushed me, Brooks, Ronde, our great defensive end Simeon Rice, all of us on those long hot summer days. We had some talent in Oakland; all we were missing was structure, discipline, and coaching.

It was the wrong situation for me in every aspect of the game. Our defensive coordinator Rob Ryan wanted to play 3–4 with Danny Clark as the middle linebacker. No knock on Danny Clark, he's a great guy, I love the man, but he was not a middle linebacker. He had never started in the NFL—suddenly he was going to be the anchor of the defense? Then they put Tim Johnson, Travian Smith and DeLawrence Grant next to him. Okay, but if you play 3–4 you're supposed to have Lawrence Taylor, Carl Banks, and Pepper Johnson or Rudy Jackson, Pat Swilling, Derrick Thomas, and Neil Smith—you got to have shutdown chillers. Please. It took away everything I did well. I mean, if you work hard at it maybe you can teach a cat to bark, but that cat isn't going to scare anybody. When I got to Oakland I had more sacks than the whole team, and they wanted to play 3–4, which basically made me a traffic cop? I did everything they asked me to do, I even played some defensive end. I sat there for the whole first year and didn't say a word. But I hated every minute of it.

Our defensive coordinator Rob Ryan was a great dude, a great football mind, and he learned all he knew from a great coach, Buddy Ryan. The problem was that with the personnel we had it was not an effective defense. But Rob's father had basically invented the damn thing, and Rob was committed to it. I never said it was bad, I just said it was bad for me. I told him, "Rob, we are trying to play the Patriot way with people the Patriots wouldn't even fucking look at."

"What?"

"The Patriots wouldn't put these people in this situation. It's too big for them. You are asking them to do more than it's possible for them to do right now. They can't think with the motion, change the call, change the stretch, they ain't gonna do it, they gonna think one way." But he was determined to teach them.

I tried to play it, but I couldn't do it. That 3–4 depended completely on having linebackers who could attack the best running backs in the league, smash them in the face mask, and then bring them down. But when I looked back there I didn't see Derrick Brooks behind me. I didn't see people who could do that consistently.

Al Davis liked to come down into the locker room and talk with his players right after a game because he wanted to hear your raw emotion. He caught me at the rawest moment. I told him, "Mr. Davis, you got to get me out of this. This is not going to work. You did not bring me here to watch the quarterback dancing around in the pocket, because rushing three motherfuckers ain't working for me. Gimme that fourth lineman. I promise you, I will take these motherfuckers down. You got to turn me loose. If you just want me to collect my check send me home, but I cannot play like this."

Rob Ryan was furious when he heard about this conversation. The 4–3 wasn't what he taught; he called it "one-arm pussy football." At the team meeting Monday morning he stood up in front of the whole squad and blistered me. I mean, this was a paint curler. He was fuming. I didn't say a word until he finished. Then I said, "Just call it. I promise you it'll work."

I looked at linebacker Kirk Morrison and said, "I'm sorry for y'all, but I'm about to start having fun. I'm gonna get to do what I do." We went out to Tennessee to play the Titans. I had three sacks, one of them recovered in the end zone for a touchdown, and we won 34–25.

After the game Rob Ryan came up to me and said, "I'll be damned. So that's why Monte Kiffin has been having such a good time all those years."

"Boss," I said, "I just asked for an opportunity. Give me four on the line and let's go." I told him, "Listen, if we had Patriot personnel I'd play that 3–4; I'm a buy-in guy. But look around you, Rob, that's not what we got."

We lost our next two games, but there definitely was a difference. We began to believe that we were going to start winning some games. Unfortunately, I tore my rotator cuff during the 10th game of the year, against Washington, and was out for the rest of the season. After that we couldn't stop anybody from running the ball against us. We lost our last six games of the season. I would have played if it was possible. I took great pride in my craft, and I wasn't getting anything done on the sideline. I played bruised, I played hurt, I played with broken fingers. I even practiced hurt. One time, I remember, in Tampa I had a hip flexor, a serious strain, and it hurt me to move around. Our trainer, Todd, told me to take a practice day off, give it some rest. I tried to do that, I went into the locker room, but I just couldn't do it. We were practicing in full pads, so I put my pads on, grabbed my hat, and went out onto the field to do my pass rush drills. We went one-on-one with an offensive lineman. Todd tried to stop me. This little fella stood in my way and said, "Where do you think you're going? You're off today."

I told him, "Get out of my way. This is how I make my money." I took my four reps and went back inside. If they could glue me together and roll me out on the field, I was going to play. But with a torn rotator cuff I was useless on the field. I couldn't rush at all. Turned out half a Sapp was actually worse than no Sapp at all.

After my shoulder surgery I was in the locker room and Assistant Head Coach/Offensive Coordinator Jimmy Raye sat down next to me and said, "Hey Big Nuts, you're the reason we're getting fired right now."

"What are you talking about?"

"Well, if it weren't for your damn shoulder going out we'd be winning some games now. We had a shot at winning this year."

At the end of the year Al Davis fired Head Coach Norv Turner and Raye and brought back Art Shell as head coach. Shell had been a great head coach in 1990, but he got himself stuck there. Maybe he figured, George Bush was president then, George Bush is president now, nothing's changed. Shell brought in Tom Walsh to be the offensive coordinator. Walsh had to leave his job running a bed and breakfast in a small town in Idaho to take the job, because there must not have been another qualified person actually coaching in the National Football League. Davis kept Rob Ryan, and on defense we played 4–3 from the jump. The 2006 Oakland Raiders had the best pass defense in the National Football League, because we were able to put on a rush, and the third best defense overall. I had 32 solo tackles and 10 sacks—and we won two games. Two games.

We had no offense. In three of our first six games we didn't score an offensive touchdown. It was so bad that when we played Denver in our sixth game we were a 15-point underdog—and the Broncos were averaging only 12.2 points a game. In practice one day I heard

Shell whisper to Walsh, "Run that play we used to run with Bo Jackson."

I said to him, "Y'all looking at LaMont Jordan and you see Bo Jackson? Are you kidding me? You people have lost your damn minds." Then I walked away. They were looking at an out-of-shape running back and seeing one of the greatest athletes God ever put on this earth. There was no way to deal with people like that.

Shell lasted that one season. This wasn't even a revolving door. The way coaches were coming and going it was more like beads hanging over the doorway. I'd read optimistic stories in the newspapers about the team that had absolutely no relation to what was actually going on. These stories made the situation seem almost sane. After Shell was fired I figured that it would be almost impossible to find a coach worse than Art Shell. But I got to admit I underestimated Al Davis.

In 2007 Al Davis hired 31-year-old Lane Kiffin to replace Shell, making Kiffin the youngest coach in the history of the National Football League. It was a surprise to everyone, maybe even Al Davis, because when he announced the hiring he even called him by the wrong name, identifying him as *Lance* Kiffin. Not only had Lane Kiffin never coached in the NFL, he had never been a head coach anywhere in the world. Not even in Pop Warner football. I don't know how Al Davis found him, but he even outgeniused himself by hiring him. The NFL game is simply too complicated to put a man who has no experience on that level in charge. Trust me, there were a lot of qualified coaches that would have taken this job. I mean, Rob Ryan was standing right in front of him, for example, and Rob was so damn big it was impossible to not see him. But instead Mr. Davis found Lane Kiffin. Kiffin had been the offensive coordinator at USC and was considered the best recruiter in college football. I don't know, maybe Mr. Davis forgot that NFL teams don't offer scholarships. I knew Lane Kiffin; when his father was the D-coordinator in Tampa he used to be around. I was the player who gave him my code to punch in so he could get into the offices to see his girlfriend. I thought he was a nice kid. Twelve years later he was my head coach.

Right from the very beginning I knew it was going to be a difficult year. A reporter told me that he'd heard that "Kiffin doesn't want anybody in camp who's older than him."

I think that was me. I responded, "That doesn't make any difference to me. Al Davis won't allow Kiffin to touch me. He told me I would die a Raider. Last time I looked in the mirror I was still breathing pretty good, so I know I ain't going no-damn-where." Maybe not right away, at least. I knew I was getting near the end of my career, and if it was at all possible I wanted to go out with 100 sacks. Athletes look at their numbers: *100* was a nice round number that was easy to remember. I worked hard that off-season. I lost 52 pounds to make sure I had my quickness. The first night I got to camp I went into Al Davis's office and said, "If you don't want me here, please let me out. I don't want to deal with this kid if I don't have to."

"Now Warren," he said. "You know I want you here . . ."

"That's all I need to know."

But when practice started it was clear they were coming at me. In practice they ran power at me nine times a day. In practice. They wanted to see if I could still hold up the double-team. I used to break it in half and look over at Offensive Line Coach Tom Cable and give him a big smile. Are you kidding me? You can't move me. I haven't been moved in 12 years, you think all of a sudden you're gonna move me? I took it as a personal challenge. I burned myself out that whole camp. I beat the shit out of my own offense. Did they really think they would be able to cut me? It wasn't going to work that way. When I was ready to go, I was going to walk out the door. Nobody needed to hold it open for me.

I wanted to win. Few fans are more loyal to their team than Raiders fans, and I could just imagine how great it would be to win in Oakland. In camp I tried to work with some of the young players—like I'd always done—but most of them just didn't want to hear about it. They already knew too much to want to learn anything. I got on receiver Mike Williams because of his weight. He came to camp overweight and out of shape, and I let him know about it. I told him I'd already made that mistake, and I knew how that worked out, so he didn't have to go through it. Told him he should be blocking rather than receiving. He didn't want to hear it. He told the newspaper, "(Warren) doesn't mean anybody any harm . . . It's more entertainment than an insult."

No, that ain't right. It *was* an insult, it wasn't entertainment at all. If I wanted to entertain him I would've sung a song. I wanted to teach him how to play football. In the middle of the season they cut his ass. How entertaining was that for him?

I worked with defensive end Tyler Brayton teaching him how to rush the quarterback. I told him, "Tyler, I love white boys that hustle, but you need a little bit of skill, and I can give you some of that." He wanted to learn; he wanted to be a better football player. I loved him for that. I taught him my five steps to quarterback, and he worked his ass off on that move. He'd smile and say, "I got it."

"No, you don't," I told him. "Those are the three worst words in football. You never got it, because it's always the next snap." A year later he was starting in Carolina.

Talent is born, players are made.

I tried everything to change the attitude in that organization. If you had been at practice you would have heard me yelling. Sometimes I'd be the only one. The newspaper wrote that "Sapp's voice serves as the soundtrack for practices." Damn right. I even got on the practice officials for not doing their job. Not calling penalties in practice wasn't doing anybody any favors. That's not how to prepare for a game. But there were too many people there who just didn't give a damn.

I will say one thing positive about Lane Kiffin: For an inexperienced not-so-knowledgeable coach he definitely had a lot of confidence. Okay, it was arrogance really, but I'm trying to be kind to him.

Maybe with more NFL experience he could have become an average coach, but at that time he didn't understand professional football. He was coaching like he did in college, and that will not work on the pro level. He wasn't even smart enough to know when he was supposed to kick the ball. One time in preseason he went for a first down on fourth and 6. You do not go for it on fourth and 6, or fourth and 4, or fourth and 3—you punt the ball or try to kick a field goal. Our kicker was Sebastian Janikowski, one of the best place-kickers in NFL history. The guy once kicked a field goal from the parking lot of a Walmart around the corner from the stadium. Into the wind. Please, let the man kick the ball. Take the points. Going for it on fourth and 6, that's ridiculous. Even the O-line has no confidence they can get those yards. When he made one of those college decisions I happened to be standing next to Offensive Coordinator Greg Knapp. I said, "Knapp, please. Do something."

Greg knew, he was a veteran NFL coach. "I'm trying, Sapp," he told me. "I'm working on it."

As bad as the situation had been my first year at Tampa Bay, this was the only time in my career when I knew we had no chance to win. Oh my God, that year was depressing. Kiffin insisted on going back to the 3–4. We just did not have the personnel to make it work. Every Sunday I'd put on my pads and a smile and go out there pretending that this was the week we were going to turn the season around. That season was going only one way. I remember telling a friend of mine before we played the Chargers that we were going to get our ass kicked. That game was the biggest setup I had ever seen in a football game. I told Kiffin during practice that if he insisted on playing that 3–4 defense LaDainian Tomlinson was going to run for 200 yards. I pleaded with him, "You know the way a defense is supposed to work. Your daddy and me built it. We just do not have the linebackers who can stop him." He insisted on playing that 3–4, and he proved me wrong. Tomlinson only ran for 198 yards and four touchdowns. It was a beatdown.

Losing is understandable and even acceptable if it is part of a development process, like it was in Tampa. If you see improvement each week it takes a little bit of the sting out of the loss. But that wasn't what was going on in this situation. We were losing because we were bad, and there was no effort to fix our problems. There was very little teaching of fundamentals going on. Give you an example: Tommy Kelly made the team as an undrafted free agent in 2004. Three years later he was starting at defensive end, but they wanted him to eventually slide over and replace me at tackle. That was good, that was the natural order of football. I accepted that and tried to teach him how to read protections, how to call a game. I wanted to pass along what I had learned in my 12 years in the NFL. I told him, "When you come to the line of scrimmage this is what should be going through your mind: What is the situation? What is that back thinking? Where are the two receivers? What formation did we just break? Let's make it easy, which way does your center slide, left or right?"

He asked, "You really want to know that?"

I actually started laughing. The fact that no one had taught him these things was ridiculous. "Are you serious? Evidently somebody thinks I got near 100 sacks 'cause I been out here guessing all these years. Yes, you want to know that. Every move a player makes affects every other player. You got to be able to see it, understand it, and adjust to it. And you got a couple of seconds to do it."

I spent that whole season preaching to those kids that they had to talk to each other on the field. We would be on the field, the offense would go in motion, and nobody on the defense would say one word. I thought, what the hell? Ain't we supposed to be checking something? Somebody say something, please. I tried to teach them that a quiet defense is a dumb defense, and a dumb defense is going to get the crap beat out of it every week. We were so loud in Tampa, we were always shouting at each other as we lined up, checking off, letting everyone know what we were doing. When it got too loud in old Raymond James Stadium we would communicate by hand signals, but however we did it, we communicated. In Oakland the defense was so quiet it was like the kids were scared they were going to get thrown out of the stadium for talking.

That was typical of the way things were done, or not done, in Oakland. I'll tell you how bad it got: The night before a game I was able to get a full night's sleep. That told me everything I needed to know. Throughout my entire career I would wake up at 4:30 a.m. Sunday morning in a cold sweat. I was always worried that I was going to oversleep and be late for work, that I was going to miss the game. And once I was awake I could not go back to sleep. Eventually I'd turn on the television. Trust me on this: The worst shows of the week are on Sunday morning. *National Geographic's Beasts of Borneo* was the highlight. But usually as it got closer to kickoff I'd start getting excited. The closest thing I can relate it to was being at Disney World and not having to wait on line for the best rides. That you just go to the head of every line.

But that feeling was gone.

In the middle of the season I walked into Lane Kiffin's office to try to understand what was going on. Every coach has his own way of dealing with his players. I've had coaches who communicated through their assistants while other coaches kept their door open. Coaches who demanded every rule be followed strictly and coaches who left some room. There is no right or wrong way; the object is simply to get everybody pulling in the same direction. I would never make a good coach because my aspirations would be too high. I definitely would be too demanding.

Maybe it was uncomfortable for Lane Kiffin to have me on his team. I had known him when he was a kid, I had worked for his father and sometimes argued with his father, and I was older than him. When

I met with Kiffin I said, "All year long you've been standing in front of the team and telling us that our objective is to 'do what we do.' What exactly does that mean?"

I knew exactly what it meant. I'd heard his father use that phrase often enough in Tampa: The way to control the game was to impose our will on our opponent by doing those things we wanted to do better than their ability to stop us. In Tampa, we did what we did best, regardless of our opponent.

Instead his answer absolutely shocked me. "Lose," he said.

"Wow," I said. "You don't have any idea what it means." I walked to the blackboard, picked up a marker, and wrote *1996–2002*. "You know what those dates are? Your dad and I started working together in 1996 when Dungy got the job." I wrote down *PPG* and underlined it. "What were the points per game?"

He had no idea what I was talking about.

"From 1996 until we won that Super Bowl in San Diego the average points per game we gave up was 16.02 points. That's why I told Dungy, get us 17 points per game, and we'll make it stick. That's what we do. So the next time you stand up in front of your football team and tell them 'do what we do,' at least know the fuck what that is.

"And let me give you a little bit of advice. You don't ever want to tell anybody you ever said that. Don't let that leave this office." Then I put down that marker and walked out the door.

I knew for sure it was my time to retire when we played Green Bay in the 13th game of the season. I was having a good year. This was my last hurrah, and I was going out and knocking down everything I could hit. Anything that was moving, I hit. I didn't even care anymore; first down, second down, I was trying to make every play. I didn't have Brooks behind me to make plays, so I had to make them myself. I was shooting the last bullets in my gun. We were in the third quarter and getting beat bad. Brett Favre came out of the huddle, and he had that look in his eyes, and he twitched. I knew instantly what he was fixing to do. Play-action pass. I'd seen that before, maybe a hundred times before. Okay, here we go.

I came up to the line of scrimmage. I lined up opposite a second-year player named Daryn Colledge. I had to look up his name. I came off the ball at the snap. Man, this young fellow jumped on my chest, grabbed me, shook me, and hitched up with me. Meanwhile, Favre did his little fake to the running back, dropped back, and cocked his arm. I was in the full lock-up mode. I couldn't get this kid off me. I watched Favre let it go, and Greg Jennings caught it for an 80-yard touchdown. The kid was still holding me. Finally I said to him, "Would you let me go now, young fella?" He did.

That was the one play that let me know it was time. I knew the play. I had the snap count. I had a good get-off, and I had no move for an inexperienced kid. There was no way I was going to spend the next two years of my life collecting a check and having to watch that kind of play on tape.

Two weeks later I played my last game of football. San Diego Chargers at Oakland. That was a hard Sunday. Before the game I told our D-line coach Keith Millard that I was going to do something I hadn't done in 13 years: I was going to take the ball right out of the quarterback's hands before he could hand it off to a running back. I was going to be so quick, I was going to beat the running back to the quarterback. "No fucking way," he said. Watch me, I told him, watch me.

Philip Rivers was the quarterback. In the second quarter he brought his cocky ass on up to the line, looked at me, and winked. He winked. Oh yeah, I thought, it's on. It is on. He snapped the ball and turned to hand it off to LaDainian Tomlinson. I got there first. I grabbed Rivers's wrist, and the ball flipped into the air. "Ball's out!" I screamed, "ball's out." I was looking all around for it, but I believe it was Tommy Kelly who grabbed it. I tapped Philip Rivers on the head and said, "You just go ahead and keep playing with that ball like it's a kids game." Then I ran over to the sideline.

Keith Millard was waiting for me, "You did it! You did it!"

For a few very happy seconds I forgot this was my last game. "I waited 13 years for that, and I got it!" But a few plays later I went from happy to the end. Right before halftime I banged up my shoulder, and as I came off the field I knew I was never going back on. I told Keith Millard, "I can't go no more." I put my jacket on and I cried.

When I didn't come out to play in the second half LT ran out of the huddle over to our sideline. "Yo Dawg," he said, "what's going on?" I told him my shoulder was hurt and I was done. "Ah, no, Sapp. That's a damn shame. It was a pleasure, man."

I said to him, "I would have loved to have seen you if I had them boys in red with me."

He laughed. "I would've loved that too. That would've been a classic." Then he took off.

In the locker room after the game I went to see Lane Kiffin to tell him I was retired. "You're not really gonna do that?" he said.

I asked him, "You've known me since you were 18 years old. Have you ever heard me say I was going to do something and then not do it? No, you have not."

After informing Kiffin that I was done I went to see Al Davis. I knew I was leaving $15 million-plus on the table, but I couldn't play at Sapp-level anymore, and I wasn't going to embarrass myself or steal the team's money. As I walked into his office, Davis was watching the end of the Patriots–Giants game in which the Patriots completed the first perfect 16–0 season in NFL history, Tom Brady broke Peyton Manning's record by throwing for his 50th touchdown, and Randy Moss caught a 65-yard pass to break Jerry Rice's record for touchdowns in a season with 23. As we watched Moss race into the end zone Davis said, "They told me he couldn't run anymore."

I said, "I just came up to tell you I'm going to retire."

"Oh no you're not," he said. "You're going to come back and . . ."

"I can't, Mr. Davis," I said. "I'm done. It has nothing to do with you, but I've had enough." I told him about the do-what-we-do conversation I'd had with Kiffin. It was a real bittersweet meeting. As we watched that football game he gave a running commentary. Listening to him, it was as if he was still living in the past, naming players who had long been retired, talking about the league as if he still was a powerful man, making promises about the future. The big bombast was still there, the bravado, just not the production. I listened to every word, just appreciating him. Al Davis was one of the most brilliant, complicated people in the history of the National Football League, and even after everything that had gone wrong there, I was pleased I'd gotten the chance to know him.

Turned out Lane Kiffin wasn't going to be there too much longer either. In September 2008, Al Davis fired him, accusing him publicly of breaking his contract by insubordination, lying, and rule breaking. He called him a "flat-out liar" and accused him of "bringing disgrace to the organization."

When I walked out of that locker room later that day I knew my career was finished. I had several friends waiting by my car. They knew too. Nobody said too much. My shoulder was killing me, and I didn't feel like driving. I handed the keys to one of those people and got in the backseat. As we drove off I sat there thinking, that's it. No more quarterbacks to sack, no more games to play. What am I gonna do now?

My career was over—but not before one last controversy.

SIX

With only six quarters left to play in my career, I set a new personal record when the league fined me $75,000 for unsportsmanlike conduct, breaking my old mark of $50,000, as well as becoming the first player in the entire history of the National Football League to be ejected from a game for nonphysical contact. I know there are a lot of people who think that was an appropriate way for me to go out.

We were trailing Jacksonville 28–3 with 21 seconds left in the second quarter. They had been running up and down the field on us, and I didn't have a lot of hope it was going to get any better. They had the ball, third and 10 on our 25-yard line, when the officials called them for a 10-yard penalty. As a captain it was up to me to accept or decline penalties. I decided we would accept the penalty, which moved them back out of field-goal range. If we held them to less than 10 yards on their next play, rather than adding another three points, they would have had to punt. It wasn't much, but it was the best I could do. I'd played the game professionally for 13 years; I knew what was going on. I looked at the referee to tell him we were going to accept it—but he was already signaling that we had declined it.

In my own endearing way I asked the referee, "Yo. Who declined that penalty?"

"What?"

"I said, who you been talking to? See that *C* on my chest? That means I'm the captain." I pointed at our two other captains on the field. "That one don't talk, and that one ain't been near the huddle in 20 minutes 'cause he plays man-to-man every snap. I'm the only one you can talk to. I know you can't decline it on your own, so tell me, who was it declined the penalty?" He acted like he didn't hear me, so I added, "You can't do that." It is possible I threw in another adjective.

This official was an African American and I knew that it was his first season as a referee. There were not a lot of black officials in the NFL, and I wanted him to do well. I figured that maybe he just didn't know how to handle this situation. But he continued to ignore me. There are a lot of different ways of responding to me, some of them better than others. Completely ignoring me ain't any of them.

So I asked him again, "Listen to me, I want to accept the penalty. Who declined it?" I walked over to the sideline, took off my helmet, and told Kiffin, "You're not gonna believe this, but that dumbass referee declined the penalty on his own."

Kiffin turned to the referee and asked, "Who declined the penalty?"

Hello? I thought I just told you who declined the penalty, Lane. That referee did. What is wrong with you? At this point I was really starting to get upset. It was a meaningless penalty in a meaningless game at the end of my career, our record was 4–10, we were already down 25 points, and trust me, we weren't coming back. But I wanted to accept that penalty. There is only one right way to play the game of football. And as long as I was on a football field I intended to play it that way. What the referee did was wrong, wrong in every conceivable way, and he needed to correct it.

I looked over at D-line Coach Keith Millard, who asked clearly, "What the fuck?"

I told him, "He declined it on his own. Didn't ask nobody." So now I had to walk back onto the field to accept the penalty I've been trying to accept. Meanwhile, millions of fans watching the game on television and my mother in the stands were all wondering the same thing: What the hell is Warren doing now?

Four seasons of frustration got squeezed into these few minutes. I went up to this referee, and said, "Yo, my man," except I didn't exactly call him *my man.* Called him something else. He looked at me like, oh no, don't tell me I got to deal with this crazy fuck again. I explained to him, "I'm just gonna tell you that you can't do that. I been on the field 13 years, and I've never seen an official decline a penalty on their own. I'm talking to you like this because you got to be the authority on the field. You can't be making calls like that. Not too many of us hold your position you understand, so you're representing us . . ."

Once again, it is entirely possible that I threw in a few more choice words. Okay, a lot more, to make my point in a memorable fashion. But that was okay, we were speaking football. He knew all the words. Mostly, I was just giving him a hard time, which is when the umpire decided to get involved.

That brought a whole new dimension to this situation. I had a history with this umpire. Seven weeks earlier this umpire, no. 53 in your program and in your heart, had been working our game with the Houston Texans. For whatever reason, most offensive linemen are white. Houston had one black player on the O-line. During a timeout in that game I was standing there looking at their huddle just in case somebody mouthed a play. I used to try to read lips in the other team's huddle. There is only one way to say *Y cross* for example. The tight end is the *Y.* If I saw somebody's mouth form a *Y* I knew it was a pass play involving the tight end. There were a few times in my career that I successfully stole a sign. This official, Mr. no. 53, was standing near that huddle. But all of a sudden they all busted out laughing. When the timeout ended the umpire moved behind me to watch the next play. I asked him, "What's so funny? I'd like to laugh too."

He answered in a whisper without looking at me, "They're afraid of you."

Five offensive linemen in the NFL were telling each other they were afraid of me? That's not the way it works. I snapped at him, "You a motherfucking liar." I resented that. I'm a man; whatever they said was not going to bother me. Just tell me to my face. Lying bothers me.

I guess that got him riled because he reached over and grabbed hold of my arm. "What'd you say?"

I looked at his hand on my arm like he was crazy. "Get your hand off me, then move way the fuck back," I told him. "I got to play football."

I got down in my stance and looked over to him. He was still mouthing the words, "What'd you say to me?"

The play ended and he came back at me. I told him, "Listen to me, whenever I've been in a situation where somebody's lied to me, like you just did, I call them out on it and that's what it is. You gonna look me in the face and lie to me?"

The referee came over and wanted to know what was going on. I told him, and he clapped his hands and said, "Let's play ball." We played ball, but that's where this confrontation got started.

It ended in Jacksonville. All I wanted that referee to do was acknowledge he was wrong. They finally did accept the penalty and moved the ball back out of field-goal range, but by this time my motor was turned on and roaring. I told that referee one more time that he was my man, except it wasn't *my man*, and no. 53 heard me. He told me, "You can't talk to him like that."

I explained the situation this way: "Mind your own motherfucking business."

I swear to you, he threw that penalty flag so high he looked like he was trying to toss it to Jesus: 50 feet straight up in the air, a new NFL record. Unsportsmanlike conduct, no. 99! I said to him, "You've been waiting to throw that flag for about seven weeks, haven't you? You happy now?" I turned around and walked back 15 yards.

They marched off the penalty against us. Instead of it being third and 15 it was now first and 10. In terms of winning and losing none of this mattered; we were going to lose this game. But it mattered in terms of respect, respect for the game of football, respect for their jobs, respect for me. Every snap of my career mattered. We lined up for the next play and . . . they blew that damn whistle. Offside, no. 58, which was the man to my right, Chris Clemons. Chris went ballistic. "Wait wait," I said. The official who called it was on the far side of the field. It wasn't even his call. I couldn't believe it. I asked, "You telling me that guy way over there made that call?"

The referee clicked on his microphone and announced, "Offside, number fifty-*six*." Fifty-six? That was Derrick Burgess. They changed the damn call. Now Derrick started yelling, and this was when the situation started really deteriorating. I pointed to the line judge on the side nearest Derrick and brought him into the argument. "And you're over there and apparently you ain't doing your damn job. If he's offside that's your call. If somebody is offside just throw the damn flag. You don't need to be sleeping on the job where one guy is declining penalties all by himself, one guy is calling penalties on anybody he wants and changing the number . . ."

The next play the officials called another penalty; I believe it was hands to the face.

By this time my mother got up to leave. As long as I was on the field my mother never left a football game. She and my aunt Ola would sit there in their Sapp no. 99 jerseys cheering. They both loved going to my games. And by this time they knew just a little bit about football. She knew that when I walked backward it wasn't a good thing. And when she saw me arguing with the officials and then walking backward she'd had enough. She didn't like those refs. She told me later, "They don't like their jobs."

The next play the officials called another penalty, offside on our right corner, Nnamdi Asomugha, one of the best cover corners in the game. He hadn't been caught offside since 1805. He wasn't blitzing, and he probably wasn't offside, but even if he was normally the official will tell the D-back, back up a few steps son. In the 13 years I'd been in the league I don't think I'd seen that call made if we weren't blitzing. Damn, there were more flags flying than at the United Nations. Finally the referee came into our defensive huddle and said to me, "I'm doing my job now."

I would say that was when I lost it. I'd just had it. The whole situation in Oakland, four years of losing and nobody caring, officials showing a complete lack of respect, I'd had it. I wanted to see what it would take to actually get kicked out of the game.

My whole team knew what was going on, and they didn't like it either. I really exploded. The officials called a second unsportsmanlike penalty on me, and then they called one on Derrick Burgess. It was fair to say that the situation was rapidly deteriorating. Our coaches came on the field to try to restore order.

Our coaching staff restoring order? Really? Where had those people been for the last four years?

The coaches and officials began trying to separate the players from the other officials. The referee claimed that while this was going on I bumped him. That wasn't true. I never touched the man. Even the television replays show that. But that was when the officials threw the flag on me for the world-record-breaking third unsportsmanlike conduct penalty.

In fact, it actually was the officials who were doing the pushing. As Nnamdi explained after the game, "I was trying to break it up, and an official came over to me. I'm asking him a question; he starts pushing me out of the way. It was ridiculous."

I almost beat my mother home. I was pretty angry about the whole thing. As I told a reporter in the middle of the next week, "I felt cheated being thrown out of an NFL game for nonphysical contact. If I was going to get thrown out, I should have at least whipped somebody's ass so they put me on *SportsCenter*. At least I'd get a little respect."

Maybe it was appropriate that there was this one last controversy in my career. I don't know another player who found himself in the middle of so many controversies as I did. I know what my reputation is; I definitely know that. It's big, big in every respect. Big plays, big mouth, big voice, big ego, big smile, big confidence, big personality, big attitude, big heart, big trouble, big target, too big to miss. My name has always evoked a reaction. Everybody has an opinion about me. It has always been that way. My whole life there were a lot of people who thought I had an attitude problem. I told those people straight ahead, "I don't have any damn attitude problem, and if you don't believe me you go ahead and say it to my face and see what happens."

To some people I was "colorful," while to others I was arrogant. Some people called me "outspoken," while others called me everything else you can think of. There definitely was love for me. In 1999, for example, I got more fan votes for the Pro Bowl than any other player, quarterbacks included, which was unusual for a defensive lineman. But there also was hate.

My reputation preceded me. In 2003, for example, *St. Petersburg Times* columnist Gary Shelton wrote, "Ever have that run-down feeling? Ever wake up feeling tired? Ever feel exhausted in the middle of a workday? Here's your remedy. Blame Warren Sapp.

"Ever have those tough, clinging stains on your floor? Ever have wax buildup? Ever wonder how to return to that natural luster? It's easy. Blame Warren Sapp.

"Go ahead: It's quick. It's easy. It's convenient. Blame Sapp for rising gasoline prices, for traffic jams and for the shortcomings of the latest *Matrix* sequel. Blame him for global warming, explicit lyrics in rap music and the suspect ratings of *Hollywood Squares*. Blame him for a worldwide glut of bad manners, bad dancing and bad choices of words. Blame him for letting the dogs out. Feel better?

"If not, blame him for that too."

I may not have been perfect, but I definitely was not one of the people responsible for violence in America, as one radio talker claimed.

For some people I was guilty even before I was accused, and I was convicted even before I was tried. In 2002, for example, Eagles kick returner Brian Mitchell accused me of spitting in his face after a return. It instantly became fact: Sapp spits on Mitchell—except I didn't play on special teams. I wasn't even on the field.

When I spoke with him about it he told me, "I thought it was you."

He had the wrong dude. There are a lot of things fans never see that go on when interior linemen visit. It isn't all fair play and good sportsmanship. It is definitely possible that in my career there were times I was talking shit and some spit came out, and if that happened it was not intentional and I was truly sorry. I would never disrespect another player by spitting on them. I knew what it took to get there. And if someone did that to me I would have been gone. I mean, gone. Spitting or putting your foot on another man when he's down will get you seen at the bus after the game. In street clothes. Those are straight violations of your manhood.

I remember that during a game against Carolina Hardy Nickerson spit on running back William Floyd. I couldn't believe it, but I was standing right there and I saw it happen. I looked at Hardy and said, "I know you didn't mean to do that, man, 'cause he's gonna come to see you after the game."

"What are you talking about?" Hardy said. "I didn't spit on him."

"Hardy, I'm looking right at you spitting on the man."

I knew Hardy didn't intend it. In the passion of the game things happen. This happened. And after the game Floyd was waiting for Nickerson outside our locker room. Fortunately I got there first. I've known

William Floyd since college, when he was at Florida State. Derrick knew him real well too. "Whoa, Floyd, we can't do this here," I told him. "Cannot. Not here, not now. I know how you feel, but this cannot happen. You come down to Tampa in the off-season, and we'll make sure Hardy knows you're coming. We'll set up a man-on-man situation."

We got it calmed down, and eventually Hardy called Floyd in North Carolina and apologized.

I definitely understood how Floyd felt. I always told people I didn't have a temper, I had a trigger—and someone spitting on me would have caused me to pull my trigger. But when Brian Mitchell accused me of spitting on him, and everybody immediately believed it was true, I really did wonder, what have I done to deserve this reputation?

At least part of it certainly came from the fact that I played the game rough and tough. NFL does not stand for *Nice Fellas League*. I always said I wanted two hits on every play—me hitting my opponent and him hitting the ground. Defensive linemen usually are neither seen nor heard. They're like the guy on a date with Jennifer Lopez: You know that nobody is looking at you. D-linemen work in the trenches and get down and dirty. But people definitely noticed me. Maybe that was because among D-linemen my 96.5 career sacks is second only to John Randle, maybe because I hit hard and often, maybe because I have never been shy about voicing my opinions, or maybe it was because of my big smile.

We can assume it was not my smile. On TV the football shows are always looking for the blow-up hit. The one that is so hard the audience has to get carried off their couch. And when they get one they show it over and over. During my career, there was none bigger or more controversial than the hit I made on the Packers' Chad Clifton in November 2002. It wasn't the hardest, it definitely wasn't the hardest, but it was in the open field and got caught on TV, and people never stopped talking about it. It became part of football history: Sapp's hit on Chad Clifton. We were in the third quarter of the game when Brian

Kelly intercepted a Brett Favre pass and began to return it. On television it looked like I came all the way across the field and blindsided Clifton, who didn't even appear to be involved in the play. And then I did a little dance to celebrate that hit. That's what it looked like. Clifton stayed down and had to be carried off the field. He was in the hospital for almost a week and had difficulty walking for several weeks after that. They showed that play on the football shows and my celebration over and over and over. Basically, the impression left was that I had mugged an innocent bystander.

My mother liked to tell me, "Don't believe anything you hear and half of what you see with your own eyes." Her meaning was that people rarely see the beginning of an event; they only see the event. They never know what led up to it. This was one of those situations. A play doesn't start with the interception. When a pass is intercepted the first thing you hear is somebody shouting "oskie, oskie, oskie," the code word meaning turn around fellas, we are going the other way. As a defensive lineman, instinctively the first thing you do when you hear that is look for someone to block. I used to spend the whole game working against two offensive linemen; an interception was my turn to hit them back. If you don't, people notice. When your team is looking at the game films the next morning, trust me, everybody is going to be watching to see who got the biggest hit on the interception. If you don't hit someone after an interception you are going to get called out in that room. So you learn to hit anybody—hit a vendor if you have to. But hit somebody.

The first thing I always did after an interception was look for the quarterback. The protection he is granted by the rules is gone. Suddenly he is just another defender. It's like Superman meeting kryptonite—his powers are gone. I'll give you an example. One time Derrick Brooks picked off a Kurt Warner pass and started running it back. The only player between Derrick and the end zone was Warner. This was not a good place for him to be. There weren't too many quarterbacks I've ever played against who had more courage than Kurt Warner. He was never afraid to stand in there and take a big hit. In this situation he knew what was coming, I knew what was coming, and he knew I knew it, but he wasn't moving off that spot. I raised my hand a little, my warning that if he didn't move I was going to have to knock the crap out of him. The man didn't move. He saw me coming and he didn't move. I thought, really? You gonna stand there? O-kay. Then I ran right over him. Actually it was more like running through him. Derrick scored the touchdown, and I reached down a hand and pulled up Warner. He was still vibrating. "I gotta give you some love," I said to him. "You weren't getting off the track."

He nodded. "I threw the pick," he wheezed. "I had to stand there."

That showed me his heart. Kurt Warner knew how to play the game. He threw the interception; it was his responsibility to do everything possible to stop the touchdown. If it meant being the Road Runner and getting rolled flat by the steamroller, that's what he had to do. "I admire you, buddy," I told him.

I sacked Brett Favre 11 time in my career, more than any other quarterback, as well as the most times he was sacked by a single player. I have a special place in my heart for him; he would hang in there. But he knew what to do when a pass was intercepted. On the Clifton play, after his pass was intercepted, Favre took one look at me and started running straight for the sideline. He knew that the safest place for him was out of bounds, where he wasn't going to get hit, and would survive to pass again. So my first target was the quarterback, but if I couldn't find the quarterback, I was going after the left tackle and then the center, in that order. Quarterback, left tackle, center. Chad Clifton was the left tackle.

Offensive players are taught that when a pass is intercepted get your head on a swivel, because now you are defending, and people are going to try to hit you. I am those people. When Favre took off for the hills I looked for Clifton, and I spotted him on the side of the field, but he wasn't running, he was loafing after the play. I was disappointed.

I had nobody to hit. Meanwhile, Brian Kelly is faking and juking across the field on the interception return. He was feeling his way, looking to pick up blockers. He didn't know which way he was going, so I damn sure didn't know it either.

There are team rules most fans know nothing about. One of them is that after an interception an offensive lineman will be fined $1,500 for not being in the frame. That's a rule the offensive linemen made for themselves. What that means is that when coaches are watching the game film they pause it when the player returning the interception is tackled—and every offensive lineman has to be in that freeze-frame. They got to be trying to make the tackle. If they're not, $1,500. Right after the interception Clifton was not in the frame—he was loafing. After Brian made a couple of moves I figured Clifton had to be chasing him. That's when I looked toward the sideline and saw him la-di-da'ing. The man was on the field of play in a National Football League game. He was a potential tackler. There is a reason my position is called *defensive tackle* rather than *defensive blocker* or *defensive talker*—my job is to hit people. So I hit him. Hit him good, the way I had been taught; the way he would've hit me if he had the opportunity.

I saved Chad Clifton $1,500 for not being in the frame. People complained that he was out of the play when I hit him. Except that's not the way football works. On an interception return the only people out of the play are on the sidelines or in the stands. If he was on the field, he was in that play. I didn't realize I was supposed to be kind to him. He was loafing across the field. After I hit him I celebrated. Did my little dance. I knew I was going to be on the highlight reel the next day. That interception was a big play for us in that game. The score was tied, and it led to the go-ahead touchdown. Damn right I'm going to celebrate it.

I did not know he was hurt when I celebrated.

What brought the real attention to it was what happened after the game. I said good-bye to my mother and did an interview, and I was walking toward our locker room when Green Bay coach Mike Sherman got in my face. "Cheap shot, motherfucker," he said. That's not what he told reporters he said, but trust me, that is what he said.

He was lucky I wasn't 25 years old without kids and a conscience. That would have gotten ugly. Instead I said to him, "What do you want to do about it?" Members of security tried to get between us, and I warned them to keep their hands off me. I told Sherman, "Say it again." I moved toward him and he cowered away. "You trying to get me to punch you in the damn mouth?" Oh man, I was overheated. I probably threw some other language in there too. The cameramen had come over to us, and Sherman wasn't saying another word. On camera he was going to be the good guy. I was livid. I said, "You're so tough, go put on a jersey. C'mon, get some." I said a few more words and then walked away. Sherman also didn't mention that two of his players were penalized for personal fouls during the game, including an unnecessary roughness penalty when his center hit Dexter Jackson out of bounds after Jackson intercepted another pass.

Sherman told reporters he was reacting to my celebration, which he "perceived as inappropriate." My response was much more reasonable, especially when I referred to him as "a lying, shit-eating hound." Later their offensive line coach promised that the next time we played they were going to cut block me and injure me. Yeah, right, I thought, bring 'em on.

My boys in the locker room were completely supportive. Brooks explained it, "When you make a hit on someone you don't know if that guy's hurt or not so you're celebrating the play." Ronde jumped in too. "There's no escaping the fact that he hit the crap out of the guy. But it was clean. Warren was just hustling more than that guy, and it showed up that way on film." And Gruden was right there too. "(Warren) has a very, very fast heartbeat during a game, and if you're going to approach him after the game about the ethics in which he plays, to me that isn't very logical. (They had) some flagrant, after-the-whistle 15-yard penalties that weren't exactly ethical, but I'm not going up to those players and asking them to please not do that." Thank you, fellas.

That play got a lot of attention, most of it negative. I did receive death threats. But after an investigation, the league put out a statement that read, "It was a legal play, there will be no disciplinary action." Three years later they instituted the "Warren Sapp rule," which penalizes players for hitting a so-called "defenseless player." Hey rule people, if you are on the field in an NFL game you are not a defenseless player.

Admittedly I wasn't always the totally innocent party. I liked to have fun on the field, although it's possible my definition of *fun* was different than other people's. That's what led to the most expensive drink of water in history.

In 2000 we were playing the Buffalo Bills in Tampa, at beautiful Raymond James Stadium. Early in the fourth quarter Brooks knocked running back Shawn Bryson out of bounds. While Buffalo's trainers were tending to him I asked one of the water boys on their bench for a cup of water. In the NFL the home team supplies half the water boys for the visiting team. Their bench, but one of our water boys. I recognized him. That's why I asked, and that's why he gave it to me. There were rows of filled cups of water sitting on the table. I was thirsty. They weren't going to miss one. But Ted Washington stepped in front of me and said, "Nope, no water for you."

"Big Ted," I said, "please. Just move out of my way."

The referee was standing a few feet away. He told Ted Washington to move, which he did. As I started drinking my one cup of water Doug Flutie, li'l Doug Flutie, protested to the referee. That man is drinking Buffalo Bills water! Whistle! Flag! Taunting! Fifteen yards! The referee told me I was inciting a riot!

Inciting a riot? For drinking a glass of water? I asked him, "You can honestly tell me that's in the rule book?"

His answer was, "I called it."

I told him, "You'll never get another drink in this stadium. I don't care if it's 120 degrees . . . You'll never ever drink any Buccaneer water, if I got anything to do with it . . . And I will enforce this rule as long as I'm a Buccaneer."

I guess that was when I swept my arm across the table, knocking off every cup. *Whoosh*, every one of them. Niagara cups. Fortunately the camera didn't catch that move, which undoubtedly would have been shown endlessly in slo-mo replay while the broadcasters analyzed my one-arm sweeping technique, which is why the league fined me only $2,500.

The question is this: Did I go over there to provoke an incident, to taunt them, or simply because I was thirsty? Here's the one thing I will guarantee you: This was not a planned play. Oh no, this was not in the weekly playbook, Hurricane Steals Water. I'd been playing hard, I was thirsty, I saw the water, I drank the water, I thought it would be fun. The fans thought it was fun and they cheered. I had no mean intentions or malice in my heart; I was just having a good time. That's why I always refer to the NFL as the *No Fun League*. But I did promise myself that from that point on, if I was going to spend $2,500 on a drink, it was not going to be water.

I did have confidence. I did like to set the tone for my team. At Miami, when the team came running out of the Orange Bowl tunnel into the smoke, that stadium would shake like it was being tickled. We literally could *feel* the cheers on the field. I had my own routine: At the corner of each end zone there are bright orange pylons, plastic highway cones, to let the officials see the out of bounds. When the team came out for our pregame stretching I would run a lap around the field, and as I passed each pylon I'd knock it over with my calf. All eight of them. I did it every game. I did it at home, I did it on the road, and nobody got upset about it. When I got to the pros I just kept doing it. To get all the pylons I had to go right through the other team's stretching formation. I used to skip right through it. La-di-da.

It was me; it was a superstition like banging helmets before a game. I admit it was not polite. Maybe it did show my attitude: Those two end zones are mine. If you want any part of them you got to go through me and my boys to get there. I did it for eight seasons. I did it at Miami when we were competing for the national championship, and I did it in Tampa when we weren't winning any games. In college nobody ever got upset about it, nobody ever said a word. In the NFL nobody complained about it—until we started winning. When we were the Yucks nobody gave a damn. But when we started winning people began complaining about me running through their stretch to knock over the pylons.

I wasn't kicking babies; I was knocking over orange plastic cones. It's a damn pylon, just stand it back up. My people in Tampa used to set it up good for me 'cause they knew I was coming for it—they would have been disappointed if I hadn't. I didn't care if my teammates ran the great circle route around the opponent's end zone. I ran my route through the end zone stretch because I have been taught that the fastest distance between two points is a straight line. Even if that straight line runs right through the Pittsburgh Steelers.

My problem started when we played the Steelers in 2002. When I skipped through their end zone I heard somebody yell, "He's running through our stretch!" Somebody call the cavalry, it's a Sapp attack! Run for the hills. Hide the women and children. C'mon, I was just having some fun. Jerome Bettis gave me a little shove. That led to a little bit of a discussion between approximately 10 tons of football players, with some skinny little officials in the middle trying to break it up.

The fifth week of the 2003 season we were playing the Indianapolis Colts on *Monday Night Football*. This was a big game; it was Colts' head coach Tony Dungy's Tampa Bay homecoming. It also was his birthday. There was a lot of anticipation, which is why the NFL put it on Monday night. Now you tell me, I *wasn't* going to skip through their warm-ups? Apparently the Colts were ready for me. Tony knew exactly what I was going to do—he'd seen me do it often enough. Apparently he told the

Colts' big center, Jeff Saturday, "He's not gonna touch anybody, he's not gonna curse anybody, he's just coming through." Then he warned Jeff that if he did anything at all he was going to fine his ass. And Tony never fined anybody. Never. Jeff told me later that he was not real happy about this, but there was nothing he could do. I went right through their stretches bopping and skipping. Tony looked at me, I looked at him, maybe he smiled just a little. I nodded to him, with respect, and just kept going.

That was some football game. At the beginning of the fourth quarter we were leading 28–7. With under four minutes left we were up 35–14. After a 90-yard kickoff return they scored again, 35–21. They recovered an onside kick. After the game the league admitted it was an illegal recovery because the ball never hit the ground or wasn't touched by a Buc. But the officials blew the call. When you're on the field in those situations you can feel the momentum shifting. Believe me, players feel it. There isn't too much you can do about it. That anxiety gets in the way. What you need is one big play, one big hit, one sack, to turn it around. We came real close to Manning; we just couldn't get him. They scored to make it 35–28. Everything was going wrong for us, everything.

They tied the score with 0:35 seconds left in the game. We had Peyton Manning down 21 points with four minutes left. What changed the whole game was that my left corner got hurt, and we had to put in a kid who didn't understand the fundamentals of the game. When we got in our huddle I asked the kid who he was covering—and he pointed to the Colts' tight end Dallas Clark. I asked him, "Then who the fuck is that behind you?"

"Marvin Harrison?" he guessed.

"That's right, Marvin Harrison. Caught 143 balls in a season. Who the fuck you think Peyton Manning's going to throw to? Dallas Clark or one of the greatest wide receivers in NFL history?" But this kid wasn't going to cover him. "That's the threat you fucking dumbass. Why would you be pointing to Dallas Clark? The prize is behind you." That was our defense in that situation: Our D-backs didn't care who was in front of them, let 'em play all day in front of us, but don't let the play go for a touchdown. We wanted to prevent quick strikes, make them throw short and eat clock. But we couldn't do it. We lost track of the fundamentals.

In the overtime their kicker attempted a 40-yard field goal—and missed it. But the official in his wisdom penalized Simeon Rice for unsportsmanlike conduct when Simeon took a running jump to block the kick. The officials claimed that our lineman was propping him up. Dumbest call ever. Happy birthday, Tony! The retry was batted, but it hit the uprights and flopped over for the game-winning points. I just stood there on that field trying to sort out all the emotions I was feeling. Are you kidding me? Penalized for running and jumping. My goodness. The last time they made that call they were playing with a pigskin still attached to the pig. A game should never be decided by a ridiculous call like that. When there is a questionable call in a game the league sends the team affected by that call a letter. We wore the mailmen out getting those letters. This time we got the letter on Tuesday, telling us that the officials had missed two calls in the game. No shit, I thought. That's what we were trying to tell you on Sunday.

At that time this was the largest blown lead in the last four minutes of a game in NFL history. Some people have called it the most spectacular comeback ever. Those were not the words used by my mother to describe what happened. Losing devastates me. Tears me up. But this loss, oh my God. What made it even worse was the drive home with my wife and family. My little girl, the Captain, she is a football fan—I mean a football *fan*. She loved watching our games so much that she would start crying when the teams left the field at halftime because she thought the game was over—until JaMiko explained to her that we were just taking a little potty break and would be back.

After every home game she would be waiting for me outside our locker room, and as soon as she saw me she would come running fast as she could to hug me, and if we'd lost the first words out of her mouth were, "Daddy, you lost!"

I was devastated after this game. How do you explain this type of excruciating loss to a five-year-old who wants to be hugged? "Yes, Captain, we did lose."

"Well, Daddy, why did you lose?"

See there were these two horrendous calls made by the officials, and then that dumbass left corner didn't know . . . no, I couldn't say any of that. Instead I said sweetly, "I don't know, Captain."

And all the way home, over and over as only a five-year-old can do: "I don't understand why you lost, Daddy. But you lost."

We definitely did lose that game, but we had help. And rather than admitting that those two terrible calls by the officials had cost us the damn game, the league warned me that I was no longer permitted to skip through the other team's stretches. Naturally I cooperated, naturally. "Tell you what," I suggested. "Draw me a diagram what route I should follow when I go to work." I wanted to see a map with my route highlighted. The Bucs' front office also asked me to stop running through the warm-ups. We had just got beaten out of an important game by two unbelievably bad calls—and the focus was on my little game. Okay.

We were playing Washington that next Sunday. Before that game the Redskins' LaVar Arrington looked right into the TV cameras and sent me a message: "Sapp, I'm going to get you. I'm expecting for Warren Sapp to cause me to grab him—because he's going to try to run through our lineup in pregame. You don't let somebody come to where your whole team is because that's a blatant show of disrespect."

When he was asked how he would feel if Gruden used me on offense, he insisted, "That's disrespectful in my opinion, too . . . I'm gunning. You come out there, you got some killers on the other side of the ball."

I always liked LaVar. The man had a sense of humor. He's going to get me? Maybe that was just his version of Dancing with a Star. Honestly, I didn't know what I was going to do when I ran onto the field. Some people were telling me to leave it alone. But there also were people like my aunt, who sent me a note telling me, "Don't stop skipping. Don't let them change you."

There have been times in my life when I can be stubborn. For example, always. But making this point wasn't that important to me. The situation had gotten way out of control. On Sunday none of that mattered, because when I ran out onto the field and looked around I felt like Custer, but instead of Indians I was looking at officials. They were waiting for me.

I did not run through Washington's warm-up. But as I ran down the sideline I brushed against the back judge, who had turned away from me and had his back to me. It was not intentional. I wasn't trying to show anybody up; I wasn't trying to make a point. I tried to avoid him. The official wasn't bothered by it, and he didn't say a word to me. If I'd hit him, wouldn't he have thrown a penalty flag on me? They'd never hesitated before. He knew I wasn't trying to show him up.

We beat up on Washington, 35–13, but on the next Tuesday I was informed by the NFL that I was being fined $50,000 and threatened with suspension for bumping the official. "It is apparent you made deliberate contact with the official . . .

"Your continuing disrespectful and intimidating conduct has no place in the game," NFL official Peter Hadhazy wrote me. "You have repeatedly abused game officials and ignored their directions and authority in at least three of the Buccaneers' games this season."

I was not happy with that decision. I think my exact words were, "It's a slave system. Make no mistake about it, slave master say you can't do it, don't do it. They'll make an example out of you." I knew when I said it that it might cause a problem between me and the National Football League. And it did. It was obvious that Commissioner Tagliabue was furious about my remarks, and to punish me the league asked me to be on the NFL Network every Thursday night. They definitely wanted to make an example of me, and they wanted millions of people to turn on *NFL Total Access* to see that.

It was ironic. Two days after fining me $50,000 the league asked me to appear regularly in a segment of that show with Michael Strahan to comment on the league. As Strahan pointed out, "Sapp is entertaining. And whatever I say or do, it won't cost me $50,000 . . . Both of us are outspoken and pretty good players, too. It should be a lot of fun."

"Outspoken and pretty good players." I guess that was a reasonable way of describing us. It was ironic. While the league was busy penalizing me for saying—and doing—what I thought, the league was also putting me on TV every week to say what I thought. They knew what they were doing. Nobody told me, "Warren, don't be yourself." The NFL successfully walks a complex tightrope. The league is marketing a very violent game, while at the same time supposedly trying to get rid of the violence in the game. They wanted me to be on their show because I was colorful, sometimes controversial, and well-known. I said what I believed, fought for what I thought was right, and tried to have a good time without hurting anybody but quarterbacks, and then they fined me for doing it.

People often ask me why. Why did you do that? Why did you say that? Why didn't you just walk away? Why are you always in the middle of it? The easy answer to that question would be my pride, but I don't think that's it. Pride is what will get you killed on Saturday night. Pride prevents you from taking a step back when it is appropriate. I like to believe my pride is at home with my kids. But respect has always been important to me. Coming from my background that shouldn't be a surprise to anyone. Respect is earned. When I feel I am not being given the proper respect, I respond. That happened in high school, and it happened in the pros. I have never judged another person by anything other than the way they treat other people. With the exception of quarterbacks, of course.

There is no one in this world I respect more than Tony Dungy, for example. I consider the man my spiritual father, but I also expected that he would respect me. During a game against Denver in September 1999, I broke two bones in my left hand. At halftime I wrapped up my hand and played the second half with two broken metacarpals. Yes, it did hurt—hurt like a bitch. I did my job, but there was no way I could play the following Sunday.

Before that game Tony stood up there and gave a speech in which he said, basically, that the team didn't need any superstars; we just needed the people on the field to do their jobs and we would win. Well, thank you very much Tony. I didn't realize I was so easily replaceable. Anybody could do my job? That bothered me, bothered me a lot. That's like telling a friend, hey we had a great party last night, and nobody even noticed you weren't there. I've never met a successful professional athlete without an ego. You got to have some arrogance when you get on the field. You have to believe you are an essential gear in the machine. The last thing any athlete wants to hear is their coach saying the team can win without you. Okay, I admit it, my feelings were hurt almost as badly as my bones. We all carry the wounds of our childhood through our whole life. I felt that Tony was not respecting me.

The next week we went up to Minnesota. We were losing 21–0 before we blinked. I told my boys on the defense, uh fellas, you might want to slow them down a little bit; right now they're on a pace to score 84 points. We lost 21–14.

Week after that Tony made the same speech. Said it again, "All we need is for everybody to do their job and we can win." Maybe he didn't say the words "without Warren," but that's what I heard. I thought, okay, you think you can win with anybody, go ahead and win with anybody. Before practice on Wednesday Trainer Todd Toriscelli asked me if I was ready to go. If we were in the playoffs I would have strapped it on. But we weren't in the playoffs. "One more week," I told him. "I'm on the bone generator 10 hours a day. Besides, you heard the man, he can win with anybody."

I did a walk-through in practice, and when we were done Tony asked me to come into his office. "What percentage are you?" he asked.

" 'Bout 80," I said.

"You know what. I'll take Warren Sapp at 80 percent over anything I got in that locker room at 110 percent."

"Well, I don't know," I said. "I'm sitting here listening to your speech, and you're saying you can win with anybody."

"I need you."

Respect. "That's all you had to say," I told him. "I needed to hear that from you, that you needed me in the lineup." I strapped it on and played with my healing hand that weekend.

I had a similar situation in Oakland when D-line Coach Keith Millard took me out of a game. Keith Millard is my man, I love him; one of the best defensive coaches in the game of football. He helped me get 10 sacks as a 34-year-old. After he left Oakland I know for a fact I helped him get a job in Tampa. They asked me for a recommendation, and I told them he will put a smile on the face of every D-lineman. No one can question my feelings about him or his ability to coach. But one time the man took me out of a game for no good reason. So when he told me to go back in I refused. "You took me out," I said. "Evidently you thought someone else could do my job, so let's watch this together."

He thought I was kidding. "Come on, dude."

I told him, "Man, you got to apologize to me before I go back in this game."

"Okay, I'm sorry."

Respect. "Thank you very much. I'm going back in now."

I demand that same respect from fans too, and I didn't always get it, which admittedly caused me to have a sometimes rocky relationship with the entire city of Tampa. My reputation in Tampa was that I was aloof and sometimes rude, that I often refused to sign autographs and almost always refused to pose for photographs. And that was mostly from those people who liked me.

In my heart I am still a small-town boy in a big-city body. The result of that is a conflict in my spirit. While I love to see people happy, and there are few sounds I enjoy more than cheers and laughter, I greatly value my privacy. I watched Michael Jordan becoming a victim of his fame to the point where he almost could not go out in public. The fans loved him so much they made him a prisoner. I wasn't going to allow that to happen to me. I have always been recognizable, oh believe me I am recognizable, but as I became more successful people began believing they owned part of my time. I must have missed that memo.

I was called a lot of names for not signing autographs or posing for pictures or sometimes even shaking hands. The problem was that it rarely was one polite request, sometimes it wasn't more polite than "sign this," and as soon as I signed one autograph a long line would start forming. It would turn into the Warren Sapp Show. And if I didn't sign every last autograph for every person in that line I guarantee you I was going to be criticized by that person who didn't get an autograph. I could sign 15 autographs, and the 16th person would describe me as an arrogant asshole. When I was in a restaurant having dinner with my family I wanted to enjoy my salad and talk to my kids, but if I refused to sign an autograph for a person who interrupted us they called me rude. In college I signed every letter I received. Every last one of them. I'd sit in front of my locker signing them and returning them. But once I got to the pros that pile grew out of control. I wasn't about to tell Dungy or Gruden that I'd like to practice today, but I can't because I got to sign all these autographs. Wyche, maybe. And I never could get used to people who would ask me for an autograph and then ask if I had a pen and piece of paper to write it on. I wasn't the only athlete who didn't sign every autograph. The great Bill Russell does not sign autographs, he wouldn't even sign for his teammates, but rather than being criticized he is still one of the most respected champions of all time.

There was a good reason I didn't like shaking hands when people came up to me. Whenever someone introduced himself to me he would grip my hand and shake it hard as he could to prove how manly he was. Even the women. They'd just grab my hand and *squeezeeeeeeeeeee*. Show me how sincere they were: "Shook that ole' Warren Sapp's hand so hard I made him scream in pain! Should a heard him yelping!" Let me confess right now: Sometimes it hurt! Playing on the D-line my hands got banged up worse than a drunken carpenter. My hands are permanently puffed up and slightly deformed. Here's the way I had to play the "this little finger" game with my kids: "This little finger went to the hospital, this little finger got 12 stitches, this little finger had a compound fracture and the bone came through the skin . . ."

I also asked that when people came up to me they were polite. Like I said, I'm good in math, but I can't count the number of times people have come up to me and began a conversation by saying, "I'm from Philly . . ." I know what comes next; that person will want to talk about the 2002 game and tell me "my bag is still packed for the Super Bowl." They always tell me that the Bucs were lucky, that it was "one of the ugliest wins ever." I've heard that phrase too many times, an "ugly win."

Do they expect me to agree with them? Hello? Instead, those times I don't walk away, I explain politely that I would rather have the ugliest win than a Picasso loss. Picasso never played football. No loss is beautiful. I don't care if I had five sacks, caused a fumble, and had 12 tackles. If we lost the game what I was going to remember was hearing my little girl saying, "But you lost, Daddy."

She never told me, "You won, Daddy, but you played for crap." No, thank you. I'll take two first downs and no tackles long as I get that beautiful *W*.

All I asked for when people approached me was common courtesy and common sense. And I found out that was a lot to ask for from some people. I had a clear rule: You do not own me. My time belongs to me. I needed that rule to survive. I couldn't go out to a sports bar with friends in Tampa and just sit there with a brew and enjoy whatever game we were watching. I couldn't have a quiet conversation with someone in public without being interrupted. At times it seemed like I was the fastest gun in the South because people seemed to want to challenge me. Like a lot of people with high profiles, there have been times I've had to turn around and walk away to avoid an unpleasant situation. Some people didn't seem to understand that when I went out with my wife and kids I actually wanted to enjoy being with my wife and kids. I wasn't at my job. I was at my other job, being Daddy. I'm trying really hard to do a better job with my kids than my biological father did with me. People would often interrupt us by saying, "I hate to interrupt you, but . . ." I would think, well then if you hate to do something why are you doing it? If you hate asparagus would you order it? No you would not. If you hate doing something, then don't do it.

I admit I may have been harsh about it on occasion, but I'm just not a mild-mannered person. Just not. It's who I am. I am sorry to those people I have offended, my mother taught me manners, but people need to understand there is a right time and right place for everything. JaMiko has always said that we were a perfect match; our weaknesses were each other's strengths. For example, JaMiko couldn't pass-rush worth a damn while sometimes socially I could be abrupt. If we were interrupted in the middle of dinner, for example, she would say softly and politely, "We're having a family dinner right now. Do you guys mind waiting until we're done, please?" Now I would make that exact same point, although I would use different words to make the point. And maybe I'd forget about the *softly* part.

I love real football fans. I am a football fan; even if it wasn't part of my job I would watch every game that I can. I'll still stop my car to watch little kids playing. I'm still in awe when I meet the legendary players who built this game. Real football fans are people who appreciate the game, root for their team, and drive home safely. They understand that the game is supposed to be fun. One time after a game in Green Bay we were in the locker room waiting for our charter flight to arrive. Our elegant after-the-game dinner consisted of a cold box lunch with potato chips. They did give us as many bags of potato chips as we wanted. Are you kidding me? I had just spent three hours getting the heck beat out of me, and as a reward they were offering a second bag of potato chips? My oh my, life is grand. No, thank you. I decided I wasn't going to eat that crap. So I went hunting for food. I went out of the locker room into the parking lot looking for a meal. It was emptying, but some fans were waiting for the traffic jam to die down. I found a Packers fan who had been tailgating in his Winnebago. If he was surprised that a Bucs player was in the parking lot he didn't show it. Instead he gave me a great big welcoming smile and said, "Hey Warren, what are you doing here?"

I told him, "I was hoping somebody had a grill that was still on. Our charter's late and I'm hungry."

He'd be delighted to fire it right up, he said. This man was a serious Cheesehead, although at that time he was not wearing his wedge. His RV was like a Packers shrine; the walls were covered with Green Bay memorabilia and tickets to the many games he'd attended. He opened a pack of brats, pulled out the cooler and a six pack, and set up some chairs. It didn't bother him that I played for the Bucs; he was a football fan. And, fortunately, a bratwurst fan. He asked me if I'd ever worked a grill, and I told him once or twice or a thousand times. Then I called my boys inside the locker room and told them, "Y'all might want to come out here." The key word I then used was *food*. They came a-running. We had a nice little gathering in that parking lot. And the man wouldn't take any money either. He said just having Warren Sapp and his teammates sitting there was enough. I didn't say anything, but I did wish I could have been there when he tried to convince his family and friends that Warren Sapp and a bunch of Bucs had come out to the parking lot after the game and had a barbecue in his Winnebago.

As I always said, I was being paid to play football, not to let people chip away at my private life. Other athletes may feel differently, and they may even be right. For them. I understand that as a professional athlete I did have a certain amount of power—and responsibility. I knew that kids looked up to me just the way I used to look up to professional football players. And while sometimes I could get irritated with adults, I always tried to use that power to do my best for kids. In Tampa, for example, I had a shoe charity. With some kids needing so much else, it seemed to me that was one important area that was being overlooked. Growing up, it was a task for me to get a new pair of shoes. I had a size-13 foot when I was 13, which definitely limited my selection to basically whatever they got that fits. A new pair of shoes, for me, was as important as a new bike or a new car. That first day of school every year if I could step out of the house with a new pair of shoes my confidence level was sky high. Check out my new bobos, man. But when we couldn't get those shiny shoes, when I had to wear an old beat-up pair with holes in the soles, my spirit felt poor. So I was always sensitive about my shoes.

I found out that in parts of Florida there were a lot of children who couldn't afford shoes. Worse than that, in some migrant families, the seasonal pickers, their kids had to share one pair of shoes. Some days the kids couldn't go to school because it wasn't their day to wear those shoes. I couldn't believe that when I heard it. We were poor, but we always had some kind of shoes. So I organized Sapp for Shoes. Payless Shoes was a big contributor, and while the program was active we gave away tens of thousands of pairs of shoes. Even now, years later, I still occasionally have people come up and tell me, "You don't know me, but my child was one of the kids who got shoes from you."

It may not seem like much, but trust me, poor kids know all about shoes.

I also used my celebrity to raise funds for pediatric cancer research. JaMiko sat on the board of St. Joe's Children's Hospital, and through her I ended up visiting some of these kids. I posed for pictures with a beautiful young girl named Autumn. Oh, I loved that little girl. Pictures of her sitting on my shoulders were on every billboard in the city. And then she died. She died.

Somehow I didn't see that one coming. I was certain she was going to make it. When she didn't it hit me hard, harder than I could have possibly imagined. That wasn't supposed to happen. So I always tried to give back to those people who needed some help, if not always to those people who needed an autograph. I also have participated in the Make-A-Wish program, for kids with serious illnesses. If it was a kid's wish to meet me I wasn't going to try to talk him or her out of it. One 12-year-old boy wanted to play a round of golf with me. Of course we did. It worked out great too—I won $50.

No, I did not. I didn't even make him pay for the drinks!

But because of my big image some people will believe almost anything bad about me. Any guy that hit as hard as Sapp has to be a bad guy. The story doesn't even have to be true. Every celebrity is a target, and because of my big image, my big attitude, and my big personality, I was a big target. I admit it, I am not perfect. I have made mistakes and I do have some regrets. Like any human being, there are places in my life where I wish I could have a do-over. When I'm wrong I apologize—but I do not apologize for things I didn't do. And I tell the truth. My mother taught me that sometimes the truth hurts, but a lie is a big old damn landmine that just might explode in your face. Probably the worst thing that ever happened to me off the football field was being accused of committing domestic violence. Accused, and while the police investigated and dismissed every single charge, there will always be people who believe it was true. No matter how often I explain what actually happened that night I understand there are people who won't believe me, but this is exactly what happened.

This incident took place in February 2010, a few years after JaMiko and I were divorced. We had the nicest divorce in history. We are still very close. I got a set of keys to the house, and I keep my stuff there, and sometimes we even go on vacation together with the kids. Her father, James Vaughn, remains a close friend and a very important person in my life. But I was single and I did go out with women. The night this happened I was in Miami for the Super Bowl, scheduled to appear on the NFL Network the next day. I had known the woman who made the complaint against me for about three years. I was at a benefit party with about 80 people to raise funds to provide aid for victims of the earthquake in Haiti. The next afternoon there was a knock on my door, and the police told me that I was being arrested.

Wow. Arrested? For what? Oversleeping? I was dumfounded. For a few seconds I thought it had to be a joke. Then they handcuffed my arms behind my back and put me in a transport truck. Nothing funny about that. I pleaded with them to let my hands loose, and eventually they allowed me to sit there with my hands cuffed on top of my head. My whole life I had stayed in control of the situation, whatever the situation was, but this time it was beyond my control. There is no way I can describe everything I was feeling as I was being driven to jail; it was some combination of incredible anger, confusion, and embarrassment. Jail. Wow. In my whole life I had never been touched by an officer of the law, and now that was gone. And worse, they were taking me out of my telecast on Super Bowl Sunday in my own city. That was going to sound great on my broadcast: "Warren isn't with us today 'cause he's in jail." My goodness.

I began to find out what was going on. This woman, who said that she was my girlfriend, claimed that I had dragged her out of bed at 6:00 a.m. in the morning, "grabbed her and began to choke her," and then made her leave the room. She went outside and left in a taxi. Then six hours later she reported it to the police. Six hours? If somebody hits you why would you wait six hours to report it? Makes no sense. Because none of that was true, that's why.

This was not my girlfriend; this was a woman I had seen a few times in the three years I'd known her. This was not a person I wanted in my life. Turns out she had other ideas. She'd called me to tell me she was coming down to Florida for the Super Bowl. Staying with a friend. Okay, good. I invited her to the party, but I was not with her. I hadn't stayed in that room with her that night. I wasn't even staying in that hotel. I was given that room by a friend in the hotel management who wanted me to have a place to stay if I had too much to drink at the party. He was trying to protect me. At one point late that night my friend got the key from me, took her upstairs, and got her situated. When I came back early in the morning I did ask her to leave. And she left.

When I got to the police station a detective began asking me some questions. He told me, "I'm going to help you out here. You've got the right to remain silent . . ." He read me my rights and then asked, "Okay, tell me what happened."

Didn't he even listen to his own self? I said, "I have the right to remain silent."

He said, "You're learning. You've got the right to remain silent."

I was learning. They put me in a little nasty orange jumpsuit. Man, I hated that color since my first year in Tampa. Now I knew why. They took my shoes away and gave me little sandals that didn't fit. I had a psychological evaluation to see if I might commit suicide. The theory was that for some people being arrested would cause a nervous breakdown and they would commit suicide.

Finally they put me in some little hole in the side by myself. I was fuming. This was not the image I wanted my kids to have of me. I'd seen too much of this kind of behavior myself when I was growing up, and I didn't intend to repeat that for my own children.

As soon as I was released I asked the hotel for its video tape of this woman leaving. I knew it was going to show her walking fine and looking unconcerned. The security would only give the tape to my attorney, to maintain the chain of evidence. Okay. He went down there and looked at the whole tape. She was not on it. They gave him the wrong tape. When they finally found the right tape there she was walking out the front door, walking perfectly fine on six-inch high heels. She was with a man, and instead of a taxi, they got into a Range Rover and drove off. On that tape she didn't show any of the injuries that I supposedly inflicted by picking her up and choking her. Soon as the police looked at that video this case was over. The newspapers reported, "Prosecution documents reveal that there were inconsistencies between the victim's statements and the physical evidence."

But it did damage to my reputation. There are people who continue to believe the whole story is true, even if the facts prove different. But that's my image.

I will say one thing about that image though—it is big.

SEVEN

After I announced that I was retiring people asked me if I thought I'd miss playing the game. Miss being double-teamed by almost 600 pounds of linemen every play? Miss being always banged up and bruised? Miss the aches and pains of getting out of bed Monday morning? Far as I was concerned there was no doubt about it—damn right I would miss it. I'd miss every bit of it.

I was playing the game that I love, that I'd been playing my entire life. I had averaged about 1,000 snaps a year for almost a decade. Ten thousand times I went hard into that wall, and it definitely wore me down. My body was ready to retire, but not my soul. I knew I would miss that feeling of being on the field for an NFL game. I would miss the camaraderie of the locker room and that feeling of being part of a team working together as a cohesive unit. Nobody walks away, or in some cases limps away, without missing the game. John Lynch told me once that he missed the competition, having to go out there every Sunday and prove yourself all over again. The competition and the hitting; Lynch loved hitting people. It didn't surprise me at all that Brett Favre kept coming back for one more year, one more year, one more year. Anybody who has played the game can understand that.

So much takes place on the field that fans know nothing about, especially in the trenches. The difference between watching a football game and being on the field is like eating a steak or looking at a picture of it. You get the idea, but not the flavor. Being in the middle of the mix was what I was going to miss most. We have our own little world on the field. It's just us, the players, the people who have spent their lives working to be on that field at that moment. It's a noisy world too; there is a lot of conversation that goes on. Most of it is just talk: Watch out, I'm coming for you. That the best you got? Yo, your team stinks worse than your breath. Mostly we're about the business down there, but there were times that I got to laughing so hard I could hardly get ready to go. For example, John Lynch's brother-in-law, John Allred, played tight end for the Bears. During a game in 1997 Allred caught one across the middle, and Lynch just leveled him. Knocked him out cold. He was lying on the field, and they brought the doctors out. The Bears' Keith Jennings was pretty upset about it, and he screamed at Lynch, "God damn Lynch, you knocked your brother-in-law out . . ."

That was all Culpepper had to hear. Before Lynch could say a word, he yelled right back, "Damn right. And he fucked the shit out of his sister too!"

In college I didn't do too much talking on the field, especially my first years. That was my learning time, and I was listening to my elders. One time we were playing Memphis State, and their offensive guard started jawing on me. I didn't say anything back to him. Finally he challenged me, "C'mon, you got no words for me, baby?"

I looked at Ray Lewis. Little ole' Ray Lewis, who barely said a word on the field in those days. He grew up to be voted one of the top trash talkers in the NFL. Made me so proud. But in this situation he just looked at me and asked, "He talking?"

The next snap I beat that guard badly and dumped his quarterback on his neck. Turned him upside down like I was emptying a pitcher. As I walked back to the line of scrimmage I finally said to him, "Now you know why I ain't wasting my breath on you, because you're so sorry."

It was the conversations that Brett Favre and I had on the field that got both of us a lot of attention. Favre loved that part of the game as much as I did. Most offensive players don't do much talking. I don't know why, maybe they're not smart enough. But the fact is that Favre started this dialogue between us. We were playing the Packers, and I'd been chasing him all afternoon. I was having a big day. I'd finish with seven tackles, three sacks, two forced fumbles, and one recovery. On the last play of the third quarter I got triple-teamed and didn't get to him. Triple-teamed. As I walked to the sideline to get my breath I heard someone shouting after me, "That's right, Sapp, go take a blow."

Excuse me? I turned around, and he had this big grin on his face. I said, "You talking to me?"

He got right up in my face. "Where you going, Fat Boy? We're just getting started."

Really? I looked at the clock and saw that there were only a few seconds left in the third quarter. I'd get my break between quarters. I waved off my replacement and said to Favre, "What's up, pretty boy?"

"Where you going? We're just getting started right here."

That's when I knew he was just like me. I wasn't used to being challenged on the field, especially by a quarterback. Quarterbacks are the piñatas of sports; far as I'm concerned their only job is to be hit. The Football Gods would have definitely advised against Favre challenging me; so would the emergency room technicians. But that's what he did. I told him, "All right, you go talk to your coach, get your play, and I'll be right here waiting for you. We got one more quarter. Let's do it. You and me. I'm gonna build my house right here . . ."

"I'm with you," he said. We slapped hands, and it was on for the rest of our careers. From that time on we were like two kids trash talking in a playground game. He went and got his friends, I brought my friends, and we went out to play. I loved him for that, absolutely loved him. He really was just like me, always looking to have a little fun.

The one person who hated our conversations was Baggadonuts, Packers center Frankie Winters. Oh my goodness, he just hated them. One time he practically ordered Favre, "Listen, you got to stop talking to him. The more you talk the madder he's getting. I got to block him. So stop it. Don't say one more word." I absolutely know he said that because Favre told me he did.

Naturally I had to share that information with him. Next time I lined up against Winters I asked, "Frankie, you telling me and Favre can't talk no more?"

"Hell no, you can't talk."

Okay. So from that moment on I always made a point of saying something loud to Favre. Knowing how angry it made Winters made it even more fun. When he complained, I asked, "Let me get this right. You saying I can't even say hello to the man?"

Winters snapped. "That's right, you don't get to talk to him at all." Well, I guess you can imagine how well that worked. It was Favre's wife who finally made him stop talking to me because she was afraid he was just getting my engines going. That eventually he was going to get hurt. In my memory I believe that was about the time I started complimenting Brett about that lovely dress he was wearing.

When you're playing 16 regular-season games there are going to be some Sundays you come in flat, and you need a little something extra to stroke you a little bit. I liked to talk. Dungy used to shake his head. That wasn't his game—he wanted you to focus in on your job—but he never told me to stop. One time he admitted to a reporter, "Not everyone can play that way. But Warren can talk to the crows and still concentrate."

Sometimes I'd begin my conversations hours before the game started, contacting my opponent by e-mail and asking, "We talking today?" Soon as I got on the field I started talking. If a player didn't want to talk to me I took that as an encouraging sign. It meant I might be able to get inside his head. Then I definitely wouldn't stop talking. I had a whole line of chatter: "You don't really think you can block me one-on-one, do you?" "I can see you're scared, that means you're smart." "I hope you got some help coming."

I loved talking to quarterbacks, loved it. I tried to put the fear of Sapp in them. And maybe even make them laugh a little. If I got a sack early in the game, for example, I'd shake my head and tell the quarterback, "You are a brave man, playing this game with what you got blocking for you. Man, those people gonna get you killed."

I'm not the only player who liked to talk on the field. We were playing Minnesota the opening game of the 1998 season, and just as the ball was about to be snapped Culpepper screamed at Vikings guard David Dixon, "Hey Dixon, watch it! Your shoes are untied." Dixon actually looked down to check his laces as the ball was snapped.

The Vikings' great receiver, Cris Carter, made me laugh harder and longer than anyone else in my career. Defensive end Regan Upshaw and I had a lot in common: We were both defensive linemen that Tampa selected on the 12th pick of the first round. But Regan had something I didn't have: A gold tooth. On a second-and-8 play Cris ran a crossing pattern. Randall Cunningham's pass was high. Carter leaped for it but couldn't make the play. "Old man," I told him, "you can't go get it like you used to. Look like you're ready to go to the age game."

As Upshaw walked up on us, Cris Carter acknowledged him. "Hey, Regan Upshaw."

"What's going on, Cris?" Upshaw said. It was pretty obvious that Regan was damn pleased that a respected veteran like Cris Carter even knew who he was. He smiled big time.

Carter asked him, "Hey man, how long you been in the league now?"

"Three years," Upshaw said.

Carter got ready to jog back to his huddle, but before he did he paused and then said to Upshaw, "Then don't you think it's about time for you to take advantage of our dental program?" Oh my God. Then *whoosh*, he was gone.

Regan Upshaw looked right at me and warned me, "Dawg, you'd better not be laughing."

Turned my head away and laughed for two quarters.

Most of the talking that takes place on the field is business. That Tampa Bay defense talked football. It wasn't chatter, trash talk, or boolah-boolah let's go get 'em guys—it was all informational. What are you seeing? What are they doing? Where you going? Who you got? Unlike what we had at Oakland, a good defense is loud and noisy. I needed to know what my boys sniffed out and what they were planning to do about it. If I felt the offense was playing a game on us I'd shout out, "Something's up, something's up. Check. Check." That put everybody on notice to pay attention.

This is the kind of talk that takes place on the field. We were playing St. Louis, and they were in the shotgun. I had watched a lot of film of the Rams in this particular formation during the week. We expected them to do this. But there was something about this particular set that just didn't feel right to me. I'd spent so much of my life on a football field, I'd seen what there is to see, so anything out of the ordinary was going to catch my attention. It's like glimpsing a demon out of your peripheral vision; you know something ain't right although you don't know what it is. "Something's up!" I yelled. "Check, check." A second later I heard someone else on the D-line yelling, "Motion." Then the Rams went in motion, and by the movement of the outside back I figured out what was happening: "Weak, quarterback throw back, quarterback throw back." Like an echo, that was repeated right down the line. We were all on the same playbook page now.

It was a trick play. Kurt Warner was going to take the snap and hand it off to Marshall Faulk, who would take a few steps toward the weak side, hoping that we would read it as a weak-side run and commit to defending it. That would bring up our linebackers, while their receivers kept motoring. Faulk would stop suddenly and lateral the ball back to Warner, who would look upfield to see who was open. Steve White was my defensive end, and he didn't bite on it. He stayed right where he should have stayed, and when Faulk threw it back to Warner, White got it stopped before it could get going.

Sometimes we communicated with sign language. At times that stadium got so loud we couldn't hear each other, so we would use hand signals. For example, if someone showed me an open hand it meant he was going through the line first. A fist meant I went first. Making a motion like I was throwing a rock meant we were all going to the right. Putting my thumbs on my helmet and waving my fingers meant something else. However we communicated, we got it done. That Tampa defense was like a symphony of violence; we were completely in tune.

What made that defense so good was that we were smart, fast, and physical. We had a lot of great individual talent, but we played as a team.

In Oakland our defense was like somebody had pressed the mute button. It was so quiet you could hear us dropping in the standings.

The offensive also communicates, and we would always listen to them, trying to pick up their signals. More than once I would be standing right there when the guard asked the tackle, "What's it on?" Hello? Don't you see my ass standing right here four feet in front of you? Do I really look like I just came out of Madame Tussauds? How does he tell him the snap count without telling me too? The only thing he can do is try to outsmart me. He can't say, it's on one or two, so instead he has to answer in secret code: "Monday." Okay, lemme think, Monday? Well, Monday is the first day of the workweek. Hmm, I wonder what that count is.

A lot of times it was very easy to steal information. For example, if I heard someone on the offensive line shouting, "Razor, razor, razor," or "Roger, roger, roger," I knew the offensive line was sliding to the right. "Laser, laser, laser" meant they were going left. When the quarterback called an audible it would go right into my memory bank, and when he called it later in the game we knew what it meant. For example, "122" meant the snap count was two, and "123" it's on three. I remember Rich Gannon walking up to the line of scrimmage in the Super Bowl and calling, "Check, check, 93 willie." I turned my head and shouted back to my linebacker, Shelton Quarles, "Quarles, right here, the three hole." If he'd said "92," it would have been over there, the three hole. Trust me, once you've played the game it just ain't that complicated. There were a lot of games that by the fourth quarter we pretty much knew every play that was being called. The quarterback knew we knew it, but there wasn't anything he could do about it. The offense almost never changed the meaning of a signal during the game. They couldn't; they didn't want to confuse their own boys. So once we picked it up we had it. We were a better second-half defense than in the first half, because a lot of times we knew what was coming.

In the offensive huddle the quarterback does almost all the talking. Like I wrote, I'd always be up on the line of scrimmage trying to pick up some information. One thing people have asked me about is exactly what a quarterback says to the player who missed his block on the 320-pound lineman who clobbered that quarterback from his blind-side. Like when I come between them. How about, "Don't do it again." Or, "If I don't make it, tell my wife I love her." The real answer is absolutely nothing. I mean, you would think that the quarterback would say a few angry words, but I promise you, that quarterback is not going to say one critical word. At that time he is much too busy trying to get his brain turned back on, calling the next play and making sure the right people are in the huddle. A football game is always about the next play, not the last play. Last play's over, done, finished. If there's a problem, get it fixed and then move on.

During a game there is so much testosterone in that huddle that the last thing the quarterback wants to do is start a debate. There is a reason no one goes into a huddle armed. Now, the film room the next morning, that's a whole different thing. That's when blame might be assessed.

When a quarterback sees how bad it was, that's when he might say something. I've seen that happen. The nicest thing a quarterback is going to tell an offensive lineman is, "You do that again, you're going to get me killed." To which the lineman might respond, "You keep standing back there holding on to the ball you probably deserve it. Just throw the damn ball away!"

For me, even when the entire stadium was on their feet screaming, once a play began I didn't hear the crowd at all. It was really weird. I'd hear the quarterback calling signals, the ball was snapped, I'd take one step, two steps, there'd be a lot of grunting and screaming, and then the world went quiet. Not completely silent, but far, far away, as if somebody was holding their hands over my ears. Then as soon as the play ended the sound burst into my ears again, as if that same person suddenly turned on my iPod. Loudly. I don't know if it was the same for other players, we never talked about it, but that's the way it was for me. I always assumed that I was focusing so intensely on getting my job done that the noise didn't register. It was there. I was fast, but not faster than the speed of sound, so I tuned it out. Basketball players use the phrase "In the zone" to mean playing on another mental level where the game comes naturally to you, and for those few seconds every play I was in the zone.

I didn't just talk to other players when I was on the field. When your career lasts as long as mine did you develop a little bit of a relationship with the veteran officials. There aren't that many of them, and over time you do get to know some of them. Most of them actually liked me. Okay, some of them liked me. Well, they didn't dislike me. I wasn't always screaming at them. I knew they had their job to do, and most of them do it professionally and very well. Being an NFL official is usually not a full-time job; officials are moonlighting from another profession. They are doctors and dentists, they have regular jobs, but just like me, football is their passion. It's a pretty strange second job. Most people who take a second job usually work as a bartender or drive a cab, but these people pick a job that requires them to spend their Sunday afternoon throwing their little bodies in between two or more large powerful men wearing complete protective gear who basically want to rip each other apart. For that they get paid between $25,000 and $70,000 a season.

After 13 years in the league I got to know several of the officials real well. No. 81 was from Ocala, Florida. No. 31 was from Palm Beach. I was on a first-number basis with a lot of officials. For example, I always called no. 99, just *9*. There's a lot of dialogue that goes on between players and officials during a game, although almost all of it was straight business. Before a play, for example, officials might warn a player that he is getting close to committing a penalty. "This is the last warning. You're too close, back up," or "Watch your hands, keep 'em down."

Players are always trying to plead their case. There were times I would turn to the umpire and complain, "Yo man, watch this hole. He's holding me." And at least some of those times he was. But it rarely made a difference. Usually the umpire would smile and tell me, "C'mon Sapp, just play the game." They knew I could take care of myself.

I probably spoke to the officials more than the other players on the defense because I was a team captain. When I was on the field I told them what we wanted to do when a penalty was called. The officials' job was to ask, my job was to respond. Long as everybody did their job we were fine. Here's the way it works when a penalty is called: The official would tell me our options, what the down and yardage would be if I accepted or declined the penalty. I rarely had to look at the sideline for a decision. Dungy trusted me with that responsibility. Generally, we accepted or declined a penalty based on the yardage. Anything that resulted in the offense needing less than five yards for a first down we didn't take. But if the result was loss of the down and more than five yards we took it. Almost always we would take the longer yards—unless it was on third down and they hadn't made a first down, or if the quarterback had been sacked on the play. We were taking the sack every time, every damn time. One time I took the sack instead of the penalty, and Dungy got really upset with me about it. We stopped them on the next play and they punted. When I got to the sideline he said, "You got lucky on that one."

"What do you mean, Coach? I took the sack."

He started to explain to me why I should have accepted the penalty. Technically, he was probably right, but I stopped him. "Coach, you got to take the sack." That was a message that came down to me directly from the Football Gods: Thou will always take the sack. Eventually Tony agreed with my interpretation of those scriptures.

The reality is that the officials easily could throw a penalty flag on every play. Every damn play. In college Mike Brown told me once, "If you ain't cheating, you ain't trying to win." I think it's fair to say that like every other player, I did whatever I could get away with to win. For example, on every play there is some holding going on. But unless it affects the outcome of a play the officials aren't going to call it. Holding in the NFL is like traveling in the NBA, it doesn't really exist. An NBA player takes 15 steps, does a little hop, skip, and jump, and no official touches his whistle. The best way for a lineman to prevent being held is to keep moving, keep juking, slapping hands, and clawing—you have to knock their hands away. Now, in addition to that there were some other things players did to make it hard for opponents to hold them. For example, I wore my uniform as tight as possible so there was no loose fabric for people to grab hold of. Some players—not me of course—would cover their uniforms with Vaseline or even silicone. Before a game they would go into a bathroom and spray down their jerseys with silicone, which made it very difficult for anyone trying to hold them. It was illegal, but the officials almost never checked. Now they will kick players out of the game if they have an illegal substance on their uniform, but at that time nobody much cared.

Now that Whitey also is retired I'll confess for him that he was one of the people who did that. He practically bathed in silicone before a game. Trust me, if he had ever tried to hug his wife before a game she would have slipped right out of his arms and gone straight up in the air. One time we were playing against a center who also used silicone. Late in the fourth quarter his team had a second-and-long on about their own 25. That center tried to grab hold of Whitey but instead ended up with silicone all over his hands. Being a dummy, he didn't call timeout. Third down obviously was a passing play so his team went into a shotgun formation. That center snapped that ball about 20 yards over the quarterback's head. We ended up recovering on their 2-yard line.

Their coach started screaming *silicone*. "Their nose guard's cheating," he was yelling. "Look at him, look at him. He's got some slippery crap on his jersey." Whitey took off running toward our bench. It was freezing cold, but he was dumping water over his head. Several of us were standing around him, shielding him from the officials. By the time the referee got there Whitey was soaking wet. When the referee asked what that was all over his uniform, Whitey told him, "What are you talking about? Are you kidding? I'm sweating. Whew, it's tough out there."

There was nothing the officials could do about it. They let the play stand, and we scored what turned out to be the game-winning field goal. After that we all would bring two jerseys with us, just in case we had to switch out of one.

The NFL outlawed defensive holding about 1997, but until then Brooks and I ran a beautiful game. On certain plays the responsibility of the guard is to block a linebacker, but to get to Brooks that guard had to get through me. The tackle was supposed to block me to clear a path for the guard. So I took on both the tackle and the guard. Instead of getting tangled up with the tackle and letting the guard slip by me, I would grab him by his jersey, pull him close to me, and spin him around. That would leave a gap for Brooks to run right through, allowing him to go hit the running back in the mouth. Offensive line coaches would scream bloody holding at the officials. In fact, there were some times when I thought my real name might be *Sapp's holding 'im*, because that's what the coaches were shouting, but it was a call the officials never made. Until 1997, when I came to camp and found out that the league had changed the rule. They told us we couldn't grab on to them anymore.

The league usually changed rules to increase safety for the players or increase scoring for the satisfaction of fans. When the league made a rule change they sent around a video illustrating what was no longer permitted. When they made the no holding video I was all over it. When I showed it to Brooks, I told him, "Now you see why you're making all them damn tackles."

In fact, pretty much every time they changed some rule and made a video to show what you could no longer do it ended up looking like my highlight reel. Defensive holding, adjusting the strike zone where you could hit somebody, running through another team's stretch; I felt like I was being trailed by the rule book. It didn't surprise me that they changed some of those rules. I pushed the existing rules to the outer limits.

When they changed the defensive holding rule I had two options: Follow the new rule or don't get caught holding. Just like a rearview mirror has a blind spot, there are blind spots on a football field, places where you can get away with things because the official can't see you. Every player knows exactly where the officials are positioned and what they can see from that spot and when they are screened. If I went to the backside of the player I knew I could still hold him a little bit without being called for it. If the NFL moved the officials just a few yards in any direction they would be calling a whole different game. Two seasons after I retired they moved the official behind the line. It makes it impossible for him to see holding inside. It was just a small change, the fans didn't even notice it, but when I read about it I thought, oh my goodness, they have just brought back defensive holding. Made me sad that I had retired.

The biggest penalty that I know for absolute certain the officials missed took place during a game we played against the Green Bay Packers. They were always our biggest rival, and those games we played against them were wars; each team was looking for every single advantage. Near the end of the first half Favre had found his rhythm. He'd moved the Packers about 60 yards downfield, and they were on about our 35, just a couple of yards out of relatively easy field-goal range. On second and long we flushed him out of the pocket, and he took off running along the sideline. Get him, get him! Even just writing this down I want to tackle his ass. Whitey caught up with him just short of the first-down marker, and the two of them went down in a jumble right at the sideline. It looked like a regular play, but next thing I knew the Packers called a timeout and reserve quarterback Doug Pederson was jogging into the game. On third down Pederson threw an incomplete pass, and they were forced to punt.

As I walked to the sideline I looked over at the Packers' bench, and Favre was just sitting there, tying his shoes. He looked fine to me. I said to Culpepper, "What's that all about? What do you think happened on that play?"

Brad had this devious little smile. "When I tackled him I ripped his shoe off," he told me. "And when I rolled over I picked it up and flipped it right into the stands. The officials didn't see it. That's why he left the game; he had to get a new shoe."

The most amazing thing about officials is how good they are at their job. While everybody complains about penalties, in fact it is very rare for a game to end or be turned around by a penalty. Generally penalties even out over the course of a game or a season. Notice that I'm writing this after I'm retired and have nothing to gain by praising the officials. The one thing that players ask for from officials is consistency. If it wasn't a penalty in the first quarter it damn well better not be a penalty in the fourth quarter. Basically what officials want to avoid is making a questionable call that turns a game around or ends it. The worst calls of all are those that are technically correct but not in the spirit of the rules. In September 2010, for example, the Lions' Calvin Johnson made a fine leaping catch in the end zone that should have given Detroit the lead over Chicago with less than a minute to go in the game. The man caught the ball, got free of the defender, and went down. Both his knees touched the ground, one arm touched the ground, and then he sort of put the ball down on the ground. Touchdow . . . Whistle! Whoa. The officials ruled it an incomplete pass, explaining that according to the rule—certainly not common sense—by laying it down on the ground he had not maintained control of the ball throughout the entire catch. The Bears won the game on that foolish technicality. It was a ridiculous call. Johnson clearly caught the pass, but technically it was the correct call.

I didn't get called for too many penalties during my career, and I never got called for a penalty that affected the outcome of the game. Well, maybe with the exception of those three unsportsmanlike conduct penalties that I got within five minutes. My penalties were usually committed out in the open, where the officials could see them. One time, for example, I had hold of Drew Bledsoe and he didn't know enough to go down, so I picked him up and put him down. Whistle! Flag! Unsportsmanlike conduct no. 99, roughing the passer. It was a good thing for me that they didn't have a penalty for trying to plant a passer.

Some penalties can't be helped. On the play that Jerry Rice got hurt I just reached out and swiped at him, and my pinkie got caught in his grill. It was a face-mask penalty, but it was not intentional. That type of penalty is almost impossible to prevent. It is going to happen. But offside? There is no excuse for an offside penalty, none, although eventually pretty much at some time in his career every lineman goes offside. And when you are called offside the only thing you can do is stand there with your hands on your hips thinking, how stupid am I, and rooting for that clock to hurry up and move so you can put a play between you and the penalty.

We spent a lot of time practicing not to jump offside on a hard count: *hut hut hut HUT*! Whistle! Fooled you, Sapp, we weren't hiking the ball. Nah nah. Five yards. Quarterbacks love to try it. And once in a while the good quarterbacks can influence the cadence and draw you in. Kent Graham was good at it; John Elway was fantastic; if he drew a D-lineman offside he would stand there beaming like a little kid who stole the teacher's Apple iPod. Steve DeBerg was unbelievable at it, Dan Marino may be the record holder for drawing people offside.

In practice if somebody on the D-line got drawn offside by a hard count, oh my God, we were all over him. How stupid are you? Why don't we just tie a string from the ball to your nose so you won't move till it gets pulled? You having trouble with thinking or counting?

Centers also tried to draw linemen offside. Baggadonuts was the best at it; he'd move the ball, he'd fake snap it, he'd spin the ball, everything just barely legal. Every single time he snapped the ball he would do the same move, maybe raise his head an instant before he actually snapped it, and eventually we would notice it and start looking for it. When Frankie moved his head, he was snapping the ball. Got it. But late in a game, when five yards really mattered, he'd make that same move—only the ball would still be sitting there. Whistle! Flag! Where you going so fast Sapp? And Frankie would stand there smiling as innocent as Jack the Ripper.

Truth is that the defense also tried to pull the offensive line offside. Here's a secret for you: Those boys on the O-line are not that bright. For an offensive line to be effective five people have to work in unison. One guy screws it up, the whole plan falls apart. To make it easy for their offensive linemen, quarterbacks try to establish a rhythm; they usually like to snap the ball on the same count. When the fans in the stadium are especially loud, making it difficult for the linemen to hear the signals, quarterbacks like to go on quick counts to reduce the chance of going offside. Don't want to confuse them boys by changing the snap count. Quarterbacks like to go on two—*hut hut*—a lot, so the D-line knew that when the offensive linemen sprinted out of the huddle and got right down on their knuckles it was going to be a quick count. I always watched offensive linemens' knuckles. If they shifted their weight back off their knuckles they were getting ready to pass block, but if I saw white knuckles they were pressing down to come forward to block for a runner. The rule is that when a quarterback is calling signals the defense is not allowed to make any noises that sound like a snap count; meaning you can't intentionally try to draw them offside. But every once in a while, a split-second before I sensed that the ball was going to be snapped, I would yell out "backSET!" real loud, and every time a guard or tackle would jump or the center would snap the ball. Calling out a word was legal; the defense was allowed to call defensive signals. Of course, *backset* didn't mean a damn thing, though it definitely sounds like it does. Everybody who moved would point at me, but they would point at me from five yards farther back. One time I made my call, and the center snapped the ball before the quarterback was ready—and fractured one of the quarterback's fingers.

Gotcha!

One thing that does happen that nobody will admit are make-up calls and home cooking. As difficult as it is for some players to accept, not me of course, officials are human beings too. Those aren't real stripes they're wearing. So when they hear the 65,857 fans, and my mother, screaming at them in Raymond James Stadium it isn't surprising when they respond. Just a little. Anybody who believes the officials don't hear the crowd needs to have a little conversation with my mother. Officials know when they miss a call, and when it does happen they will be a little extra careful. So no one on the field is real surprised when they make a call that hasn't been made since the Canton

Bulldogs played the Rock Island Independents in the NFL's first season, 1920. They may not be exactly make-up calls, but an official might hesitate to throw a second flag, or they might look a little harder for a holding call. It isn't that they're trying to cheat—they are not, absolutely not cheating—instead they're just trying to balance the playing field.

There is a legendary story they tell in the NFL about the Immaculate Reception. Who knows if it's true. In the 1972 AFC playoff game played in Pittsburgh, the Steelers were losing to the Raiders 7–6 with 22 seconds left in the game. They had a fourth-and-10 from their own 40. Terry Bradshaw threw it up, and halfback Frenchy Fuqua and Raiders' D-back Jack Tatum collided on the Raiders' 35-yard line. The ball bounced off someone, and just before it hit the ground running back Franco Harris plucked it right out of the air and ran it in for the game-winning touchdown. A lot of people believe that was the greatest play in NFL history. The Steelers even put up a statue of Harris making the catch outside their new stadium. The problem was that nobody knew if the catch was legal. The rulebook said it was illegal for two offensive players to touch a forward pass without it being touched by a defensive player. So unless the ball bounced off Tatum before Harris caught it, the catch was illegal, two Steelers had touched it without a Raider touching it, and Oakland won 7–6. There was no instant replay rule back then.

With the whole season on the line the officials huddled up, and the referee called up to the press box to speak with the supervisor of officials. But supposedly, while they were waiting for a decision, with the whole stadium just a big roaring bowl of noise, one official said flatly to another, "You do know that if we change this call we're never gonna make it out of Pittsburgh alive!"

These officials had to make a very difficult decision: What city did they prefer never ever being allowed to visit for the rest of their lives, assuming they lived, Pittsburgh or Oakland? Because whatever call they made their names were going to be printed in the newspaper

Monday morning. Finally, they ruled touchdown Steelers! No kidding. And they all lived happily ever after. Well, they were officials, so at least they lived.

There was one thing that the officials did that I just could not deal with. It drove me crazy. Here's the situation: Third down and 2. The running back takes the ball into the line, and the entire Mormon Tabernacle Choir falls on top of him. I mean, that pile is so high it's snowing on the player on top. An official digs out the ball, then flips it to another one, who takes three steps and puts the ball down. Then they bring out the first-down chain and they measure—the tippy-tip of the football is just beyond the marker. Like two inches over the first-down line. The official signals first down, and the offense gets a whole new set of downs. Then the whole crowd reacts.

Are you kidding me? Two inches? Ten inches? There is no possible way those officials can determine a runner's forward progress under that pile. Then they pick the ball up and toss it around like it's on fire—and finally they put it down careful like they had determined the exact spot with a slide rule. That kills me. I put my whole body in front of that man, I absorbed the best blow he could give me, I held most of my ground—and the officials give him an extra two feet through my stomach. Oh my goodness, why did I even bother? The ref at the top marks a spot with his front foot, the official at the bottom marks it with his back foot—and then they put it in the middle. When I hated the spot the officials gave us I'd complain to them, "Oh c'mon, how do you mark that ball right there. At the end of this drive that's going to mean something. Y'all don't get it man."

My complaints never made an inch of difference. They had put that ball down just like they actually knew where it belonged, and nothing I could say would change their minds. To me, the way officials marked the ball was the most frustrating part of the game. Everything else I could deal with. Every other call they would get mostly right, and when they were wrong they usually were wrong evenly for both teams.

The penalty calls I could deal with even when I didn't agree with them, but oh those spots. We'd fight the whole game for a couple of inches, and then the officials would just give it away. It made me sick.

Unless the spot went our way, of course.

The one play I hated more than any other was third and inches. Third and inches, can we stop them? Can the defense rise to the occasion? No they cannot. I hated that play. We almost never stopped them on third and inches, and unless it was on the goal line it made no difference. The only way to stop it was to chop down the center and the two guards so our linebackers could see where the ball was going and step over the top to get to the ball carrier before he reached the line of scrimmage. We had to submarine in there and cut their legs off. That gave me a headache and I hated it. One inch, two inches, the quarterback sneaks straight ahead and disappears under a pile. And that official is going to mark him shy an inch? No, it did not happen that way. I always wanted to tell them just go ahead and call it a first down, and let's line back up and play the game.

Now on the goal line, that's different. Those inches of real estate in front of the goal line might be more valuable than downtown Manhattan. Goal-line stands are so tough that defensive players remember them the same way offensive players remember long touchdown runs or great receptions. The greatest goal-line stand of my career took place on September 9, 2001, at Cowboys Stadium. The very first series of downs of the first game of the new season, Dallas' new quarterback Quincy Carter moved them down to our 1-yard line. Maybe even our half-yard line. First and goal at the one-half. This is the first set of downs of the season; the last thing you want to do is allow a touchdown. It just doesn't feel right to start the season that way. But back there in the Cowboys' backfield they had Emmitt Smith, one of the best running backs I ever played against. And blocking for him was Larry Allen. Are you kidding me? Emmitt Smith had 94 touchdown runs of one yard or less in his career. Larry Allen was one of the greatest and strongest players in league history; the man once bench-pressed 692 pounds. Trust me, you did not stop Emmitt Smith on the 1-yard line with Larry Allen blocking for him.

Except this time. First down, Emmitt ran into a wall. I mean, an immovable wall. Nothing. But now we had his attention. On second down, Carter ran a little bootleg, and we stopped him before he could get outside. I loved that call. You got Emmitt Smith standing there, and you let Quincy Carter run with it? Thank you very much. Third down, Carter handed the ball to Smith. No kidding. Emmitt went outside. I came up out of my block and took off after him. Brooks was coming too. Lynch was right behind us, but the only player who had a real shot at him was our little cornerback, Brian Kelly. Brian Kelly was 5'11", 193 pounds, and he was a good kid, but he was not known for being overly aggressive. There was no malice in his heart. But Brian put up one of the best fights over one yard I have ever seen. He refused to yield, holding him up long enough for help to arrive. Brian dropped him for a 3-yard loss. That goal-line stand on the first series of downs turned out to be the difference in the ballgame. On fourth down Dallas kicked a 21-yard field goal. That was the closest they came to a touchdown—and we beat them 10–6.

One brief conversation I did have with an official I'll never forget took place inside Seattle's Kingdome. I put a slick move on the guard, faked going inside, and when he leaned that way I gave him a little push to help him along and went to his outside shoulder. Then I ran up quarterback Jon Kitna's numbers. Kitna had his back to me; he was looking for a weak-side receiver so he didn't see me coming. The only thing between me and Kitna was time. There is that one instant surge of excitement when you realize, he is mine, but you got to get to him before he releases the ball. Most of the time you don't. But for that one split-second, when the quarterback is holding the ball up by his shoulder, it looks as big as the Thanksgiving turkey sitting on a serving platter. Your eyes laser in on it just sitting there. In Tampa we used to practice hacking at a quarterback's arm. Marinelli actually had a hacking drill where we'd whack away at the quarterback's arm trying to cause a fumble. There were some quarterbacks who held the ball loosely. Drew Bledsoe, for instance, until he learned the death grip, we could always slap the ball out of his hands. But on the field you've got less than an instant to decide whether to go for the body or the ball. Most times you don't go for the ball. The ball and the man are equally valuable, and you don't want to miss the man by going for the ball and maybe letting him complete the pass. Basically, you reach for the closest body part and hope it's his throwing arm. But you'd happily take a head.

On this play, instead of sacking Kitna I dragged down his arm, and just before he hit the ground I grabbed the ball right out of his hand. I took it right out. It was instinctive. The official was on the other side, and I was afraid he had been screened and missed it. So I looked right at him and said, "You saw me take it, right?"

"Yes I did, son." Thank you very much, I thought, you are a fine man, and I did my little *Dancing with the Stars* audition.

A D-lineman can't accurately be defined by statistics. Every move a quarterback, running back, or receiver makes on the field has some kind of number attached to it: Carries, yards, attempts, completions, drops, first downs, longest catch, yards after catches, total offense, touchdowns, sneezes, yards in the red zone, yards out of the red zone, third-down yardage, speeding tickets—everything is recorded and compared. Even defensive backs can be judged by how many times the quarterback threw at him, how many completions he allowed, and for how many yards. At most positions the game can be measured statistically, but not on the line. Not really.

As far as fans are concerned, our performance is judged by those things they can see and hear: Tackles, sacks, fumbles caused, and interceptions. And big hits, of course. Some teams keep track of pressures, but in Tampa we didn't, because *pressure* means you didn't actually get there. Close, but no quarterback. Me and Whitey used to dream about hitting for the cycle: Sacking the quarterback, causing him to fumble, recovering the fumble yourself, and taking it in for a touchdown. I never managed to do that. The best I managed was three out of four. In addition to Kitna, I caused fumbles that I recovered. I just never scored. Came close, real close. One time against the Chiefs I put a nasty move on Will Shields and got to Elvis Grbac just as he was reaching back to throw. I slapped his arm and the ball came loose. It hit the ground, bounced straight up into the air, and fell right into my hands. That was the picture on my football card one year. Against the Bears I hit Erik Kramer's arm, and the ball went flying up in the air. I caught it and took off running. I was on my way to my first career cycle: I got the sack, fumble, recovery, and I was chugging toward the end zone. I was on my way to a career highlight. The big fella was about to make the opening of *SportsCenter*. Instead, Erik Kramer tackled me at the 10-yard line and brought me down. The quarterback tackled me. That couldn't happen: Quarterbacks don't tackle nobody. They are warned not to risk hurting their pretty little selves, and they certainly do not tackle a 300-pound D-lineman pounding his way to glory. But when Kramer lost that ball he must have lost his mind too—he threw himself at me and made the cycle-saving tackle. And just in case I didn't know who it was that brought me down my teammates were very happy to remind me. And remind me. "Who was that who caught you again?" Ten yards, that's how close I came to hitting it.

Instead of getting on *SportsCenter*, that fumble recovery actually cost me $2,500. My homeboys were sitting in the end zone, so after I got tackled I tried to throw them the ball. The league fined me $2,500 for throwing a ball in the stands. Now that was really unfair; I didn't throw it in the stands. My pass didn't even reach the stands.

I almost had another triple against the Falcons. In October 2002 we were in Atlanta for a nationally televised game, and those idiots had waxed the field to make it look nice and shiny on TV. You understand what I'm saying? They shined the football field. As a result it was like trying to run on glass; we were slipping all over the place. We had to put on our turf shoes to get any traction at all. In the fourth quarter we were winning 13–6 when Atlanta got the ball deep in their own territory. Their quarterback, Doug Johnson, dropped back and in my mind I can still see Simeon Rice and Greg Spires converging on him like two pieces of bread about to become a sandwich. It was all happening in slow motion. He's gonna get hit, I thought, and that ball is coming out here somewhere. Just as Johnson got set to release it . . . oh my goodness, they hit him. The ball came wobbling toward me. I jumped into the air and caught it, officially an interception, and took off for the end zone. I was a few yards out when a guard grabbed my leg and held on, and suddenly I heard the greatest voice I have ever known shouting, "Doom! Doom! Doom!" It was Derrick Brooks; we called each other "Room Doom." I didn't even look back; I just pitched it to him. He caught it with one hand and ran it in. Touchdown! Touchdown: 20–6!

Atlanta coach Dan Reeves threw the challenge flag. It slid about 10 yards on the polished field. He was furious and claimed I'd lateraled the ball forward. He had nothing to lose by throwing that flag. He had a challenge left, and he couldn't take it home with him, couldn't use it at the store, so he might as well spend it here. I shouted over to him, "Buddy, I don't know what y'all challenging for. That's a touchdown." And that was the call.

There are just no statistics that accurately measure the contribution made by a D-lineman during a game. Squeezing a block, for example. Offensive linemen try to create a hole in the line for the running back by establishing position on either side of that hole. What defensive linemen try to do is close that hole, or at least condense it, by pushing the offensive lineman into it. That enables someone else to make the tackle. The best running backs I played against were Emmitt Smith, Barry Sanders, and Marshall Faulk. All of them had the ability to take it to the house on any play. They had the ability to see a hole and be in it before it closed up and then make their cut. And if there was no hole they could make one. They were always moving, always shaking. As far as I was concerned they weren't down on the ground until we were lining up for the next play. Barry Sanders especially. What made him so difficult to bring down was that he was unbelievably quick and totally unpredictable. He was the only back I ever played against who could go full speed in one direction, then reverse like he'd smacked into a wall, then be going full speed the opposite way. Tackling him was like grabbing cotton candy. What he could do that made him especially difficult to bring down was create his own holes. Ball carriers usually follow their blockers—not Barry Sanders. If he didn't like the way the play was developing he'd go his own way. We'd hit him behind the line of scrimmage for a two- or three-yard loss, and next play he would hit us for 80. We tried to stop him by squeezing the hole and funneling him directly toward John Lynch. There is no stat for squeezing a hole, no way for the fan to know what happened on the field, but doing it correctly and repeatedly will make a huge difference in the outcome.

There is a completely different scale by which linemen should be judged, a scale that records all those intangibles the fans don't see. In Tampa, Rod Marinelli's grading system accurately measured a lineman's impact on the game. This scale included things like factors, loafs, penalties, OG (or on ground), missed assignments, missed gap, missed tackle, and mental errors. These are the real requirements of the position.

After a game the first statistic I looked at was my factor grade. Most fans never even heard of it, but to me this was the number that defined how well I had played. The factor grade measures the number of plays in which a player was a factor. One play out of four is considered a pretty good factor grade. My objective was always one out of three, which meant I played a role in at least one play every series of downs. The 2000 NFC Championship Game against St. Louis was one of the best games of my career, although statistically it doesn't look like I even bothered to show up. I had a triple 0 that game; on the stat sheet it read: zero/zero, zero, no tackles, no assists, no sacks. But I can watch that tape over and over proudly because I was so solid in my assignment. The only people who knew that were my coaches and teammates. We went into that game with a specific defensive strategy designed to stop Marshall Faulk. It required me to shut down my side. It wasn't glamorous; I basically just had to protect my territory. By staying home I allowed the rest of our defense to fulfill their assignments. Oh my goodness, at times I was so tempted to go rogue, to go get a sack, but I didn't try it. I knew that if I went rogue our entire defensive scheme could collapse, and Marshall would bang his head on the goal post maybe three times. That was an example of the discipline that the coaches demanded in Tampa. The fans looked at the newspaper, saw those numbers, and probably wondered, was Sapp away on vacation? He must have had another appointment because I don't see any numbers next to his name. But in that game I fulfilled my assignment, and I got a strong factor grade.

As much as I wanted to be in the middle of every play, that was impossible—although at the beginning of my career I definitely tried. I never slowed down. I went 110 percent on every play. I was a proud Miami boy showing no signs of distress. Every down I would sprint toward the football to try to disrupt the play. I was trying to win the damn game by myself. I had to learn that there were times to hit the highway and times to pull into that rest stop. Most fans believe players go all-out all the time, but that's a myth. Marinelli had to teach me that there were times you just went through the motions and breathed to block another day. On a hot day in Tampa in 1997 Barry Sanders broke loose for an 80-yard touchdown run, and I chased him every step. Trust me, I knew I wasn't going to catch Barry Sanders, but I didn't know any other way to play. The reality is that on every play as many as five people on the defense will not be involved at all. Marinelli took me aside and told me that there are "ungettable plays, plays on which there is no way you can get to the ball." Instead of expanding all that energy, and, admittedly, after chasing somebody for 80 yards it would take me two or three plays to get my wind back, he wanted me to make the initial effort, but when it was clear this one wasn't coming my way, I should just ease up. It took me a little while to accept the fact that at times it is not only permissible, but it is desirable to give a medium effort.

At Tampa we had tremendous confidence in each other. On a pass play I would turn and make sure somebody was there to make the tackle before I took off hell-bent for glory. There wasn't any sense in pursuing a play that Brooks or Lynch or Ronde was going to make. No need to race over there just to congratulate them. What I did on those plays was take my two hard steps, that's what we demanded, two hard steps, moving toward the play. The maximum I was going to go full-out was 10 yards. After that I wasn't going to catch up anyway so I went into conserve gear. The same thing was true when the offense ran a play to the weak side of the line. Within a second it was obvious I wasn't going to be involved in that play so I would take two hard steps and then shut it down. The offensive lineman knew he wasn't going to be in the play either, so the two of us would la-di-da it a little bit, but we wouldn't give it the all-out rocket-blasting rip-'em-apart attack. People in the stands wouldn't notice any difference, they didn't even notice us when we were in attack mode, but as Rod used to tell on some plays it was perfectly fine to keep my motor running in neutral because, "I'm gonna need you in the fourth quarter to be that dynamic rusher in our two-minute drill."

I hated being taken out of a game, but I trusted Marinelli. There were games when I'd be in the rhythm, I was feeling the protection, I knew what the offense was trying to do to us, I'd gotten a couple of good whacks at the quarterback, and suddenly on third down Rod would grab me and tell me, "Take one."

What?

"Take one."

I understood, but our agreement was that if they made a first down or if they moved inside our 40-yard line I was putting myself back in the game.

The important thing was to know when to conserve energy. Doing it at the wrong time was called a *loaf*. Oh, I hated those loafs. A loaf was when you didn't go full force, or didn't turn and chase a ball carrier, didn't follow a play when you had the opportunity to be a factor. At the most I would end up with two or three loafs a game. If I had four that was a bad day for me. Sometimes Rod and I would pleasantly discuss this. At times every player has to make a deal with the devil and go a little softer to keep some fuel in the tank.

There also was a category called *OG*, on the ground. That meant that somebody put your fat ass on the ground. *On the ground* basically meant beaten, defeated, knocked down. There is no way you can make a play when you're on your stomach. For me, *loaf* and *OG* were the worst things on Rod's sheet.

I also hated those MEs, mental errors. There is never an excuse for making a mental error. No matter what broadcasters like me tell you, for a lineman the game is not that complicated. A mental error is like being a blind dog in a meat house; it means you got no awareness of what is going on around you. For example, failing to recognize a screen play. There was also something we referred to as *rushing behind the quarterback*, which was considered a mental error. Our rule at Tampa was that a rusher never went deeper than the quarterback. Once you got on the same plane as him, you stopped; so even if you couldn't get to him he couldn't go outside. It was a way of directing the play into the middle of the field. To stop a great scrambler like Michael Vick, for example, we had to take away parts of the field, funneling him into tacklers. So rushing behind the passer was an ME. One time we were watching film, and defensive end Eric Curry was 17 yards up the field. That is not an exaggeration; he was 17 yards behind the line of scrimmage. What was he doing way back there, completely out of the play? The only person he could tackle from back there was the referee. No quarterback in history has ever dropped back 17 yards on a pass play. That was considered an ME.

Most people don't realize it, but I did compile some impressive offensive statistics too. In fact, it's completely accurate to say that I am one of the most proficient pass receivers in NFL history, thank you very much. I had four passes thrown to me, I caught all of them, and I took two of them for first downs and two of them for touchdowns. Maybe I'm no Mike Vrabel, the Patriots linebacker who caught 10 passes for 10 touchdowns, although most of those were in postseason games. But among linemen I'm right up there with the legendary Fridge, William Perry, who caught one touchdown pass and rushed for two more. I had a perfect record, four for four with two TDs. I didn't even do that well playing on the Dust Bowl. I averaged 9.8 yards a catch, with my longest being 18 yards. Go ahead, name me one other handsome D-lineman who scored on half of all his receptions.

Looking back over my brief career as a receiver I made my most difficult catch in New Orleans. Brad Johnson was our quarterback. This was appropriate since Brad Johnson is still the only quarterback in NFL history to catch his own batted pass and take it in for a touchdown. But on my touchdown the ball was snapped and I missed my block. I kept going into the end zone. Brad just threw it up. I leaped up into the air and I reached for the ball—then I lost sight of the damn thing in the Superdome's lights. I knew it was out there somewhere so I just reached out for it. I finally saw it as I started to come down. I grabbed it, kicked it up into the air once, kicked it again, and then held on to it. Complete! Touchdown!

I ran up to Brad, and the first thing he said to me was, "You missed your block."

"No shit, but . . ." I explained to him that I had two guys on me. "I had to take the inside guy, he's more dangerous. You never would have gotten your head around."

"You missed your block," he said again.

"I knew once you got turned around you'd throw it, and I was out there wide open."

He agreed. "I didn't see you at all. I turned around, and all I saw was the outside guy in my face. I just told myself, I hope he's out there somewhere."

That was our strategy for that play: Hope he's out there somewhere. Even with all the planning, the meetings, the practices, the studying, watching the films, sometimes that's what the game comes down to: I hope he's out there somewhere.

Go ahead and ask Eli Manning if he ever saw David Tyree when he threw that pass that ended up winning the XLII Super Bowl.

There definitely were some aspects of the game I was not going to miss when I retired. Basically, I was banged up, bruised, and played in some type of pain for my entire career. That's true of every football player. To play the game you have to learn to ignore pain. The way we described it was, "You don't make the club in the tub." The last thing I did every week before running out on the field every game was go see the doc and tell him, "Hit me." He'd give me a shot of Toradol, with a little B12 in it, which made me a little numb and dulled whatever pain I did have. Whitey would get injections in his knees and his feet so he could play. Other players would take as many as four Advil before a game to prevent or at least reduce the impact of a headache. Once you got a headache during a game there was no way of getting rid of it.

Unless a body part is broken, pulled, strained, snapped, cut, or diced, players rarely show pain during a game. That's the warrior mentality we all try to portray. But believe me, inside we are all wincing in pain. Basically, the rule is that if it's an upper-extremity injury you have to stay on your feet, but anything on your legs you can lay down.

Fingers, shoulders, arm, elbow—get your ass up. Thighs, quads, knees, ankles, toes—you can lay down.

I had an agreement with our trainer, Todd Toriscelli. When I got hurt the only thing I wanted to know was whether or not something was broken. That happened once, when I fractured two metacarpals in my hand the third game of the 1999 season against the world champion Denver Broncos. This was totally my fault. The Monday morning before this game Tony walked into our D-line meeting and said, "Fellas, I have some good news and some disappointing news. I'll give it to you straight. You got a great challenge coming up this Sunday to contain Terrell Davis. You know what the challenge is Warren?"

The walls at One Buc were really thin. You could hear right through them, and I knew that Brooks was meeting with his people on the other side of that wall. So I banged on the wall and answered Tony loudly, "Yeah, don't run past the draw Brooks!" Denver liked to run Davis on the draw, so Brooks had to be real careful not to be sucked in.

He responded through the wall, "Shut up, Sapp!"

Tony continued, "The good news is on third down you can forget about rushing the passer. They're not going to expose that young quarterback to you. That's when they're gonna run Davis on the draw." The young quarterback was Brian Griese.

On a second-and-7 deep in their territory I lined up over Mark Schlereth, who called himself Stink. I figured, considering the down, yardage, and location, it had to be a pass. Got to be a pass. Then I second-guessed myself. I remembered Tony's words: "They are not going to expose that young quarterback to you." Watch out for the draw. It's a draw, I decided—then I talked myself out of it. I decided to rush Griese. If I'd have played the draw and stayed back, I wouldn't have gotten hurt.

The ball was snapped and I took off. I beat ole' Stink off the ball. When he turned his shoulder toward me I grabbed it with one arm, pulled him back across my body, and then I jumped in the hole. It was a draw. Terrell Davis had the ball and was just about through that hole. I wrapped my arm around his chest from behind, held on to his jersey, and started to pull him down. Then I looked up—John Lynch was barreling straight at Davis. He had his nasty on. Oh my God! I felt like a door waiting to be hit by the battering ram. *Boom*! Lynch hit Davis right in the chest—and hit my hand with the top of his helmet.

I felt like my hand was on fire. Shit! I rolled over and got up. "I'll be right back, y'all . . ." Even before I got to the sideline I was yelling, "Get me a bottle of water, get me some water." One of our assistants handed me a bottle of water. I screamed at him, "Take the top off." I poured that whole bottle of ice-cold water over my hand. It made sense to me: My hand was on fire and I was putting it out.

Oh man, that hurt. Todd cut the tape off and took hold of my hand. As he did I heard *click click*. I knew that wasn't good. My hand wasn't supposed to be making *click click* noises. "You broke it," he said.

Shit. I looked over at my mom, and I mouthed the words, "I broke it." That made sense too. Who else do you turn to when you break something?

We had it X-rayed. I'd suffered a clean break of my third and fourth metatarsal. It was only a broken hand, nothing serious. At halftime Todd put a padded cast on it, and I played the second half.

The other time I broke bones in my hand it was a lot easier to diagnose—the bone was sticking clear out of my pinkie. This was in 1997 and we were in Detroit. I already had sacked Charlie Batch twice—I sacked him eight times in his career, second to Brett Favre,—and I had another clean shot at him. I missed him, and I hit the ground and landed on my hand. When I got up a bone was sticking out of my pinkie. There was just a little blood and the pain hadn't hit yet. I trotted to the sideline and showed it to Todd. As I did the TV cameras showed it to America. The announcers had to apologize. I told Doc

Diaco, "This is a two-cigarette job." We went inside, and he put the tendon back in and sewed it up. Then he gave me 1,000-mg Tylox, the big red pill, to dull the pain.

Next thing I knew I was as high as Georgia pine. I could barely stand up. Now, I'm not saying it felt bad, but it hit me. Todd asked me, "Your head all right?"

I smiled, a big wide smile, "I'm good!"

Going into the locker room to be X-rayed during the game was a weird damn feeling. I could hear the crowd reactions, the cheers, ooo's and ahhhh's, and I tried to follow the game by sound, but I really didn't know what was going on. Crowd noises give you a lot of general information but no details.

I never had a single concussion. Concussions in the NFL are about as common as oranges in Apopka. There's definitely no shortage of them, but I was lucky in my career. My first few years in the league I wore the heaviest helmet that was ever invented, Bike's Air helmet, which had a little air cushion inside. In 2000 they introduced a composite helmet with a foam pad about three inches thick. I liked it because when I stuffed my braids inside, it almost felt as if I was wearing a pillow on my head. The one time I should have suffered a concussion that helmet saved me. Here's the thing I learned that day: Fat boys shouldn't jump. We were in Minnesota. Vikings quarterback Warren Moon threw a little slant pass, and I jumped into the air to try to bat the ball. Defensive linemen are taught that there is no reason to leave your feet on a football field, but I jumped. While I was up in the air, running back Robert Smith took my legs right out from underneath my ass. I landed on the back of my head on that hard fucking Hubert H. Humphrey Metrodome floor. It was about as soft as cement, and I whacked the hell out of my head. My body folded over on top of me, and the next thing I knew I was eating my thighs. My stomach hit me in my face. That one hurt. Fortunately, the helmet absorbed some of the impact. When I got up on my feet the sideline turned vertical on me. The whole stadium was spinning. I thought, wow, I must be drunk. I felt seasick. Brooks asked, "What the fuck?"

"I'll be right back," I told him. "I just gotta put my head back on." I wobbled over to the sideline, and Todd grabbed hold of me.

I didn't have cobwebs in my head; I had chain-link fences. But it cleared up pretty quickly, and I was able to go back into the game. Since then the NFL has become a lot more careful about letting people play after a head injury. But at that time there was no problem. Long as you could count to five getting the numbers pretty much in order they cleared you to play.

I know how fortunate I was to play 17 years of major college and professional football without suffering an injury that would affect me for the rest of my life. I see people I played with and care about hobbling. I know the physical damage the game can do. While I did see some people get hurt, Rich Gannon was the only player who suffered a career-ending injury. And even he was able to walk off the field. In fact, the injuries I saw in high school were more severe than almost anything I saw on either the college or professional level. In the NFL I think the only person I saw carted off the field was Chad Clifton, and he came back to become an All-Pro.

Only one time did I laugh when someone got injured on the field. I was the Bucs' emergency place-kicker. Trust me on this, it would have had to be some emergency for me to actually get to kick in a game. But every once in a while I'd kick a few in practice. In a December 2003 game against Houston we scored late in the fourth quarter to go ahead 16–3. The game was pretty much decided, and Gruden had taken out most of the starters. But suddenly I heard him calling my name. Martin Gramatica felt a little twinge in his leg and couldn't kick off. But that was not when I laughed; nothing funny about your kicker hurting his leg. "Sapp! Go 'head and kick off." Oh boy, here we go. My chance to boom one. I took off my jacket, grabbed my helmet, and got set to run out on the field—but John Lynch stopped me. "I got it," he said.

I shrugged; it didn't really make any difference to me. "All right, go 'head."

Lynch asked me, "You okay with this?" Sure, I told him, and he went racing out there. The kickoff team lined up, and Lynch booted it—and started limping down the field. He'd pulled a quadricep. Oh my God, I'm still laughing. Even John Lynch had to admit it was pretty funny.

After a game you actually don't even know how badly your body is damaged until you get in the hot shower and start soaping up. That's when you felt that first sting. And second, third . . . Oh, that shower hurt. Every little nick and cut started barking. I usually didn't even notice when I got most of those nicks. Bumps, bruises, and cuts are so common you don't even notice them during the game. The good thing was that I was so banged up the pain was evenly distributed. It seemed like everything hurt evenly. So in addition to taking painkillers, the first thing I always did when I got home was have a nice stiff alcoholic beverage.

The biggest challenge Monday morning was getting out of bed. Sometimes I had to begin the day by apologizing to my body. From my head to my toes I was feeling every last play. Even after a game in which I barely got bruised, my hands, wrists, and ankles would be throbbing, and sometimes my elbows. Elbows can get scraped, especially on an artificial surface, and they burn like hell. I never did like playing on an artificial surface; it made you feel like you'd played two games. By the time I got to the job Monday morning there usually were so many people in the training room I practically had to take a number. We would all climb into the whirlpools and start talking about the game, talking about the little hurts and the big hits. Nobody got any sympathy; nobody was feeling sorry for anybody else. A lot of big-bang stories were told in those cold tubs. That's where I really got to know our special teams players. Trust me, as bad as my D-line people got banged up, the special teams personnel got whacked a lot worse.

The weather also affected how I felt Monday morning. I'm a Florida boy; I love the heat. For me, the warmer it was the happier I was. A man works in the good Lord's sun. That's the way it is supposed to be. I remember one time Monte Kiffin thought it was too hot to be practicing outside during the day so we worked at night. I explained to him that we were playing our games in Florida, that other teams would not be used to playing in the heat, and it would wear them down. He paid no attention at all. I always heard people saying seriously that 15 degrees was football weather. I'd hear that and I would think, you must be out of your mind. Hey, I'm freezing to death, it's a great day for football. If that was true we'd be playing football at the damn North Pole. Where did that thought come from?

When the schedule was published I'd look at it, and if we were playing in Green Bay or Chicago in December I'd be dreading it for months. Of course I loved Detroit and Minnesota because we played indoors—it was always a perfect 70 degrees with no chance of rain. There were some players who didn't mind the cold. In the locker room before a game in the cold, for example, Hardy Nickerson would rub Vaseline on his arms and challenge us, "I know it's cold. But I'm going out there without any damn sleeves. Who's going with me?"

Uh, no. Sorry there, Hardy. That would not be me. Instead, I would put on every piece of clothing I could find. Monte Kiffin used to complain that I was wearing so many layers I couldn't move. I told him, "I don't tell you what to wear when you're calling plays, so you don't tell me what to wear to go play."

Coldest temperature I ever played in was a wind chill of minus 11 on the field in Green Bay. I'm sure some newspaper was reporting that the Bucs had never won a game when the temperature was below minus 10. It was just brutally cold. I never experienced anything like it. Before the game started I went up to the referee and handed him four hot pockets, bags of a liquid that generated heat. I told him, "We got to work together today because it is cold out here. Keep these in your pockets, and when I ask you for one, you hand it over. If you're busy just tell me to wait, but when I need my hands, I need my hands. This way you're going to be half warm, and I'm going to be half warm."

"Warren," he said thankfully, "we have a deal." And it worked just fine.

It was so cold in Green Bay that day that I cracked my helmet. Literally, I cracked my helmet. I had just started wearing the lighter composite helmet. During the game I came over to the sideline, and our equipment manager told me, "Lemme see your helmet." He looked it over, and the next thing I knew they were changing the shell. "You cracked it," he said.

Cracked my helmet? I knew that wasn't good. I had never heard of that happening. "The company called us," he explained. "They warned us that their helmets can crack in the extreme cold if they get hit hard enough. You've been hitting with your hat."

Like a lot of players, I was a little superstitious about my hat, but I was a lot more superstitious about playing with a cracked helmet. "Go ahead and fix it," I said. For the rest of the game each time I came off the field they would inspect it. It cracked just that once, but once was more than enough.

Worse than just cold was snow. Oh my God, did I hate playing in snow. It is wet, it is slippery, it is nasty. My game was speed and foot-work. When I had to play on a wet, slippery track I got turned into an ordinary player. One time in college we played in a snowstorm in Pittsburgh. We were dominant that day. I had two sacks and definitely could have had more. Instead I told Dwayne Johnson, who was back-ing me up, "You see that stuff coming down from the sky? No, thank you, you go 'head and take it. I'll just stand over here on the sideline."

I loved playing in the heat. Naturally. My very first home game in Tampa was also the hottest game of my career. It was about 115 de-grees on the field. It felt like the field was on fire, like the devil himself was on the 50-yard line welcoming me to the NFL. It was like playing inside a light bulb. I had grown up in Florida. I had lived there my whole life, and that was the hottest day I remember. It actually was worse on the sideline than playing in the game because if I stood in one spot too long my feet started burning right through my cleats. On the field, at least, I was moving around. I spent the whole game pouring water over my shoes.

Actually playing in the heat wasn't difficult. I kept hydrated and took a lot of potassium to prevent cramping. By the fourth quarter that day people were dropping, but I still had fuel in my tank. The mental part of the game is being able to perform consistently at a high level in any type of conditions. To me, practice wasn't only for working on plays. When I was coming up I always looked to the people who had been there before me to see what they did, people like Hardy Nickerson, so when I got established as an All-Pro I knew I had to set an example for other players. If they saw me sweating and bleeding and busting it in practice the smart ones were going to do the same thing. There are a lot of people who had long careers in the NFL because they followed my example. Every single coach I played for in the NFL will agree that I never gave less than a total effort in practice. I'm not bragging about it, I'm stating a fact. Even when I let myself get out of shape I practiced hard. It wasn't always easy, there were times I got my teammates angry by pushing them too hard in practice, but those long days on a boiling-hot field in August translated into having your legs in the last two minutes of the fourth quarter of a game in November. Practicing in terrible conditions on Wednesday prepared me for whatever was coming on Sunday.

While showing no signs of discomfort.

In fact, as defensive captain I liked the heat so much that I would not allow them to turn on those big cooling fans on the sideline. I wanted my boys hot and ready; didn't want them cooling down and comfortable. One time in Carolina the people on the sideline insisted on turning on those fans. I explained to the individual in charge that we did not use them, we did not want them, and asked him very kindly not to turn them on. He turned them on. I explained once again that we would not be needing them and asked him politely to please turn them off. He told me that it was stadium policy that they had to be on. At which time I walked over to the fans and ripped the power cord right out of the back of the fans. "We won't be needing these things," I said.

There was one weather condition that I was not prepared for. We were getting ready to start a game in Denver when there was a flash of white lightning followed almost instantly by the loudest thunder clap I have ever heard. It shook the stadium. It literally shook the stadium. Thank you very much, I'll be leaving right now. Us Florida boys know all about being outside during a thunderstorm. Trust me, there ain't gonna be no fried Sapp. We ran back into the locker room and waited there for the storm to pass. The start of the game had to be delayed. That was fine by me.

When I finally accepted the reality that it was time for me to retire I told my mother that I just couldn't go anymore. I'd had enough. But it affected her life too. For nearly two decades she and my aunt, Ola Jones, had been going to almost all of my games. My mother attended several hundred football games, and when we look back on it, we both can say with pride that she never physically fought anybody.

She never did like flying very much, but no matter where we were playing she and Ola would get on an airplane and follow the team. I always rented a car for them so they could be on their own, but we usually had dinner together on Saturday night. My aunt was always their designated driver, because no matter how much traffic there was Ola would keep up with me. Keep up? My sweet little auntie could have been driving for NASCAR. When she was following me, she didn't let anything get in her way. If I happened to cut through a couple lanes of traffic, she'd be right behind me—even if sometimes that meant going up on the median. She stayed with me bumper to bumper. Ola philosophy of driving was pretty simple: "Don't worry about me, Warren. Whatever happens I know you'll always be there to bail me out."

If I wasn't playing my mom wasn't going to go to the games, and for almost two decades those games had played an important role in their lives. Maybe I was hanging up my uniform, but she was hanging up her signs. She was going to have nobody to yell at from the stands. All she asked me was, "You're sure now?"

I nodded, "It's time."

She thought about that silently for a few seconds, and then she said, "You know what, maybe I'll just go on out and watch Mercedes's soccer games."

Uh oh. "Mama?" I said.

"Oh, don't you go worrying about it. Maybe I'll just bring one little sign."

EIGHT

I wasn't going to have football to kick around anymore. For just about my whole life everything had revolved around the next practice, the next game, the next season. And for the first time, there wasn't going to be a next season. Believe me, playing in the NFL does not prepare you for anything except playing in the NFL. I had mastered my position, but the problem was that I had a complete set of skills, which were not transferrable. In almost any other profession when you take a new job you can utilize at least some of the skills you learned at the old place. But if I ran up to some guy in the street, knocked his briefcase to the ground, and then dived on it, chances are pretty good I would have been arrested. I mean, you can't sack a salesman.

If you've been a successful professional athlete there is no way to prepare for the rest of your life. You can't practice retiring. Besides football, the only thing that I had ever thought about doing was law enforcement, and even if I had wanted to do that I was too old and too big to start all over again. Culpepper had been a little different; he had earned his law degree while playing in the NFL. I had spent almost 40 years doing the one thing that made me happiest, and suddenly it was time to find the next thing.

That can be real tough. For a lot of athletes the adjustment is hard, and the outcome isn't always great. There is a lot of temptation in this world when you got money in your pocket and time on your hands. In 1994, I remember, I was with some people in Miami one night when somebody walked in and said, "Y'all ain't gonna believe this, but Mike Tyson is on his knees in a tuxedo shooting dice out in the air." We got into our cars and raced over to 15th Avenue to see this. It was just like the man said; there was the past and future heavyweight champion Mike Tyson on his knees on the sidewalk, wearing a tuxedo, playing craps. Obviously Tyson was still fighting, but there was something sad about that scene.

Finding my future was a real challenge. I've always had a lot of interests, a lot of ways of filling my time. I play a little trombone and keyboard, but I was never going to be in any band. Warren and the Sacks? I don't think so. I love fishing, oh I do love fishing, but I knew I couldn't spend my life fishing. Growing up, my grandfather and my brother Arnell would always ask me if I wanted to go fishing with them. Fishing? I told them, "I don't like fishing, I like catching." When I go fishing, I come back with a fish. I don't have any "one that got away" stories because when I put my hook in the water they do not get away. Fish and quarterbacks best beware of Warren. When I went fishing on ESPN's *Outdoor Sportsman* I caught a 165-pound bull shark. But the one I remember most was a little bitty one. I was down in Key West with my boys yellowtail fishing. That is gentle fishing; you lay out your line and wait. Suddenly, a couple of seconds apart my friend Ricky Bonvie and I both got a hit. We were standing back to back and pulling. He pulled, I pulled. "Uh, Rick," I told him, "I think we caught the same fish." No way. "I'll show you." I pulled my line up and his line went down. That couldn't be a coincidence. We pulled the fish out of the water, and this yellowtail no bigger than my hand had both hooks and lines in its mouth. That was either the dumbest or the greediest fish I ever saw. So I love fishing, but I knew I wasn't going to spend the rest of my life throwing a line in the water.

There was some talk that I should try professional wrestling. I did wrestle a crocodile once. A big one. Before wrestling a crocodile you have got to learn the strategy. The strategy is, don't get bit. That's it, that's the strategy. Otherwise you can do anything you want to do. My old Miami teammate the Rock made a good living at wrestling, but it definitely was not my future.

I went skiing for the first time with my family. Skiing had always looked like it might be fun to me, except for that part about the snow. Growing up in Florida skiing did not come naturally to me. Not only do we not have snow, we don't even have mountains. I lived my life at sea level, I do not like heights. I don't even like balconies, so going all the way up to the top of a mountain where it was really cold just so I could slide down the mountain did not really appeal to me. Thank you, but I'm already down. I'll just wait right here by the beer. But JaMiko had a great argument: Mercedes and Warren II, the Captain and Deuce. If I wanted to spend time on vacation with my kids, I was going skiing.

We went to Beaver Creek, Colorado. JaMiko and the kids were all good skiers. To prepare for the trip I went to the ski shop and bought, basically, one of everything in the place. I had thermal clothing, waterproof clothing, jackets, gloves, hand warmers, wool caps, and a unisuit to cover it all. When I put it all on I looked like the Michelin Man. I waddled out to the slope, and JaMiko asked me, "Why are you wearing all that stuff?"

I told her, "I don't want to get cold."

She looked me up and down, shook her head, and said knowingly, "Oh, I wouldn't worry about that." Then she asked me why I had ski poles.

"For skiing," I said. I mean, excuse me, but they are called *ski* poles, right? You got to have those poles to hold you up.

"Ski poles aren't used for balance," she explained. "The first thing you have to learn is how to stayed balanced. Then you can use those poles."

I didn't care about all that stuff. I told her, "I want to have the look."

JaMiko and the kids had been working with the same ski instructor for about five years, Jan from the Czech Republic. He looked at me and said to my family, "Oh my gosh, this is a big guy."

"Jan," I pointed out, "I'm standing right here."

"Ya, but you're so big. I think maybe you should start on the beginner's slope."

That wasn't happening. I wasn't going to start on no baby hill. I was going to be skiing with my kids.

JaMiko tried to convince me. "Warren, I know it looks easy, but it really isn't. You're carrying a little extra weight. Maybe it would be better if you started on the little stuff."

Right. I looked Larry Allen right in the face and beat him. I went helmet-to-helmet with Randall McDaniel. I practically took on the whole city of Philadelphia. Did she really think some little mountain was going to scare me? As I found out pretty quick, there is a big difference between being a good skier and being a good sport about it.

My kids were going to ski on the intermediate trail. I figured, if little kids can do this, so can I. We took the lift up to the top of the hill, all the way up to the top. I got off and looked around at the beautiful Rocky Mountains. I looked down the hill, and all I could see were trails running between trees. And I had just one question: How the hell was I going to get down that mountain? The big fella does not do trees. As far as I was concerned there was only one way to get down from there. Like I explained to JaMiko, there's a reason that ski lift runs in two directions. I was the only person on the lift going down the hill. When I finally got down the people waiting on line to go up asked me what I was doing. I told them, "That's the way I come down the slope."

I didn't quit though. I just decided that maybe Jan was right, maybe I should try to ski easier trails first. But even there my first few attempts did not go exactly as I planned. I think JaMiko's description was, "You looked like a snowball just getting bigger and bigger as you rolled down the hill."

"My body was going everywhere," I said.

"Believe me," she told me. "We all saw your body going everywhere."

The good news was I never did get cold. It was amazing how well all that insulated clothing holds in your body heat. All your body heat. And I generated a lot of body heat. I was standing in the freezing cold sweating like a furnace. But within a couple of days I actually was making it down the intermediate slope without a Red Cross escort. The boy from Florida was a skier.

Played some golf too. I was a big hitter, hit it long and far and pretty much anywhere it wanted to go, but mostly right at Fred McGriff's house. Crime Dog, his nickname when he was a star in major league baseball, lived in a house right next to the golf course. Man, I could hit that house from about half the holes on the course. I had a nasty slice, and whenever I hit it, it would go toward his house like a cop to a Dunkin' Donuts. When he'd see me out there on the course, he'd scream at me, "Sapp, get out of here before you hit my house again."

Swish! Uh oh, watch your head, Freddy. Can I have my ball back?

So unless they moved McGriff's house to the center of the fairway I knew my future was not in playing golf. Mostly I would play in charity events, like raising money to repair his windows.

During my career, because of my reputation as the latest big, tough, lovable, scary black football player, I got a lot of invitations to appear on television. Television was easy for me: Stand there and talk? I could do that. I was slimed with Michael Strahan on Nickelodeon, I was Warren Sapp to block on *Hollywood Squares* ("Who preceded

Henry XIII on the throne?" "Oh, *that* throne."), and I was Punk'd. *Punk'd* is a cable show where they play practical jokes on people. I think I surprised the producers on that show. I was at a restaurant with three friends, and all around us diners were getting huge portions. But when our meal came out it was basically scraps. They gave me two little pieces of lettuce, three calamari, and a tiny glass of water. I looked at the waiter like, are you kidding me? I wouldn't put this portion in my little girl's fish tank. When I pointed out to the manager that the table next to us had also ordered calamari and "half the Pacific Ocean was on that plate," he explained that those people were friends of the owner. Looking around the restaurant it seemed pretty obvious that the owner had a lot of friends. Then the waiter told me that large order was "off the menu." Off the menu? "Let me get this, you hand me a menu, but you have *off the menu*?" Um, are you kidding me? Actually, the answer was yes, that was exactly what they were doing. They were 'punking' me.

I don't know how they expected me to react. I probably was supposed to display the well-known Warren Sapp temper, maybe flip over the table, attack the wise-guy waiter, and rip the walls down. And then everybody would have laughed. Good old Warren, just because we insulted him he ripped the whole restaurant apart. Instead I was totally polite. And I think they were disappointed by that. Imagine how excited they would have been if I erupted: This is great, Warren Sapp sacked the manager. That was my image; I was the tough guy with a heart of cold. That was what they expected, probably wanted, but as this little episode proved it wasn't me. My mama raised . . . ah, you know that one. But I never even raised my voice in that place. I wasn't happy, though. There is nothing funny about messing with a hungry man's food.

Now I'm going to admit something: I knew exactly what was going on. You, reader—that's right, you—are the only person I've ever told this to. But does anyone really believe I would sit there pleasantly while I was being disrespected like that? I don't need to explain how I knew, but I knew. The person who told me was worried I might destroy the restaurant and my whole future career if I didn't get enough calamari. So I knew in advance something was going to happen, although until I was in the middle of it I didn't exactly know what it was going to be.

The hardest part of it for me was acting like I didn't know that I knew. Or not acting like I was acting. I didn't want to turn the tables on them. Literally. I thought about going off the reservation, about digging into the plate of the little old lady at the next table or intercepting a tray, but if I had gone too far they would have realized something was wrong. Instead I just did what I'd been doing my whole life, I played the game.

Donald Trump even asked me to be a judge for the Miss USA Pageant. There was one rule he made about that: I had to bring my wife. That was fine with me, but I didn't understand it. When I asked why, he explained, "I don't want anybody accusing the girls of trying to influence the judges." Let me see now, 50 beautiful women threatening to use their charms to try to influence the judges? Nah, I wouldn't want that either, Mr. Trump.

JaMiko! We're going judging!

The reality was if I couldn't play football anymore there was one thing I could do: Talk about football. I'd been doing that my whole life too; there was no reason that couldn't continue. There's no tackling in talking. And in my life one thing I had never been accused of was not talking enough.

I had some experience talking about football. I had started my broadcasting career while I was still an active player, doing a radio show in Tampa called *Warren's World*, with Jeff Ryan on Tampa Sports Radio 1010. This came about because I had been appearing regularly on the Bucs' radio show without running out of opinions so the producer offered me a one-hour, once-a-week show. He asked me, "Can you talk for an hour?" I laughed. With my mouth tied behind my back. My only stipulation was that I was able to talk about anything I wanted to talk about and change the subject when I wanted to change the subject.

We did the show from a different public location each week for six years. We did it at Lowe's Home Improvement, we did it at car dealerships, we were all over the state. Sometimes I'd have to drive hours to get to the location, but I was never late. Naturally the only place we couldn't do a sports show from was a sports bar. I was told that football fans were too rowdy. I did the show for six years and the entire time we only had one problem. From the very beginning Jeff wanted me to take phone calls from listeners either stating their opinion or asking me a question. I didn't want to take calls; I didn't believe we needed to do that. Jeff insisted, I resisted. Finally I surrendered, told him we'd try it. We'll do it once, just to see what happens. I figured, what could happen? It turned out that this was the week after I broke my hand. One of our very first callers asked me, "Warren, now that you broke your hand let me ask you: Can you jack off with your other hand?"

Thank you very much. Jeff, we won't be taking any more calls.

My career as a TV reporter started at the 2004 Super Bowl in Houston, when the NFL Network hired me to be a roving reporter. My job was to rove. They put a live mike in my hand and told me to find people to talk to. Probably my biggest strength as a broadcaster is that I do not embarrass easily. When I was asked if I was nervous I explained, "Actually, when I put the microphone in front of somebody, they're the one who should be nervous." Super Bowl week is a convention of football history; every time you walk around a corner you might bump into a legend. So naturally my first interview was with Beyoncé. Made sense to me. If you had to choose between Deion Sanders and Beyoncé, who would you choose?

She was singing the national anthem so I asked her inside national anthem singing questions. I asked her if she had seen beautiful, late Whitney Houston singing it in Tampa, which remains the greatest national anthem performance in history. No argument. Then Beyoncé asked me to do my famous end zone dance for her, and although naturally I was reluctant, I did it for her.

I had such fun that week. One time I saw the CBS broadcast crew across the room and snuck up behind Phil Simms and Dan Marino. I grabbed both of them and announced, "Two quarterbacks at the same time! Oh! Got 'em!" From the very beginning working on the front side of the camera felt natural to me.

Of course I did manage to stir up a little buzz too; if I couldn't be in the mix, I didn't mind stirring it up. The Patriots were playing the Panthers, and Russ Hochstein was starting at guard for New England in place of the injured Damien Woody. The Bucs had drafted Hochstein in 2001, and I had gone up against him in practice. I was an expert on the subject, I'd played against him, and I thought he was a step down from Woody. Maybe more than a step, maybe a whole escalator ride down from Woody. I put the microphone in front of my face and said, "He is what I call a plus-minus. We got a plus for beating him in drills and a minus for even having to go up against him." I thought he created more of a problem for the Patriots than for Carolina. Tedy Bruschi got all mad at me for criticizing his teammate, like he should have, but I responded, "I know him better than you do. You look for a weakness in the machine, and in my media opinion Hochstein is a screw that's a little loose." The Patriots won the championship 32–29, but people seemed surprised that I was willing to criticize another player. I just told the truth—out loud—and later the producers would remember that.

Lots of professional athletes do local TV commercials in their city. Buy this car, eat at this restaurant, put your money in this bank. My reputation didn't help me get a lot of TV commercials in Tampa. The city of Tampa had a love-hate-love relationship with me, so I wasn't the safest choice for a local business. But I did do several national spots while I was still active. Nike had me pulling a Mardi Gras float in one spot and knocking down a goal post in another. You know, the usual quiet intellectual stuff. The best commercial I did was for Jordan brand athletic clothes. I am a member of Team Jordan. Always have been. I met Michael at the Super Bowl in 1999 when they were debating about who was going to be the first football player to wear Jordans on the field. I settled that question by showing them a photograph of me sacking Brad Johnson in Minnesota in 1996, when we were still wearing those ugly-ass Creamsicle orange uniforms. Look at my shoes, patent leather Jordans I pointed out to them. I don't know for certain that I was first to wear them in a game, but I haven't found evidence that anyone wore them before me. I love my Jordans; they used to make them special for me. They put cleats on a pair of Space Jams. They made me a pair of all-white ones too. I got a whole roomful of Jordans, so when they asked me to do a commercial for them I was excited.

At the beginning of the first spot Michael Jordan is poised to run through a row of blocking bags. *Bang!* As he moves down the row knocking them off to the side his voiceover says, "I am not Michael Jordan. I am not graceful and elegant. I am not smooth and refined. I don't care what people think about me. I don't care what people say about me. I am not 216 pounds . . ." And then for an instant Michael is hidden behind a bag, and I emerge and say, "I am Warren Sapp. His alter ego."

I loved that commercial, loved it. Michael Jordan doing the stunt work for me. I had six words to learn, and I was on the screen maybe five seconds. No problem. Nice, very nice.

While I was in Oakland I did a commercial for the NFL Network. My whole acting job consisted of standing there in my Raiders uniform smiling. I could smile—but I couldn't move. That was great direction: "Don't move Warren. Can you do that?"

"You mean you want me to do absolutely nothing?"

"Can you do that?"

Of course I could, I was an actor. I could do nothing. So I stood there while my voice was heard saying, "People sometimes ask me, they say, 'Warren what are you laughing about? What's so funny? Let us in on the joke.' Usually, I don't say a word. I just smile and keep 'em guessing. I'll fill you in on a little secret. Even though I've knocked the pretty-boy QB on the backside over 90 times in my career, each time I do it . . ." Then I got to move a little. I stopped smiling, frowned in the most threatening way possible, and said in a deep voice, "It's hilarious." Hilarious, maybe not? Amusing?

I did a commercial for Hungry Man foods. As I walked down the supermarket aisle pushing a shopping cart and not saying a word an announcer explained how delicious and filling these dinners were. As he did I stopped in front of a frozen food case and opened the glass door. But instead of reaching inside and taking out one dinner, I grabbed the entire case and tipped it over so that hundreds of Hungry Man dinners fell into my cart. That was the funny part, right there at the end.

It was the damndest thing: One commercial wasn't me, another commercial I didn't move, and another commercial I didn't speak. I didn't do one commercial in which all the moving parts of me appeared with my voice. I was also an animated character on probably the most watched episode of *The Simpsons* ever. Truthfully, it wasn't only the fact that my voice was on the show that attracted that huge audience; it probably also was the fact that it was broadcast right after the 2005 Super Bowl. They called it "Homer and Ned's Hail Mary Pass," and Tom Brady, Yao Ming, LeBron James, and Michelle Kwan were also characters. The story was that we hired Homer to help choreograph our victory dances, so you knew it was fiction. I had one line, and I was in the studio with seven-time world figure skating champion Michelle Kwan. Seven-time world champion, that's an impressive resume. I'd like to do my line for you right now: "Hey, Michelle, you got a boyfriend?" That was it, that was my appearance on *The Simpsons*.

On the way over to the studio I stopped at a traffic light. Waiting for it to change took longer than it did for me to do my part.

Doing that show was strange. The day after it was shown a lot of people told me, "Hey, Warren, I saw you last night on *The Simpsons*."

And then I had to tell them, "Uh, actually, no you didn't."

By that time I was used to being an animated character. I'd already been a player in several NFL video games. I used to play EA's Madden football when it was only three buttons. Man, we played that game all night. I was tough to beat—but then it went to PlayStation, and they started adding buttons and triggers and it got too complicated. The people who played the game all the time found the little glitches, and by using them they could beat you to death, so I stopped playing.

It was a strange feeling seeing no. 99 on the TV screen and being able to manipulate the figure. Press a button, get a sack. For the first time I knew how Tony Dungy felt. It was me, but it wasn't me. I'd watch myself putting a move on an offensive lineman, and for an instant it was like looking at films. It seemed almost real. It's hard to relate to, because not many people get the opportunity to play with themse . . . let me put that another way, not many people get the opportunity to manipulate their character. Imagine if lawyers had a video game, for instance, and they could try their own cases. They'd never lose a case. Or plumbers had a game fixing pipes; there would never be a leak. That's how good I was when I played Madden football. Rush that quarterback, sack his ass. What you got to say about that, Favre? I didn't care if he got rid of the ball or not, just hit him again. From 1996 to 2006 my character was a very good player on Madden. My overall rating never went below 90, and I was considered a badass, Warren Badass Sapp. People would come up to me and tell me, "I got 14 sacks with you. You had a great season." One person actually complimented me on how good I was in the game, telling me, "I really love the way you play on Madden. Those guys at EA make you a real killer." Well, thank you, I think. In the Madden Legends game I am a badass player, and I will be a badass player forever. Madden is a beautiful thing: You never get old on Madden, you never have to retire, and after playing a game you wake up without a single ache or pain.

I met some of the people at EA Sports in Orlando. I'd talk to them from time to time, maybe suggesting that I was actually a little quicker than they rated me, had some better moves. Thanks, Warren, we'll get back to you.

I actually was on the cover of an ESPN first-person game. The player was supposed to be me, and the player's point of view was from inside my helmet. It was what I liked to call a déjà *view*. In some ways it did look like the player was on the field, but until they invent 300-pound TV sets on wheels that run into you and claw you with their remote they will never be able to reproduce the actual experience of being on the field.

It was probably a combination of my big personality and my big mouth that made the NFL decide to invite me and Michael Strahan to comment on events for the show *NFL Total Access.* They put the two of us together because they expected some sparks, like rubbing two very big sticks together. The controversy between us had started at the end of the 2001 season, when Strahan needed one sack to break Mark Gastineau's single-season record of 22. The Giants were playing Green Bay, and before the game I called Favre and told him, "Don't you give it to him, make him earn it. If he gets you, he gets you, but don't just give it to him."

With less than three minutes left in the last game of the season the Packers were leading 34–25 and had the ball, so the game really was over. Packers win. I was watching at home, and according to reports Favre said something to Strahan before the play. I didn't see that. But Favre faked a handoff and rolled out to the side with no protection; it's a naked bootleg called *belly weak*. Strahan had a clean shot at Favre, but Brett sort of slid down and Strahan landed on top of him. A new record! Yea! Everybody was cheering. They even dragged Gastineau out of the stands to congratulate Strahan.

I hated it. It was so obvious that Favre was handing him the record. Favre ran four naked bootlegs that game, the first play of the game was a naked boot, and Strahan couldn't catch him once. Earlier in the game he came close to a sack, but Favre got rid of the ball. This game was Strahan's last opportunity to break the record. I have so much respect for the people who played my game that I didn't want to see a great record broken like that. If he had broken it cleanly I would have been the first person to call and congratulate him. Like a reporter wrote in the *New York Times*, "Yes, Mr. Favre, Strahan deserves the record, but handing it to him the way you did, as if you were throwing change into a Salvation Army bucket, is the kind of mistake Favre may never live down."

That's what I thought too. I know what a sack looks like; I had 96.5 of them. Michael Strahan had 140; he was a great player, he just needs to take that one away. So I called him out on it. "You don't get a sack on that play," I said, when asked about it by a reporter. "Who was the intended receiver? You don't have to be a rocket scientist to know this. I'm from Florida, and Cape Canaveral is right around the corner from my home. But I don't build rockets, and I don't know how they fly rockets. But I do know what belly weak looks like. And I know what a sack looks like. That wasn't them. Thank you . . .

"It was my boy that gave it up. The hardest quarterback in the league to put on the ground . . . I watched the whole thing. This is not a debate."

Strahan did not like that. In addition to calling me a "jackass," he also criticized my diet, which he claimed basically consisted of McDonald's. But what actually bothered me was that he also said I'd quit playing hard in our playoff loss to Philadelphia. I didn't mind the McDonald's, because at McDonald's they love to see you smile, but I did not like being called a quitter. "(That record-breaking sack) was unbelievable," I said on the air, and I was right because no one believed it was real. "He has to admit that last one doesn't count. I'll give you the first 21½ because you went and got those. That's a man's game."

I said those things because too many people have worked too hard for too long for one of the greatest records in the game to be handed over. Earn it, the way Gastineau did. We are all supposed to leave the game better than it was when we got into it, and that didn't happen in this situation. And I was right, more people remember that phony sack than honor the record. At the time it took place Strahan and I went back and forth on it, so naturally the brand-new NFL Network thought we would be arguing all the time, which is why they asked us to appear together. Two people getting along does not make good television. As I said at that time, "It's one of those deals where we can't physically choke each other, so it'll be all right."

Michael and I did the show for two years while we were both active players. I was in Florida, he was in New York. What was most surprising to me was that the league never stopped us from saying anything we wanted to say. The league never said one word about toning it down or pushing it up; they let us do our own thing. With the NFL supposedly guarding its image so carefully, people might have thought that was surprising. But they knew exactly what they were getting when they put me and Strahan on the air. If they had ever tried to tell me what not to say, that definitely would have been the first thing that I said. I probably would have run out on the air to say it. The league knew that: It's called *reverse mikology*.

When Michael and I got on the air neither one of us backed down from this subject. When Strahan was asked about Favre, he said, smiling that gap-toothed smile, "According to Warren, he's easy to sack. You got to have a sense of humor about it, Warren."

"Still won't face reality on that, will you."

"Lighten up, man," he said seriously.

So I asked him straight up, "Why won't you admit to all of America tonight that it was a gimme sack."

"I will admit to all of America that Michael Strahan did his job."

We were two kids on the playground. "Gimme sack!"

Then all-of-a-sudden Favre butted his ass into this conversation. "For Warren and Michael I'm glad I'm the butt of your jokes, but Warren, me and Michael have one up on you if you know what I mean."

That was as close to a confession as we were going to get. Strahan knew it too, telling Favre, "That's all the ammo you need to give Warren 'cause now Warren's going to run with it. Whoever's at the NFL Network who came up with the idea to have him (Favre) say that, I'm coming for your ass. Yes, I said *ass* on TV."

One time they asked Michael and me who we most wanted as a guest on our segment and we decided unanimously that it should be Halle Berry, J-Lo, or poster girl Vida Guerra. As a consolation prize they gave us Jerome Bettis. "Oh man," I said. "We asked for a nice fine Volkswagen, not no bug." Eventually they surprised us with Vida Guerra—although she was on the set with Michael in New York. Now what was fair about that?

Instead of waves, we made nice ripples. We had a lot of fun, talked a lot of football, helped the NFL Network get established, and it was very good training for both of us. It got me very comfortable in front of a TV camera. Obviously somewhere in our minds both Michael and I were hoping we could work in television when our careers ended.

When. It happens fast. As an athlete you're always looking ahead, looking ahead, looking ahe. . . . *Boom*! You hit that wall, sometimes even before you see it. It doesn't seem possible that it could be over so quickly. It seemed to me like I was just starting, and then it was over. And football, unlike some other sports, when it's over it is completely and permanently over. A basketball player can always go out and shoot some hoops, play some pickup. A baseball player can have a catch or go to a batting range. But a D-lineman? Over is over, and when I walked out of Al Davis's office my career was over.

When I retired I already had six years of experience hosting a radio show, my two years on TV at the NFL Network, plus many other TV appearances. I had done *The Simpsons*, and I had been dealing with the media for almost two decades. So naturally the first request I received was to go dancing.

There is a woman named Tracy Pearlman at the NFL who matches players and events. If they need football players for a charity golf tournament, a TV show, Tracy puts it together. There was a little group of people that she called regularly, including Tony Gonzalez, Michael Strahan, Eddie George, me, Johnny Randle and a few others. I was getting ready to go to China with my little girl's singing group when Tracy called me. "I know you're going to China in a couple of days . . ." she started. "But I want you to think about something. How would you like to be on *Dancing with the Stars*?"

Wow. *Dancing with the Stars*? I had never seen that show, but I'd read about it and I knew how popular it was with women. So I didn't even have to think about it. "No way," I told her. "That's a girl's show. It's not me." I rarely say no to an opportunity or an adventure. I've eaten dried chicken feet and sipped the Komodo dragon wine; about the only thing I refused to do was ride the zip line with my kids across the forest canopy in Costa Rica. The opportunity to glide several thousand feet through the air on a wire high above the forest didn't interest me. Climbed down nice and safe on that one too. *Dancing with the Stars* didn't seem like a good fit for me. Maybe if they had wanted me for *Tackling the Stars* I would have said yes instantly.

Tracy was persistent. "Warren, have I ever given you anything bad?"

No discussion there. "No, Tracy, you haven't."

"That's right. Don't commit yourself. Just think about it for a couple of days and let me know."

I walked into the living room. JaMiko was in the kitchen, and I told her, "Guess what? Tracy just asked me if I wanted to be on *Dancing with the Stars*."

There is a large couch in the living room. The back was facing me so I didn't know Mercedes was lying on it. But all of a sudden this little head pops up, her eyes wide open, and she asked, "What'd you say, Daddy?"

I looked at her. "What's the rule in this house?" I'd learned growing up that when an adult is speaking the children do not interrupt them.

She ignored me. "You said *Dancing with the Stars*, and that's got kids on it. What did you tell them?"

I looked at JaMiko for help. "It does have kids on it," she agreed. Some help.

"It's got kids on it? Well, they asked me to do it."

My daughter jumped up. "You're doing it," she said. Then she ran upstairs and called both her grandmothers, her cousins, her poppa, her friends, and then my phone started ringing. My entire family decided I was going to be dancing with the stars.

We talked about it while we were in China. Mercedes's school chorus was representing the United States in a kids music festival, and we all went along. We visited a lot of museums on the trip, and several times the tour guides mentioned homes that were built for concubines. Finally at one of these places six-year-old Deuce asked out loud, "Daddy, what's a concubine?"

One thing for sure, my son was having a whole different childhood than I did. I tried to figure out a good way of answering the question without being dishonest. "It's girls," I said. "Ladies, a lot of them."

Deuce didn't understand. JaMiko was laughing at me being uneasy, until his 11-year-old sister explained, with a little frustration, "That's a prostitute, Deuce."

The worst thing was that he nodded and said with understanding, "Ooohhhh."

By the time we got home it was an accepted fact that I was going to be dancing with the stars. The show was filmed in L.A. My partner was a bubbly blond from Australia named Kym Johnson. My competition included stand-up comedian Jeffrey Ross, whatever-it-is-she-does Kim Kardashian, Olympic volleyball star Misty May-Treanor, singers Toni Braxton and Lance Bass, the chef Rocco DiSpirito, Olympic sprinter Maurice Greene, 114-year-old sexpot Cloris Leachman, the beautiful TV personality Brooke Burke, and actors Susan Lucci, Cody Linley, and Ted McGinley.

At first I didn't take it very seriously. There were a lot of things going on in my life at that time that were more important to me than whether or not people thought I was the best dancer on a TV show. Looking over my competition, I figured I could beat the comedian, no cook was going to beat me, I knew I could beat the entire Kardashian family, I probably could beat the old lady, and football has a lot more fans than volleyball or sprinting so I could beat Misty May-Treanor and Maurice Greene. My guess was that eventually Toni Braxton would get me; she is a beautiful and talented woman. So I anticipated staying on the show for about six weeks.

There could not have been two people with less in common than me and Kym Johnson. She is from Sydney, Australia; I'm from Plymouth, Florida. That was the distance between the outback and the outhouse. We met for our first rehearsal at a dance studio next to the Empire State Building. It was a little awkward at first, but then we discovered we had a lot in common: We both had the same cell phone, and we're both afraid of heights and snakes. We just hit it off right from the first *cha*.

I found out quick that Kym was as competitive as I am, and at first she thought they stuck her with a big, clunky guy who couldn't move real well. But she started showing me some moves which I picked up pretty quick; she realized I could move a little bit. When she found out that I was well known and had some people who liked me, it was oh

Daddy! We can win this thing! I never let her know, but at the beginning I was a little unsure of dancing. I wasn't sure my club moves translated to TV. Fortunately, we started with the cha-cha, which required a lot of footwork and hip movement, and those were my strengths. For me, I began to understand that this show could take the claws out of my image of a big angry dude who came into your city to kill your quarterback and rape your cattle. It would give me the opportunity to show the world my gentle, loving side—it was making my sweet little girl smile—so Kym and I set out to demolish our competition.

I began to believe we had an opportunity to win this whole thing. I had a lovely partner who was as tough on the dance floor as I was on the football field. She was a Dancer of Steel. I told her to go for it, teach me everything I need to know. I am your piece of clay, go ahead and mold me. Practice never scared me. We're here to win, baby, win!

The costume department was amazing. They could put together an outfit in 20 minutes. Right at the beginning I met with them and told them that there were only two things I would not wear. "The big fella don't do yellow, and I don't do ruffles. Anything else we can go 150 miles an hour. Dress me anyway you want." Ruffles were my limit. I knew if I wore ruffles I would never hear the end of it from my boys. Nice ruffles, Warren, perhaps a little puffy? No thank you. No ruffles, and yellow is just my bad-luck color. Otherwise, I let the makeup people do whatever they wanted to do. I mean, what harm could they do? I even wore what I called *manliner*, which was eye highlighter. I never did tell that to Culpepper though. That would fall into the category of TDMI: Too damn much information. It was a need-to-know basis, and there was no way anybody needed to know that.

Our first week on the air was the first fall Sunday in 14 years that I hadn't played pro football. It required a completely changed mentality. As we were waiting for the taping to begin my testosterone level was so high I felt like I was ready to explode. I was right on the edge. I had my game face on, although this was the first time that I needed makeup. I was sitting at a table eating my game day meal, meats and salads. Cloris Leachman came over and wanted some of my food. I loved that woman—she reminded me of my grandmother, and we had our own little friendship going on—but that didn't extend to my food. It did not. She reached over and took something off my plate. I told her, "This is the plate of a 300-pound man who needs every last bite. You reach in here again, I will cut off your fingers."

She thought I was being cute. Cute? Good thing she didn't go for any more food.

Then Maurice Greene came on by and dropped one of the L.A. newspapers on the table. "You are 17-to-1," he said, "17-to-1."

I picked up the paper, and there it was: The odds against Kym and I winning were 17-to-1. I thought about that for a minute. We were competing against 12 other couples, how could we be 17-to-1? Who were these dead people we were competing against?

Maurice didn't let up. He kept yelling the odds at me: "17-to-1, Sapp, 17-to-1."

I told him, "That is all I needed to hear from y'all. I am locked in now. I am on target." Winning on this show somehow temporarily replaced what I was missing being out on the field. It was on—I was dancing with the stars.

I really got into this competition. It surprised me how thrilled I was when the judge Bruno Tonioli said, "Big boy can dance," or judge Carrie Ann Inaba complimented me, "Someone brought his sparkle back on the floor."

Trust me, I had to work to find my sparkle. Rehearsals were time consuming and intense. Kym was tough on me, which I wanted her to be because I knew I could get lazy. When Coach Kym got in the mood, she could tear my ass up. The hardest thing for me to learn was the drop-step-kick *annnnd* doub-ble kick! My entire career had been spent moving forward, everything I did on the football field was going forward, so as long as we were dancing forward I eventually could figure it out. Turned out Kym and I could do a mean hustle, but our strength was our tango. That was when my inner Carlos came out, and I dug deep for my Spanish roots. That tango earned us our first 10.

I never realized dancing was such a tough sport. Seemed like our cast suffered as many injuries as a football team. Jeffrey Ross got poked in the eye by his partner and scratched his cornea; the doctors wanted him to drop out, but he danced hurt! Misty May-Treanor ruptured her Achilles tendon the third week and had to drop out. Brooke Burke landed hard and banged up her foot and was questionable but showed up. Susan Lucci fractured two bones in her foot. Professional dancer Julianne Hough had to have her appendix removed. Lacey Schwimmer had endometriosis but danced through it. I had to check the injured list every week just to see who was going to be there for step-and-kickoff.

My partner on the NFL's *GameDay*, Marshall Faulk, used to give me a real hard time about the competition. After watching the show he told me he suspected that my dancing was enhanced through the magic of television editing. He thought that by changing angles and varying the shots, they could edit me into a passable dancer. But one week he came to the studio and watched us dance. "You know what big fella," he said after that. "I got to give it to you. I thought it was all camera tricks, but you are working."

I said, "I told you that. If I was cheating, I would tell you I was cheating. I am always honest about my cheating!"

One by one our competition started falling. The comedian went first. I guess he danced funny. The second week Kym and I did an encore of our Paso Doble; I couldn't even pronounce it, but I could dance it. Kim Kardashian went the third week. I guess she had to get back to doing whatever it was that she was doing. Each week Kym and I were getting better and better. Like I explained to the host Tom Bergeron, "The QB killa has become a dance floor thrilla!" Cloris went the sixth week, bye-bye Grandma! Before she went she had to be bleeped for cursing out the judges. Loved that woman.

Tuesday night, November 4, 2008, the United States elected Barack Obama president. We danced Wednesday night. That afternoon I told Maurice, "I hope you brought your dancing shoes, because you know what tonight is, don't you?"

"What's that?" he wanted to know.

"There are two black men and one stage. One of us is staying. This is the vote for the second most popular black man in America." Oh, I had my tango on that night. We rocked that stage to the "Theme from Peter Gunn." I didn't pick the music. When I came off the stage I looked at Maurice and told him, "You can go home now." Then we also did the jive. I think I wrecked his whole world that night. The man still doesn't talk to me nicely.

We went into the finals against Brooke Burke and Lance Bass and their partners and those couples brought their A-dances that night. By this time the competition had turned into Sunday afternoon for me. I wanted to win. Throughout the eight weeks Kym and I usually had been one of the last couples to dance. For whatever reasons the producers held us back. While we were waiting I would be sitting there chilling, totally relaxed, while Kym would be hypernervous, telling me, "C'mon let's practice it again."

I would explain to her, "This is a one-shot. Once I say I got it, I got it. When it's time to perform, it's time to perform. You don't want to leave your legs on the practice floor. So just calm down." There was no faze in my life; I was completely unfazed.

Until the night of the finals. By this time Kym was used to my preparation, and she would sit with me. But this time, as we sat waiting backstage, I said to her, "C'mere."

"What?"

"Just come on over here. We got to go over this step one more time because . . ."

"No way," she said.

"We need to," I told her. "I don't feel comfortable with it."

She said flatly, "We're going. What's going on with you? You've never done this before."

"I know," I admitted. "Of course it doesn't matter at all to me, but I know how much this means to you, and I don't want to screw it up!"

We danced our heart out that night. About 30 million people voted. We finished behind Brooke Burke and her professional partner Derek Hough by about .36 percent of the vote. The producers showed me where the votes came from. Kym and I were strong in the heartland: Kansas, Missouri, Alabama, Mississippi, Georgia, all the way up to Michigan; we owned that. But the coasts beat us. Within a few years I would have more than 810,000 followers on Twitter, that's @WarrenSapp, and if I had those numbers when the country was voting we definitely would have won it all.

I think, more than anything, I was really pleased at the response I got from those people who didn't know about me from football. To millions of people I was Warren Sapp, the dancer.

Dancing with the Stars introduced me to a whole new audience. One time I was in Philadelphia in the winter. I was all bundled up, I was wearing a heavy jacket, I had my hoodie over my head, I was wearing a face mask, even my mother wouldn't recognize me. When I walked out of the Four Seasons Hotel into the Philadelphia cold a group of older women were waiting out in front. Suddenly one of them looked at me and shouted, "Look girls, it's Twinkletoes!"

Twinkletoes? Do me a favor please; if Ray Lewis doesn't read this book, don't tell him this story, okay? Twinkletoes. Sure, I was light on my feet, but . . . They closed in all around me and started asking questions. One of them ran into the gift shop and bought a disposal camera. Given the situation there really was only one thing old Twinkletoes could do: I gave each of them a twirl for the camera.

In some places I am better known for finishing second on that show than for my 96.5 sacks, seven Pro Bowls, and one Super Bowl championship. Especially in Philadelphia.

When I retired from the NFL I just naturally assumed my life would get easier. That's what's supposed to happen when you retire, right? But suddenly I found myself busier than I had ever been in my life. In addition to *Dancing with the Stars* I was doing two weekly football shows. All day Sunday I did *GameDay* on the NFL Network, and Wednesday nights I was doing Showtime's *Inside the NFL.* I was living on airplanes. I always had two different tickets in my pocket because until the voting was done there was no way of knowing if we were going to be eliminated. I didn't get any sleep at all.

Believe me, I hadn't planned it that way. Just before I had started dancing the producers I'd worked with when I was a roving reporter at the Super Bowl called to tell me they were putting together a Sunday morning preview show for the NFL Network. They wanted to team me with Marshall Faulk and Spero Dedes, then the radio voice of the Los Angeles Lakers and currently with the Knicks. There were some people who were surprised that after all my problems with the league, after claiming the NFL was "a slave system," that I would be hired. I was told that decision went all the way up to Commissioner Roger Goodell, and everybody approved it. I hope that they looked at my whole career and saw that I had always played hard, I had loved the game, and I loved talking about it. And they probably suspected I might say one or a thousand things that would draw media attention to their new network.

Deion Sanders was the person who convinced me to pursue a broadcasting career. "Are you crazy?" he asked me. "They are paying you a king's ransom for sitting in an air-conditioned environment talking about football."

The NFL Network actually was an on-air trial. At the beginning we weren't on enough cable systems to make a difference. If we tanked, only a few people would see it. I had absolutely no training for the job. Every other job I've had in my life they told me, we're trying to get from here to there and this is the path we intend to follow. Not this time. This time they just sat us down at a table and turned on the camera. When they hired me they said, "We believe in you; we think you can be good at this." Well, my little boy believed in the tooth fairy, but that didn't make it real. They just threw me in there and said, "Talk." But what they really meant was, "Be controversial."

John Lynch told me once that he was more nervous before he started his broadcasting career than he was before he played in an NFL game. "I always slept pretty well the night before a game," he said. "But early in my broadcasting career I had a lot of sleepless nights. I stressed over everything. I'd be obsessed over the fact that I was facing a live open mike, and I didn't know what I was going to say. What if I suddenly froze up?" I found out exactly what he was talking about before my first show. I probably was more nervous that morning than at any time in my playing career. Marshall Faulk had been doing TV for about three years, and Spero was an experienced broadcaster. I'd spent my career focusing only on my team and my next opponent. Suddenly I had to study all 32 teams and find something interesting to say about each game without being repetitive or covering the same material as my cohosts. And that was a serious challenge because we were all getting our information from the same sources.

During my career I was always confident I was prepared to play on Sunday. I had done my homework, I had practiced hard, and I knew what to expect and how to respond to it. But for this show my preparation was making sure my tie was straight and reading as much material as possible. The show was broadcast from Los Angeles, which meant we started at 6:00 a.m. so we would be on the air at 9:00 a.m. on the East Coast. When our theme music began I took a deep breath and got my game mouth on. I am my mother's son.

If there was any doubt about the tone they were trying to create, they opened our first program by showing the tape of me picking up Marshall Faulk on *Monday Night Football* and slamming him down on the turf. As the tape concluded I remember looking at Marshall, sitting just a few feet away—he was glaring right back at me. I thought, wow, this ain't good.

The first few weeks Marshall and I just went at each other. He said Steelers, I said Dallas. Both of us thought that's what the producers wanted, so we tried to give it to them. About the third week of the season the Packers were playing at Tampa, the first time Chad Clifton had been back there since I'd put him in the hospital. Our reporter, Lindsay Soto, ended her report by saying, "Some people expected Sapp to apologize for the hit, and he did not." She was sitting at the same desk with me, and when she finished she turned to me and asked, "Do you still hear about this a lot from people? And do you think the reaction surrounding this situation is fair?"

Do I still hear about this from people? Only when they show the clip on TV, which was exactly what they were doing at that very moment. But before I could respond Marshall said, "He's a cheap-shot artist. That's what he is."

I looked up just in time to see that big old bus passing right over the top of me. I looked at Marshall and thanked him, "That makes it all worthwhile." Then I told Lindsay that I didn't spend much time thinking about it, explaining, "We had one little encounter (after that) when we slapped hands. He was back healthy, I was back healthy, we were playing football."

It was obvious the producers wanted the show to be as controversial as possible. I didn't know if it was working because instead of getting any feedback from them, we got bagels and coffee. I wanted to get better, and I knew I had to work at it, but I needed feedback. So at one point I asked a producer, "Tell me this: Am I better now than I was when I walked in the door?"

"The same," he said.

No, I thought, that's not possible. You wake up in the morning, and you're either going to be better or worse than you were yesterday. I understood my role. I was supposed to be a big personality on the air, big mouth, big opinions, draw an audience. It wasn't hard for me to do that—but I didn't want to say things I didn't believe just to attract viewers. I understood the NFL Network—channel 212 on your DirecTV dial and number one in your heart, and if we're not on your local cable system yet we will be soon—was trying to build a brand, but I was trying to get good at my new profession. Build my own brand. And I needed the feedback from professionals. Finally I found a couple of people there who gave me an honest opinion about my work.

As I listened to them I thought, wait a second, I didn't mean *that* honest. But their advice was good, and I took it and tried to use it. One thing I'm smart enough to know is what I don't know. And I try to find people who do know it and will teach it to me. My mother taught us that we were supposed to learn at least one thing new every day. When we came home from school the first question she asked us was what did we learn and what does that mean. I am a quick study, if I have a teacher. So I found a teacher, I listened, I learned, and I got better.

It took some time for all of us to find our roles on the show. At one point the producers decided I should only talk about defense. Hello? Am I supposed to sit there like a Sapp on a log while other people discuss offensive football? Hey, I *played* offense, I worked against the offense every single day in practice, I sat in on the quarterback meetings, I know what the offense is supposed to be doing thank you very much. That was a brief experiment.

Maybe we didn't look at the game films every Monday, but everyone paid attention to what we were doing. We talked about it, and gradually the whole show got better. Eventually Michael Irvin and Steve Mariucci, Kurt Warner, and a cast of thousands, or at least a couple of other people, joined us. The show stretched to four hours on the air, and then me and my boys got to sit there and watch the great game of football on eight television screens. There are few things more fun than sitting in our "living room" with Marshall Faulk, Mike Irvin, Deion Sanders, Rich Eisen, Steve Mariucci, Kurt Warner, and whoever else shows up watching a day of football. Are you kidding me? We pick the games, and we argue about them the same way it's going on every place that people gather to watch the games. If people think we are passionate about our game while we're on the air, they should see us while we're watching a whole Sunday's schedule. Most people probably think we do that show for the money. Well they're right, we do; that's our job, and man, how lucky we are to have it. I'd spent my whole career voluntarily giving my opinion, and suddenly I was being paid for it. In fact, they wanted more of my opinions. The next best thing in the world to being paid to play football is being paid to talk about it. But we also do it because we love it. If I weren't being paid to sit and talk football with people who know just a little less about it than I do, I would be sitting somewhere else, watching the same games, having the same conversations, amazingly enough, also with people who know just a little less about it than I do. If it's Sunday in America, you got to be talking football.

The amazing thing to me is that with so many football experts in the same room how many different opinions we have. We look at the same teams, the same facts, the same players, and see completely different outcomes—and can always make a pretty good argument to support our position. I don't want to tell tales, but usually Michael Irvin is what we refer to as *DFL*: Dead. Fucking. Last. Or as we say to him sympathetically, "DFL, Michael! DFL!"

Just like little kids, Marshall, Kurt Warner, and I are still arguing about the *Monday Night Football* game we played in December 2000. That game was a war; both teams needed it to guarantee a spot in the playoffs. It's considered one of the best *MNF* games ever played. The lead changed six times, and we won on a broken play. Shaun King pitched out to Warrick Dunn—who got trapped 15 yards behind the line of scrimmage—and as he was going down for that big loss he lateraled it back to King, who ran 29-yards for a first down. We scored 38 points, our offense scored 38 points, which shows how bad the Rams defense was that night. Of course, they scored 35 points against us, and Marshall Faulk scored four touchdowns. Naturally, I don't talk too much about that. I always give Warner his props; he earned them that night. The weakness in our defense was the slant across the middle, but only if the quarterback had the courage to stand there and get hit. It was a three-step for Warner. We took away his first option, and then we took away his second option, which meant his third option was going to be there for him at almost exactly the same time I was arriving at his front grille. He knew that every time he waited for that third receiver he was going to get hit in the mouth as he let the ball go. But he stood in there the whole game. We hit him all night long. Bounced him off the turf like a rubber ball, and he stood in there waiting for that third receiver. If the fans didn't appreciate the beat down he took for those five or six yards, we definitely did.

At about the same time I was getting started on the NFL Network's *GameDay Morning*, I was asked to join the crew on *Inside the NFL*. This was the show that HBO had been doing for 30 years, starting in 1977. It was the longest-running show in cable television history. When HBO dropped it in 2008, Showtime swooped it on up and immediately hired Mr. James Brown, Phil Simms, and Cris Collinsworth to host it. CBS was producing the show. The original plan was to rotate the fourth chair every week. Bring in a new opinion. NFL Films President Steve Sabol didn't like that idea, so he put together a reel of my TV interviews and made CBS Sports President Sean McManus look at it. McManus offered me that fourth chair. Whoa! I have this saying, if you shoot for the moon and miss, you're still among the stars. For me, *Inside the NFL* was the moon and the stars. I'd watched it growing up. I loved it then, loved it while I was playing, and I love it now. The only thing I don't love about it is that we do it on tape, and there is only a four-minute slot to talk about the games. I wish it was live, and I wish we had more time to really discuss whatever comes up. James Brown, Phil Simms, and Cris Collinsworth had been doing this work for a long time; they knew how to dissect a highlight clip. I needed help to learn how to do that, and they gave it to me. I don't want to say they carried me, I still weigh about 300 pounds, but maybe they just pushed me down the hill.

Phil Simms had been a quarterback, but I liked him anyway. That first year he was incredibly supportive. In Tampa, I had taken his son Chris under my protection, and I think he appreciated that. The fact is that Jon Gruden could be a tough mother, tougher even than my own mother! He'd systematically bang on people to test their strength. He wanted to know their breaking point. The Bucs drafted Chris Simms out of the University of Texas, and Gruden really tested him. I remember sitting in Chucky Doll's office early one morning listening to him complain about Simms. "I'm just gonna eat him a new ass," he said.

"About what?"

"He's lazy," he said. "I need to shake him up. The attention to detail isn't there. That boy needs some tough love, and then we'll see what he's got going."

Gruden walked into our next meeting and started running film. It did not surprise me that the first player he called on was Chris Simms. "What's our first play?" he asked. The answer was 93 Willie. I knew that because I always memorized our first 15 charted plays, so I would understand our strategy. Simms didn't know the answer, so Gruden called on me. "Ninety-three Willie," I said.

Gruden shook his head and snapped at Simms, "How the fuck does a defensive tackle know that and you don't?" If you showed any weakness to Jon Gruden he would pounce on it like a cat on meat. Just rip you apart. He wasn't just driven, he was driving, and the only people he took along with him were those people who could keep up. To Gruden's credit, he was one-faced; he never said anything behind a man's back he wouldn't say to his face. I remember him telling a player he was a "seven-on-seven guy," meaning he was a good practice player, but he wasn't ready to play on Sunday. "Put 11 people around you, and you'll pee on your leg," he said, but he said it with a smile.

He definitely tested Chris Simms. I used to talk to Chris about it, trying to pump him up. I explained, "Listen man, he's coming after you because you showed weakness. He thinks you're not paying attention. You got to get on top of it because he is not giving up on that. Once he tastes weakness he comes back, so you got to be ready for him. Trust me, he's coming back."

When I joined *Inside the NFL* I think Chris told his dad that I'd looked out for him. I also suspected Lawrence Taylor might have said some nice things to Simms about me. LT and Simms had played together and remained friends. LT and I had definitely partied together; we'd hung out with the owls, soared with the eagles, and howled at the moon. I don't know exactly what happened, but Phil Simms allowed me to catch my breath that first season on the show. I felt I had to prove to James, Phil, and Cris that I was not my rough-edges image, that I brought more to the desk than big opinions. I was a natural athlete, but I had to work to become a football player. I was also a natural talker, so I knew I had to work to become an analyst. I worked with a, excuse me, vocal awareness coach to squeeze all those, you know, little slang thingys out of my speech patterns. I like to believe I have improved every year. One thing that surprised me is how much television is a team game. The best broadcast is one in which everybody plays to their strength but contributes to the whole program. On the set, similar to being on the field, you really can feel it when everybody is working together. Not just the on-air talent, but the entire production crew. As much of a cliché as it is, I had to learn how to let the broadcast come to me, rather than trying to impose my presence.

I learned some important lessons about being a broadcaster during my playing career, and the most important one was simply to know the hell what you're talking about before you open your mouth. Opinions are fine and fun to have, when it comes to who's going to win the next game my guess is only slightly better than yours. But that's only part of the talking game. I remember in 2001 the Pittsburgh Steelers came to Tampa. Late in the third quarter they ran a counter, and Jerome Bettis ran through the A-gap for a 46-yard touchdown run. The A-gap was usually my responsibility, but on that play a linebacker had the A-gap and I was supposed to go over the top and fill the B-gap. Don't worry if you don't understand it, you're not supposed to, you're not a broadcaster. But the TV people, they should know this. On *SportsCenter* Tom Jackson told the world it was my fault.

I got big shoulders. I take responsibility. But on Monday morning the whole world was waiting for me in front of my locker to find out why the big guy screwed up and cost his team the game. I had a choice: Go at my teammate or go at Tom Jackson. Those were my options: Leave tire tracks over a teammate I was going to be playing with or go at Tom Jackson. Some choice: A broadcaster who doesn't know what he's talking about or a linebacker who wasn't man enough to accept responsibility?

Yo, Tom. When you're on TV, you need to watch what comes out of your big mouth. Maybe I didn't say it quite that nicely. But I never would have had to make that choice if he had done his job correctly. So a few years later, when I was sitting in a position somewhat similar to Tom Jackson, I remembered how he hung me out there without even bothering to check with my coach. Not pleasant at all.

My biggest strength as a broadcaster is the thing that got me into trouble as a player: I say what I believe. The difference between being on the field and in the studio is that now I am encouraged to say the same things that I used to get criticized for saying. I have a much bigger platform than ever before in my life—and now I communicate my thoughts in complete sentences. You can't trash talk a camera. I don't think anybody was surprised that sometimes my opinions generated some controversy. But man, I love this game, and when I see players disrespecting it, I can't keep my mouth shut. For example, some people were upset when I criticized Albert Haynesworth for his lack of commitment. My first week on the air I put it out there that he was a useless lump. Oh my goodness, did I hate watching him dog it on the field after signing a huge contract, and I wasn't shy about saying it. "He doesn't care how many plays he plays," I said. "He has no awareness of where the ball is. He doesn't care. So if we're talking about evaluating his play compared to the check that he's getting, he knows what it is."

The second week he was playing against the Ravens and his *bizak* hit the ground, which would be the back of his neck and butt. I challenged Phil and Cris, "I got 13 years of film in this league, I want you to show me one play where that happened to me. One. Not five, not two, one time. You will never find me going ass over tea kettle, no way, no how."

Another time we put on a tape of the first three plays of a Redskins–Cowboys *Monday Night Football* game, and what we saw was a damn shame. On the first play he got blocked off his feet, and as I described it, "We're waiting for Albert to make some plays and oh! We call that *OG,* or 'on the ground' for a defensive lineman. First play of the game." The next play he was fooled on a little screen, and as I pointed out, "C'mon Albert—let's use some effort. It's the second play of the game! It's *Monday Night Football*! COME ON! JOP! We call that 'jump on pile.'"

When Darrelle Revis, who was under contract, refused to report to the Jets' training camp unless his contract was renegotiated, I was critical of him. I looked at him, and I remembered Derrick Brooks playing three years under a bad contract and showing up to the job every day without once complaining. Maybe another person's money is not my business, but I wasn't talking about his money when I said on the air, "I tell everybody, you have a situation in the NFL that unless you're Peyton Manning or that pretty boy in Boston, Tom Brady, you're not hitting a home run. So take a stand-up triple. It has to be the perfect pitch in the perfect situation, and that doesn't happen for all of us."

I have learned how to draw on my own experiences as a player—and my reputation—whenever it's possible. For example, on Thanksgiving Day 2011, I was watching the traditional Lions–Packers game. On the opening series of the second half Detroit stopped Green Bay on a third-and-goal. In a big pileup near the goal line the Lions' All-Pro defensive tackle Ndamukong Suh got tangled up with the Packers' Evan Dietrich-Smith. But as Suh was getting up it looked like he shoved D-Smith's helmet into the turf and then stomped on his right arm.

As I watched the replays over and over I knew exactly what that meant: I was going to have some explaining to do.

Here we go, I thought. And within a few seconds, literally within seconds, my iPhone practically exploded with messages. People who watched that play instantly thought about me. Even before this incident fans had compared the two of us: Big tough D-linemen who played hard and sometimes pushed the rules. Except Suh wasn't pushing them, he was stomping on them. Sitting there on my couch, I knew that I was going to have to comment on Suh's actions. That's my job.

I definitely could speak from my own experience. I would have told Suh that he has to learn how to keep his emotions under control on the field. Now please, stop laughing. I did have to learn that lesson. And he needs to say, "I don't want to be up here answering these questions because I'm sorry I put my foot on that man. I'm sorry D-Smith, I'm sorry Packers fans, but I'll tell you what, I'm going to play football, and I'm going after those guys. I promise you I won't put my feet on anybody, I won't be ripping anybody's head off, but I will be putting my foot up your ass all day long." That's what Suh should have said.

Isn't maturity wonderful.

There are other things I could teach him too, things I could teach any young player that I had to learn the hard way. A lot of the young players aren't interested in hearing about that. Apparently they already know everything there is to know about the game, otherwise they wouldn't be in the NFL, so they don't need to listen to people like me.

You have to self-evaluate yourself in this game. You have to be able to look in the mirror and not just be in awe of what you see bouncing back at you. That was the biggest thing I had to learn after my rookie year when I had Sam Wyche running his three-ring circus. My rookie year I started my first five games, played on and off through the rest of the season, and then the whole coaching staff was gone. That was one full year when I didn't learn a damn thing. I knew it. I had to look at myself and figure out how I was going to get better. I knew I needed to be stronger, and I knew I had to work on my conditioning and my pass rush. I spent that off-season working on those things. I found out that the Subway was going to be open after I'd finished my work. Suh has ability, no question about that, but if he's going to show it in this league he needs to self-evaluate and put in the necessary work.

Now if Suh had asked me for advice that's what I would have told him. I didn't spend all those years in this league without learning something.

I went through the same learning process when I started working as a broadcaster. I promise you I have never stopped asking myself— and the people around me—how to get better. One thing I've learned is how to handle controversial or at least sensitive situations. One of the biggest stories of the 2011 season was the remarkable achievements of Denver quarterback Tim Tebow. In the entire history of the NFL, there had never been a player quite like him. He is an extremely religious person, and during a game he often got down on his knee and prayed right there on the field. As I knew from my own experience there have been a lot of religious players in pro football, but until Tim Tebow came along we had always had separation of church and football.

We had to talk about it on the air, but it was a sensitive subject. This was an opportunity to draw on my career. As I said, on every NFL team I played on we had both individuals who loved the Lord and believed in Christ the Savior and other people who did not believe that or followed their own religion. But before every game we all got on our knees as a team and said the Lord's Prayer. Those people who did not believe respected the beliefs of their teammates. Maybe they were praying to the Football Gods, which are known to be a lot less strict than Jesus. Personally, I never felt the need to look around to see who wasn't praying. We also had chapel and Bible study for those of us who wanted to go. But the one thing that we all had in common was the ability to play professional football.

The thing that has made this story so interesting is that there is a certain level of skills necessary to win in the NFL: Arm strength, foot speed, physical prowess, something. Tim Tebow doesn't really have those skills. But he does not possess the skills at a level usually associated with success in pro football. That's what I said out loud, that was my opinion. I had been around the NFL long enough to understand that there was no rational explanation for his success. First, he wasn't supposed to be drafted in the first round, but he was. Second, everybody agreed he did not have the skills to become a starting quarterback in the NFL, but he did. And third, everybody agreed he was not good enough to win games with his ability, but he has.

How did I explain the phenomenon that is Tim Tebow? For him, the answer is God. And I certainly wasn't going to tell anybody anything different. His belief system provides for him a high level of self-confidence, and self-confidence is a truly important factor. Do I believe I can beat you? Do I believe I can win this one-on-one? Self-confidence is the foundation of success—but you still got to have the skills to perform. For a lot of people, in addition to Tebow, since his success could not be explained rationally, it had to be attributed to the sweet baby Jesus syndrome.

Do you really think I would disagree? My mama is watching. And one year as a birthday gift, or maybe that was a Christmas gift, she gave me a beautiful Bible with my name embossed on it. Am I going to be the one to doubt Tim Tebow? Not on your Showtime I'm not.

I understand my opinion may not always be right, I've proven that, but that has never stopped me from giving it. Although I have to admit that as a player there were some times I was pretty sensitive to broadcasters' opinions. That started when I was in college. My junior year we were playing Syracuse, and Lynn Swann, Brent Musburger, and Bob Griese were doing the game. It was an important game for me. Our public information director, John Haun, was campaigning for me to get the Heisman Trophy, and the game was going to be broadcast on national TV. Lynn, Brent, and Bob Griese came to Miami during the week to prepare for the game, and one night Lynn Swann wanted to have dinner at the famous Joe's Stone Crab restaurant. He couldn't get a reservation at the time he wanted, so he told John Haun, "If you can get me into Joe's and Sapp makes a big play at the beginning of the game, I'll put the words *Heisman Trophy candidate* up on the screen, and I'll use my vote to put him up as a candidate."

John did the exactly right thing: He asked me to get that reservation for Lynn Swann. Lynn then made the promise to me, "You get me in there and you make a big play at the beginning of the game, I'll put those words right under your nose."

"Go start typing," I told him. My man Bones, who worked the door at Joe's, took care of the reservation for me. The third play of the game Syracuse quarterback Marvin Graves came running down the line. I jumped over the center, put down my hat, and hit him in the chest. The ball came flipping out over my right shoulder, and Ray Lewis, who was right behind me, picked it up.

Swann was true to his word. Right under my picture they put the words *Heisman Trophy candidate*. And later that night, as I sat with friends watching a tape of the game, I heard Bob Griese say, "Well, I don't know about that. I don't know if he's really a candidate for the Heisman."

There are laws against sacking broadcasters. Fortunately, Bob Griese's son, Brian Griese, was a quarterback in the NFL. Every time we played him, I remembered his father's words. So believe me, I knew there were consequences to every word I said. It didn't even slow me down though.

After the Steelers' first game of the 2011 season, for example, I pointed out that "Mercedes Sapp can cover (wide receiver) Hines Ward right now . . . Mercedes is my 13-year-old daughter. She covers Hines Ward in a heartbeat." To be fair, I have to report that Hines Ward and Kym Johnson won the 2011 *Dancing with the Stars* trophy. So I probably should have said that Kym Johnson also could cover Hines Ward right now. Hines Ward had been a great player in the National Football League for 13 seasons when I made that comment, the man had caught a thousand passes, but trust me, I know how 13 seasons add up. So naturally the producers set up an interview for me with Hines Ward. I didn't back up from what I'd said. In fact, I asked the old fella, "When you're out there on the practice field and you see those young guys taking off do you sometimes feel that they're at the racetrack and you're on a bicycle?" Oooo.

Hines didn't agree with my suggestion that my daughter could cover him—but he's never seen her play. I explained to him, "You're a Hall of Famer and you've caught a thousand balls, I'll give you that. But trust me on this, based on true athletic ability she's bigger and faster!"

One week I was stunned almost speechless when Donovan McNabb admitted after playing an overtime game that he didn't know an NFL game could end in a tie. Are you kidding me? Not know the rules? "When I heard him say that I almost passed out," I said on the air. "This will follow you for the rest of your career. Your legacy in the league, Donovan, will be throwing up in the Super Bowl, Rush Limbaugh, and now, 'I didn't know there are ties in the NFL.'"

I think what bothered me most about McNabb's comments was that it was typical of the lack of knowledge about the game I see among the younger players. When NFL Network analysts Sterling Sharpe and Mike Mayock criticized Brandon Marshall's effort in a game Marshall responded, "I don't think those guys were elite players, including Sterling Sharpe. I've got to turn on the film and see what he could do . . . My understanding is he's not a Hall of Fame guy."

Oh my goodness! The fact that Brandon Marshall did not know about one of the greatest people ever to play his wide receiver position really made me angry. The man didn't know about Sterling Sharpe? Here, let me help: He is the first 100-catch receiver you dumb ass. I don't care how many 100-reception years Brandon Marshall has, he might want to pay homage to the dude who made that number important. Not a Hall of Fame guy? Only because he got hurt too soon. Sterling Sharpe is the first receiver to have back-to-back 100-catch seasons, and the fact that Brandon Marshall has so little knowledge about the history of his profession, his specialty, and didn't seem to care to know more, made me furious.

My biggest criticism of younger players is that they don't appreciate the people who laid down the road on which they're traveling. I don't mean me; that road was paved before I got there. But when I was coming up I knew I was playing in the shadow of Deacon Jones, Bruce Smith, Reggie White, Chris Doleman, Kevin Greene; the people who helped build this league, who made it possible for me to enjoy the type of career I had and be paid so well for playing football. I know what those people did for me and for my game, and I honored them for it. I wanted to be in their club. Even with all the awards I won, there was nothing that made me more proud than to be considered a player of their caliber. So I didn't know how to respond to the lack of respect for the game from younger players.

I do believe the young players have been spoiled. The rules have been changed to make the game as safe as possible, the equipment continues to improve, and the benefits are the best they have ever been. But I also suspect every generation of players feels that way about the people who followed them. Probably those people who started the league were complaining about the people who followed them. "Helmets? Who needs them damn helmets? They call themselves football players!"

As I got more experience working as an analyst I like to believe that I learned how to talk a good game. Like I did when I was playing the game, I keep plugging away at it.

I also had an opportunity to act in a movie. After that experience I think it's accurate to say that as an actor I am a great pass rusher. My movie acting career started when a friend of mine named Todd Boyd, a USC professor, called and asked me to be in a movie a friend of his was making. He told me I was exactly what they were looking for to play this role: I worked cheap.

The movie was titled *Our Family Wedding*, starring Forest Whitaker, America Ferrera, Regina King, and Carlos Mencia. It was a comedy about what happens when a black man and a Mexican girl decide to get married—and then tell their families. Naturally, there was a goat involved. I played Wendell Boyd, Forest Whitaker's brother. No Wendell jokes, please. They gave me three lines. The only advice I got from people before making the movie was to act naturally. Act naturally? How do you do that? If you're acting, it isn't natural, and if it's natural, you aren't acting. I decided I would just act like I knew what I was doing.

My first day on the set was the wedding reception, which consisted mostly of dancing and eating, fortunately two of my areas of expertise. What surprised me the most about the business of making movies was how much food there was on the set. Are you kidding me? Food all day long. The second day we shot my scene with Forest Whitaker. While I was having breakfast he sat down with me and asked, "How do you want to do this scene? Which way do you think it'd be funnier?"

Forest Whitaker asking my opinion about acting? I told him, "You're kidding me, right? That'd be like me asking you the best way to rush the quarterback. You just do it whatever way you usually do it. I'll come back at you."

He nodded, "Yeah, I like that. No thought process." And he walked away.

Just like that he had identified my whole acting technique; the no-thought-process school of acting. I was excited about it. Soon as he walked away I sent out a tweet, "Forest Whitaker asked me which way I think the scene would be funnier? You kidding me?"

We did several takes of my scene. I had all my lines down. I was waiting for his line, and then he gave me a good fake; he came at me with a wild line. I just responded. That's the way we did my scene; all those few minutes of work memorizing my script, gone. They shot the same scene from several angles and we were done. I had to leave all of that food behind.

The film was released in 2010 to what could accurately be described as some reviews. Let me put it this way, even I haven't seen the film.

There is only one thing that all the things I've done since retiring have in common: Nobody is blocking me. The fact is that the Football Gods have been very good to me. They let me play my game in college and in the NFL for almost two decades and walk away from it. While I've got my bumps and my knees know when it is going to rain, beyond some fingers that point in different directions, I suffered no permanent injuries, and the recognition I received allowed me to start a new career.

So when people ask me what I miss about playing football, I can tell them honestly: All of it. Every little bit of it. I am proud of the fact that I played hard every game of my career. I am proud of the fact that there is not one player who can put on a tape and tell people, look at this tape; this is where I kicked the crap out of Warren Sapp. Where I manhandled him. Where I panacked him. Where I drove him to the ground. The eye in the sky don't lie. My whole career is on film, and trust me, that tape does not exist. I've heard Mark Schlereth sit there on ESPN and tell people he played one of his best professional games against Warren Sapp. I heard that, and I said, please put that tape on, show me that tape, because I don't remember that game you're talking about. Put on the tape, let's have a cold one or two and some popcorn, and let's see who won. I promise you, the answer is not Mark Schlereth.

I've played the game on every level possible. I played on the Dust Bowl, I've been a proud Blue Darter from Apopka High School, and I played on the biggest stage in sports, and inside me there still is a little kid who is ready to go get my four friends and you go and get your four friends and we'll meet you in the park and play till the sun goes down.

Or at least until I hear my mother calling.

ACKNOWLEDGMENTS

I've been so fortunate to share my life with so many wonderful people. To thank everyone would be impossible, but I know you all know how much I love you and appreciate what you've done for me.

Annie Roberts, Rosie Lykes (RIP), Ola Jones, Lisa Lykes, Melissa Sapp (the five women that raised me). My three brothers and heroes, Parnell Lykes (RIP), Arnell Lykes, and Hershel Sapp, who grilled me in the backyard. Winning there was tougher than Super Bowl XXXVII.

Clemy and Lois Harper, Troy Rainey, and Tony Washington. James Dowe, Arthur Coston, Cadiliac 3000, Flip, Theanthony Curry, Kenny Ladler, Thad Rivers, Santana Melvin, and James Jackson. Demarcus Patton, DJ Selfborn, James Roberts (good buddy), George Chien, Elinor Fukuda, B, Jay Grdina, and the rest of Team FatBoy!

Chip and Carolyn Gierke, Brad, Shane, Casey, Phil King and Family, and Bill Buckhalter—who came up with the name *Sapp Attack*. Will Carton and wife, Bill Long, Mr and Mrs Billy Dean, Endenburg, and Kramer! Ms. Tasinburg, Ms. Perry, Mr. Jadenoff, Mr. Coffee, Mr. Levine, my swim coach, and Mr. Rodriguez, in track, who called me "Sugar."

My third grade teacher, Ms. Williams; fourth grade, Ms. Graham; fifth grade, Mrs. Lee; sixth grade, Mr. Kuveact; and my seventh grade teacher, Ms. Smay. My eighth and ninth grades was a blur.

Uncle John T. Lykes and family, Uncle Aspor Dawson and family, and Auntie Lela

Merriman and family, Nina and family, Gio and family, and Jack Stewart (RIP).

Auntie Ola and James Jones as well as Jonathan Jones (Tyjuan), and the rest of my clan—too many to name you all!

Steve Miller, Pee-Man Wilton, and Jon Jon (Pee-Man's little brother). Marcus Webb, Atresa Grubbs, Carol, and Chase.

My roommate Ellis Johnson. Derrick Alexander, Devin Bush, Howard Green, Tommy Johnson, Kevin Carter, Derrick Brooks, James Stewart, and the rest of the 1991 Florida team and coaches at the FL/GA All-Star Game—6–3—we won!

To all my teammates from Apopka High to University of Miami to Tampa Bay and Oakland—it was my pleasure to have played with you guys!

My roommates—Ryan Collins, Alan Smyenette, and Robert Woodus (RIP).

James Stewart, Pat Riley, Rohan Marley, Syii Tucker, Sean James, Shanon Tresvant, Jason Owens, Allen Hall, Willie Phillips, Travis Cooper, Derrick Harris (Big D), Chad Wilson, Jesse Mitch, Kevin Brittworth, Dan Prutt, and Omar Andres—brightest class under the sun. No one outshines the Class of '91.

Coach Dennis Erickson, Greg Olsen, Arnold, Bob Karmelowski (Karm), Ed Ogercon, Sonny Lubbick, Greg Mark, Greg McMahon, Ramsey Shannon, Tommy Tuberville, Rick Peteif, Art Kehoe, Mike Short, Todd Torsielle, Brad Roll, Dana LeDuke, Mike Short, Bobby Rivera, Maryna, John Hahn, Linda Unsen, and the whole P.R staff—you're all great folks!

Anna Price, Robert Bell, Dean Butler, and Dr. Wolf.

The Glazers family, Tony Dungy and family, Rich McKay and family, Tim Ruskell, Tom McEwen, Jill Hobbs, Nancy Hassleman, Dave Levy, Chris Bryan, Pat Brazil, Rob Julian (Getter Done), Reggie

Acknowledgments

Scott, Rod Maranelli, Joe Burry, Mike Tomlin, Herman Edwards, Lovie Smith, Tim Sain, Todd Toriscelli, Pat Jernigan, Scott Trulock, Dr. Diaco, Dr. Zujac, and Dr. Janecki

Last Be Surely Not least—the great Al Davis and all those who worked under him—it was a pleasure to have worn and represent the Silver and Black, the Raider Nation! Thanks!

David Fisher would like to acknowledge the assistance of all those people who so willingly gave their time to contribute to this book, among them John Lynch, Brad Culpepper, Ray Lewis, Jon Gruden, JaMiko Vaughn, James Vaughn, K. C. Jones, and John Haun. I would also like to thank Warren's assistant, Elinor Fukuda, for being there at all the right times. As always, it is my great pleasure to work with the great editor, Peter Wolverton, and his associate editor, Anne Bensson, as well as the tremendous support staff at Thomas Dunne Books/ St. Martin's Press. And also, as always, I want to thank our agent, Frank "Frankie Books" Weimann of The Literary Group and his assistant, Elyse Tanzillo. I also want to make a point of saying how delightful it has been to get to know and work with Warren Sapp. The best way of describing him is that he is, in every circumstance, a stand up guy. I'm very pleased that we have become friends. Finally, nothing I do works without the love and support of my wife, the world's greatest health and yoga instructor, Laura Stevens, who makes my life better every day in every way.

INDEX

accomplishments, 160
  in college, 13, 42, 54–55, 59, 62, 66, 77
  on *Dancing with the Stars*, 295
  in high school, 25, 26, 28–29, 71
  in NFL, 6, 27, 60, 84, 133, 169, 171–72,
    177, 181, 295
acting, in movie, 312
adolescence
  aspirations during, 11–12
  friendship during, 18, 20
  racial identity in, 16–18
agents, 68–69, 70
Ahanotu, Chidi, 161–64
Allen, Larry, 251–52, 275
Allred, John, 233
Alstott, Mike, 141–42, 143, 150
analyst, occupation as, 6, 53, 168, 278–79,
    288, 296–300, 304–5, 312
Anderson, Willie, 180
anger, 127–28, 202
Armstead, Jesse, 38, 51, 52, 56
Arrington, LaVar, 218–19
Asomugha, Nnamdi, 205
Atkins, George, 183
Atlanta Falcons, 101, 254
autographs, 223–24

Baltimore Ravens, 305
Banks, Carl, 186
Barber, Ronde
  appreciation for, 186
  blitzing by, 135
  competitiveness of, 150–51
  confidence in, 258

  Super Bowl and, 153
  support from, 212
  tough defense and, 130
Bass, Lance, 290, 294
Batch, Charlie, 263
Bednarik, Chuck, 126
Belichick, Bill, 74
Bergeron, Tom, 293
Berman, Chris, 114–15, 116
Berry, Halle, 287
Bettis, Jerome, 215, 287, 304
Beyoncé, 147, 279–80
Big East, 16, 38, 55–56
Biletnikoff, Fred, 183
birth date, 3
Bledsoe, Drew, 93, 118, 246, 253
blitzing, 135, 136
boosters, at University of Miami, 58–59
Bowden, Bobby, 33
Bradshaw, Terry, 249
Brady, Tom, 198, 282, 305
Branch, Cliff, 185
Braxton, Toni, 290
Brayton, Tyler, 192
broadcasting
  drawing from playing experience for,
    306
  lessons about, 303–4
  self-evaluation in, 307
Brooks, Derrick, 84, 104, 110, 114, 123,
    127, 135, 148, 149, 166, 167, 183,
    209–10, 213, 265
  accomplishments of, 140, 171–72
  appreciation for, 186, 187, 305